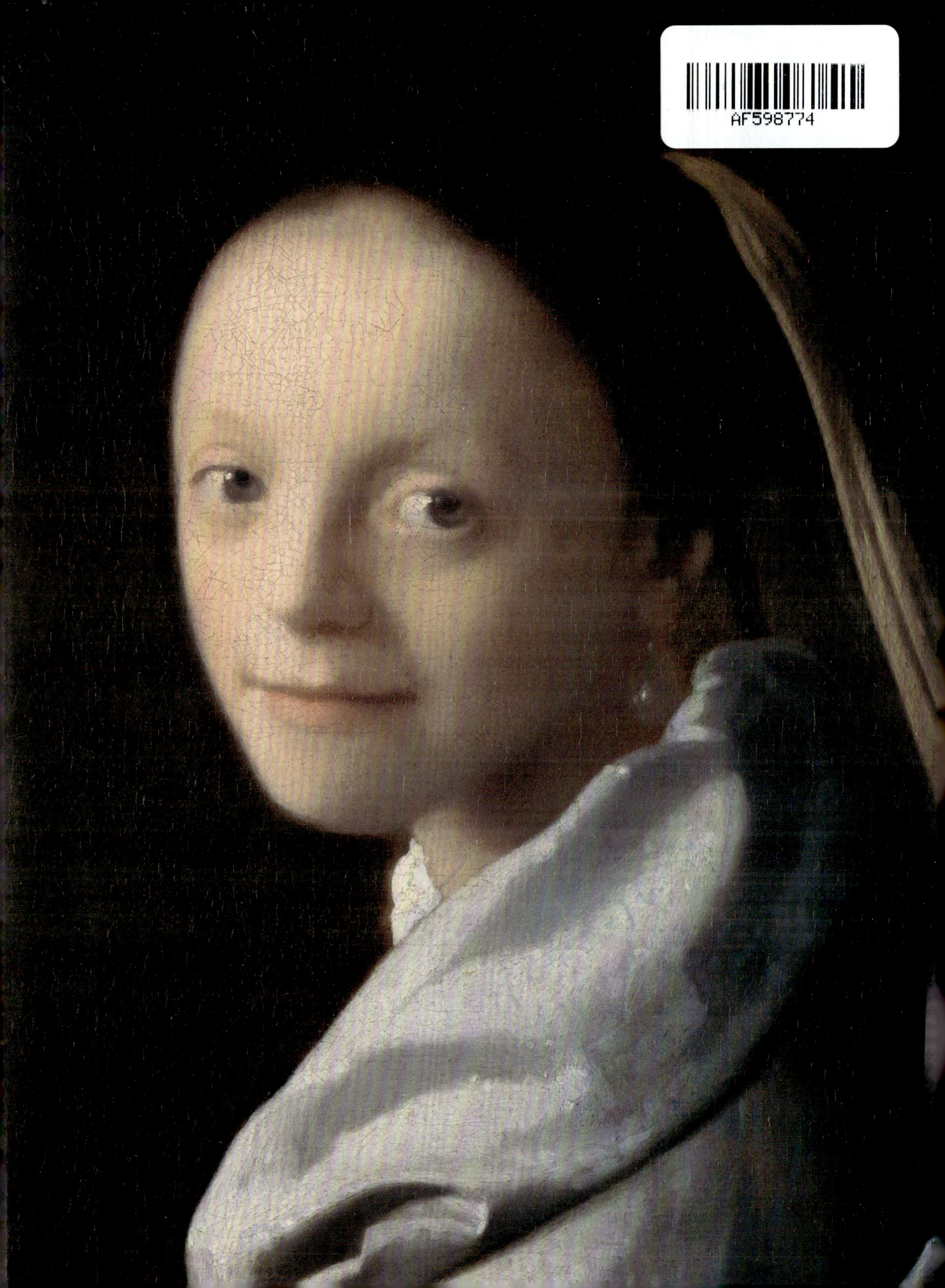

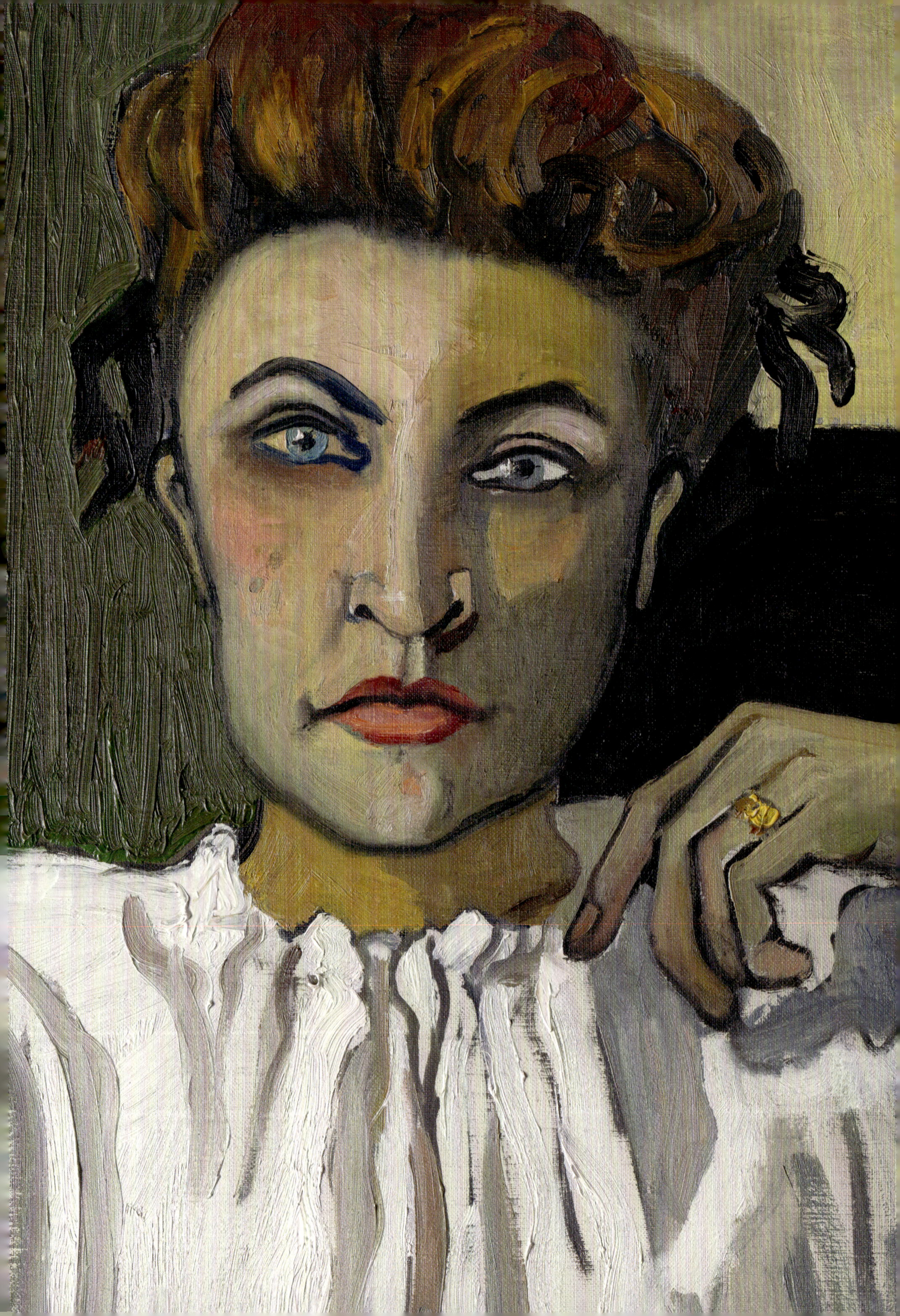

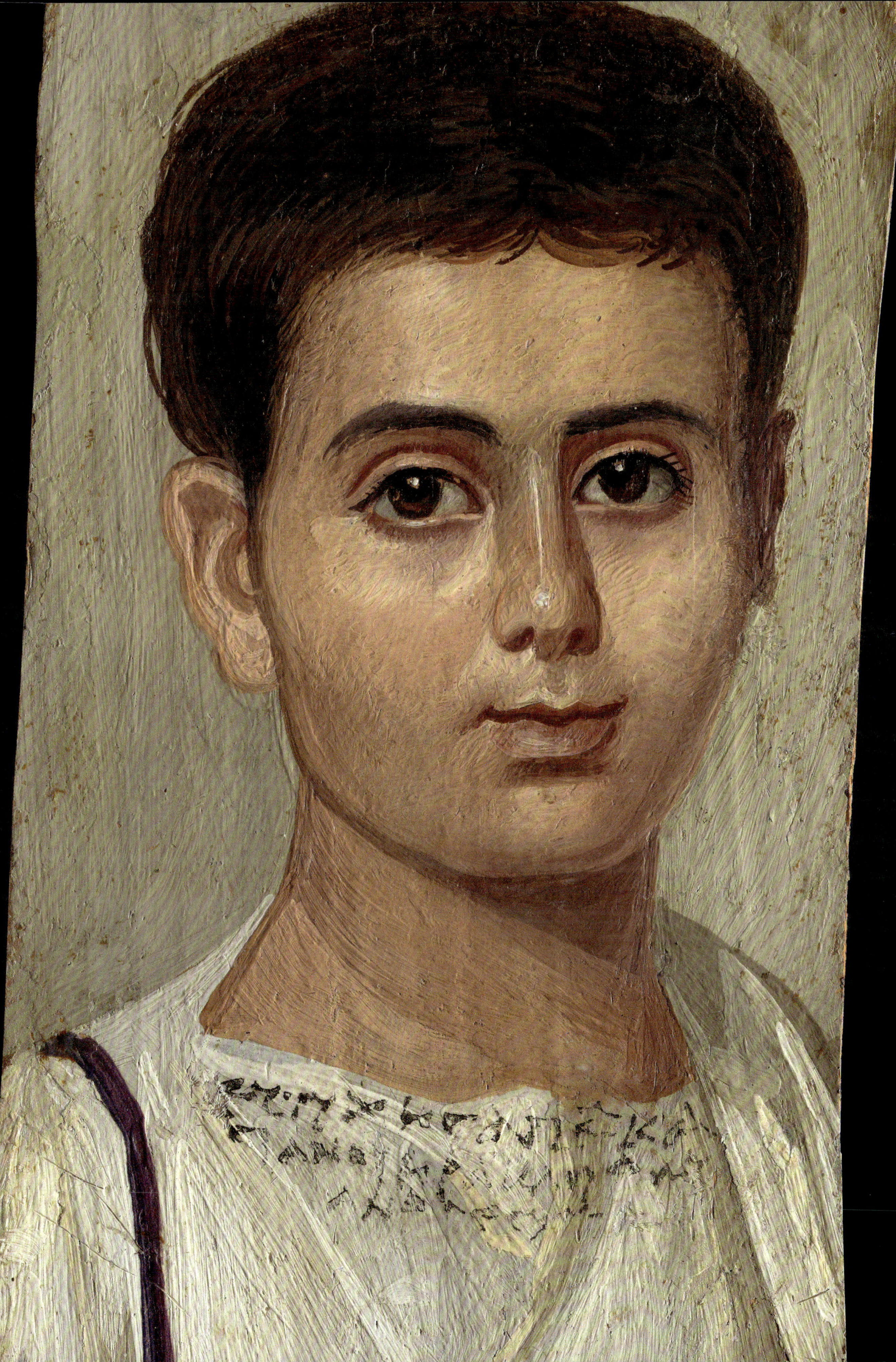

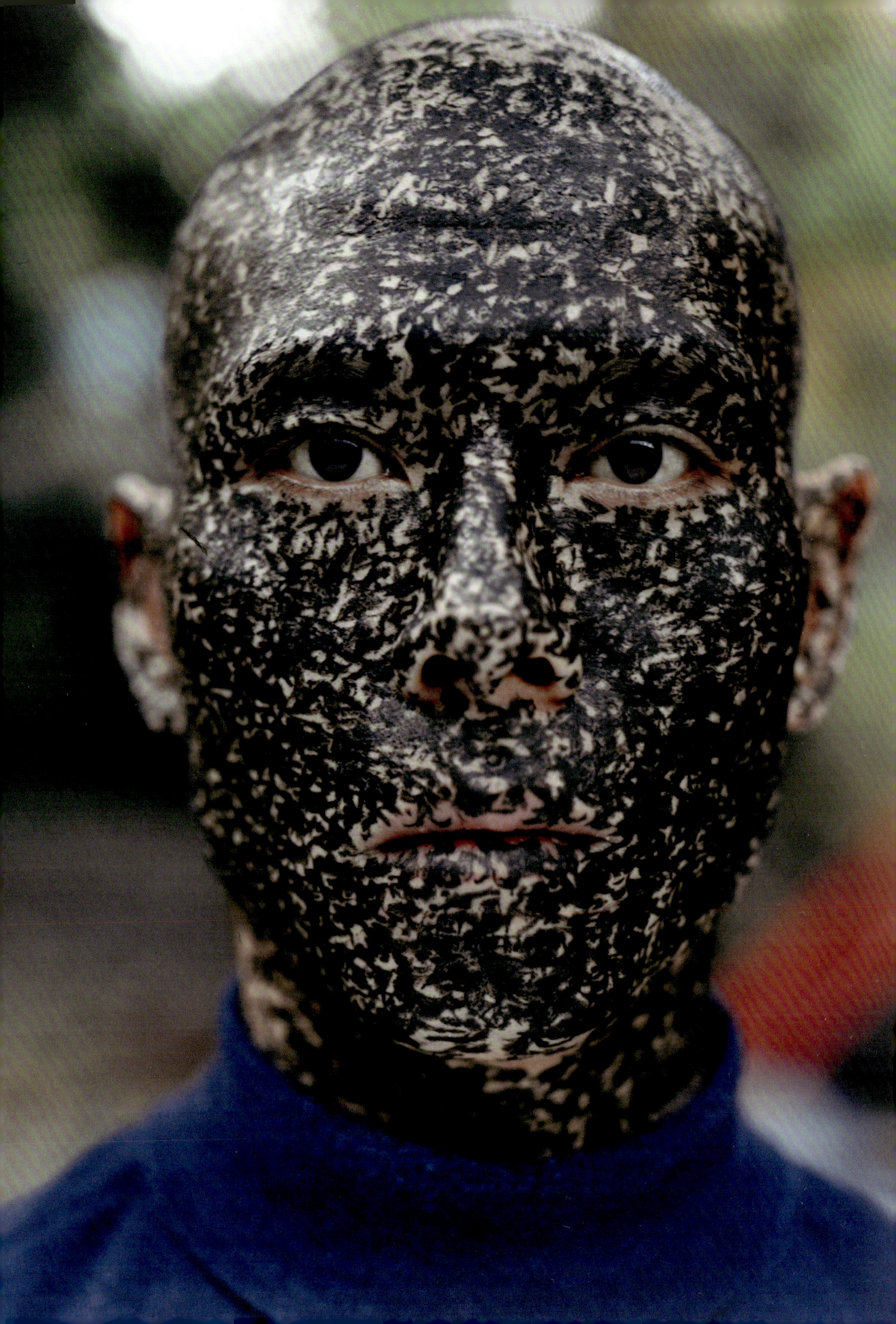

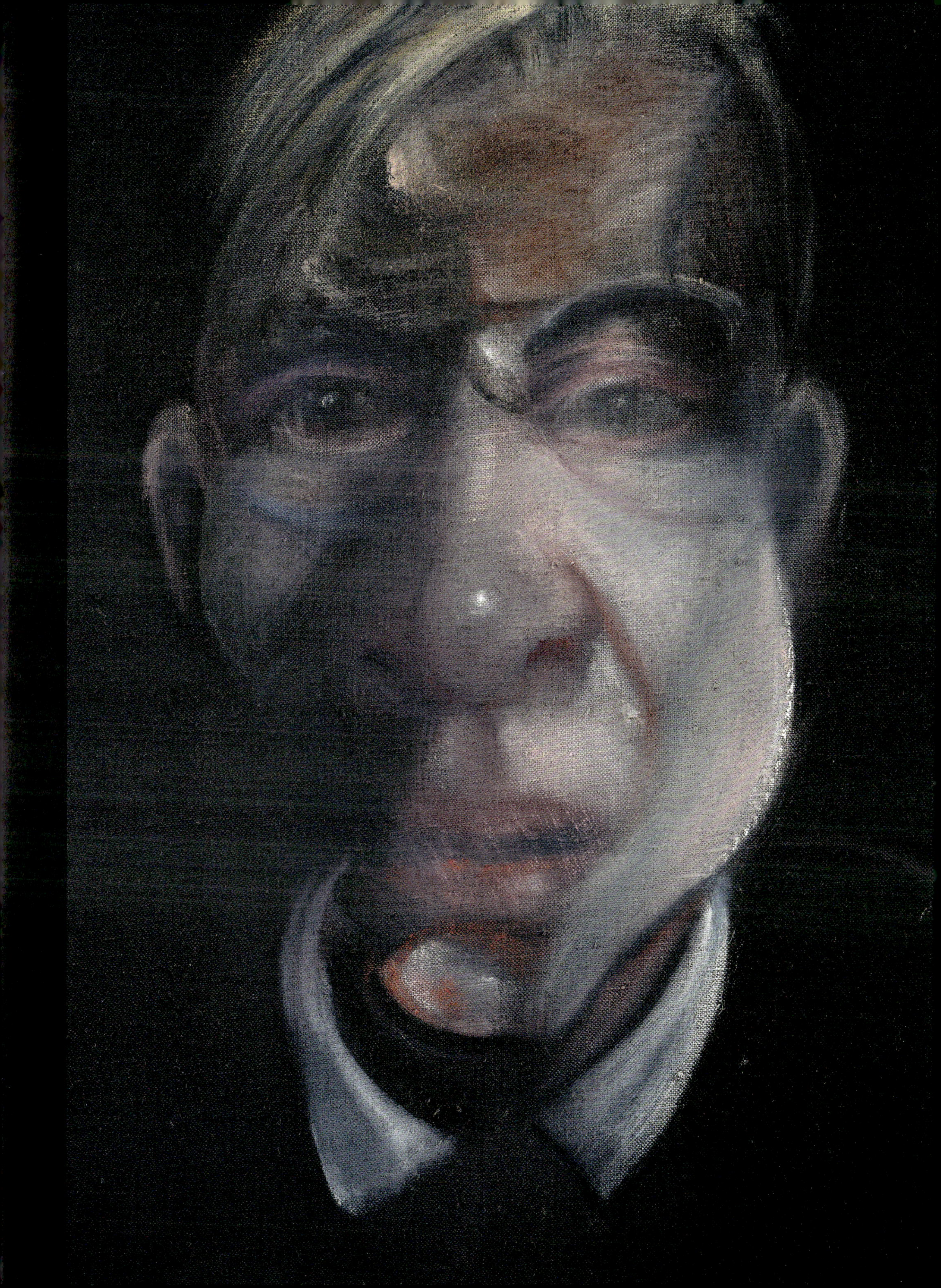

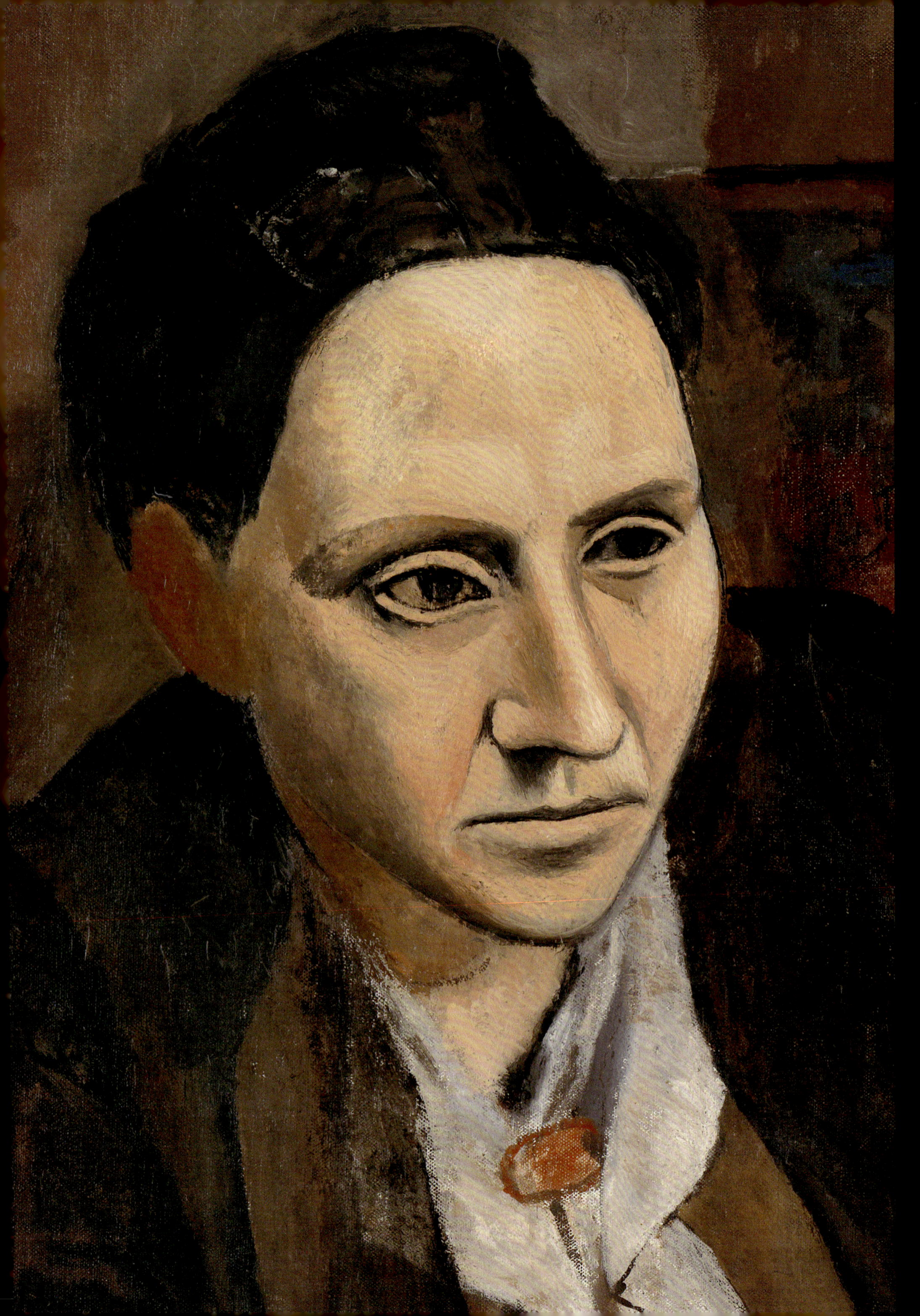

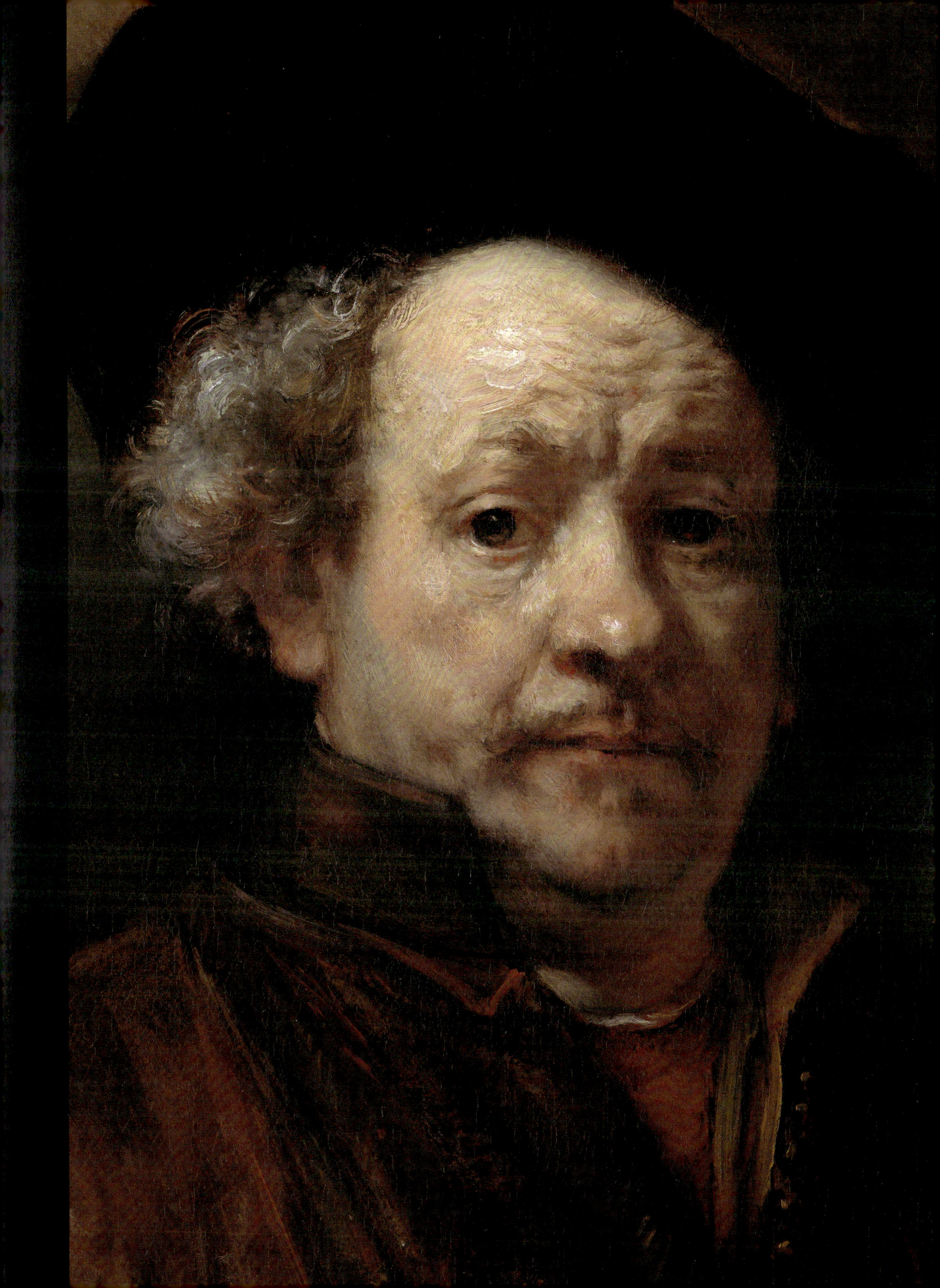

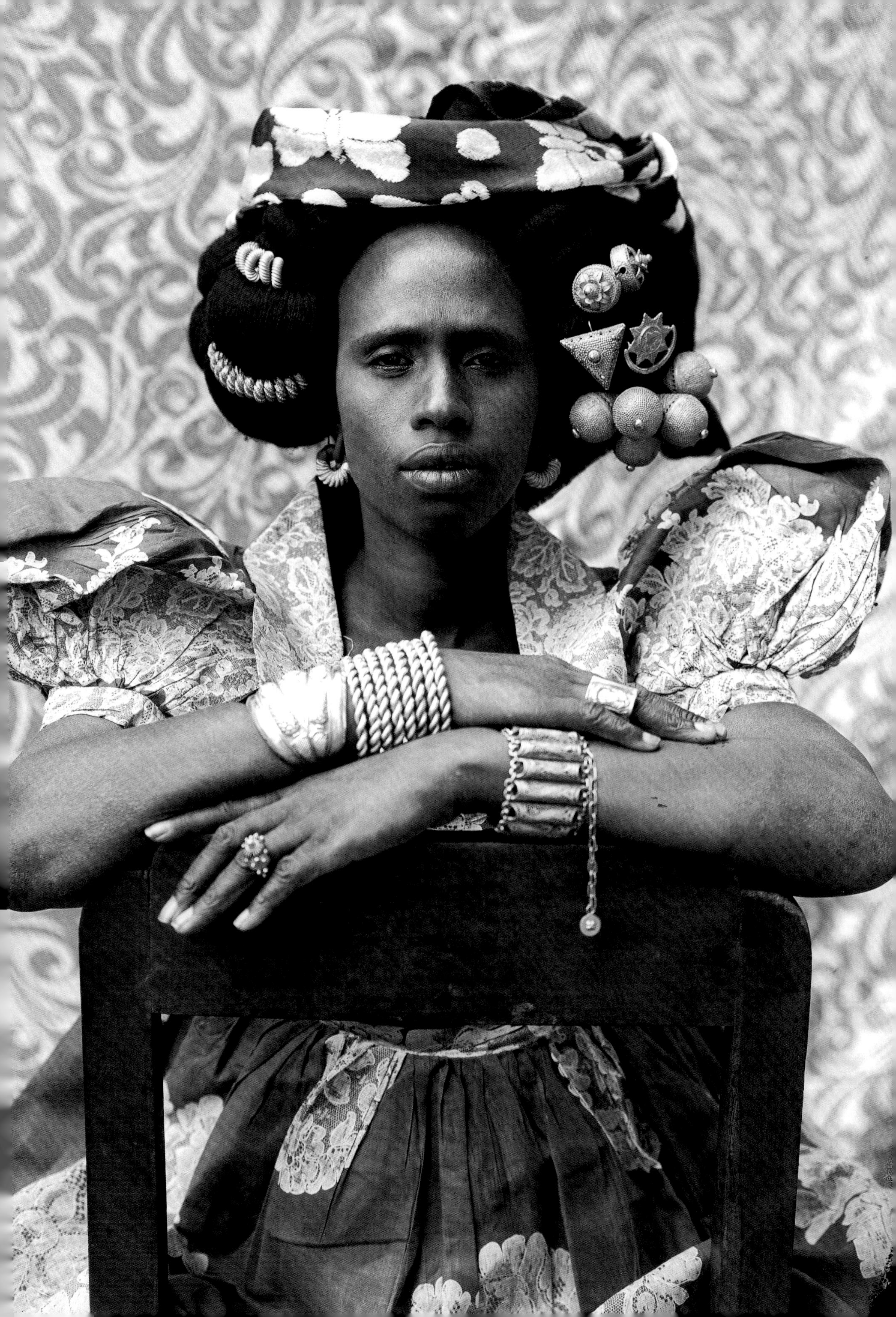

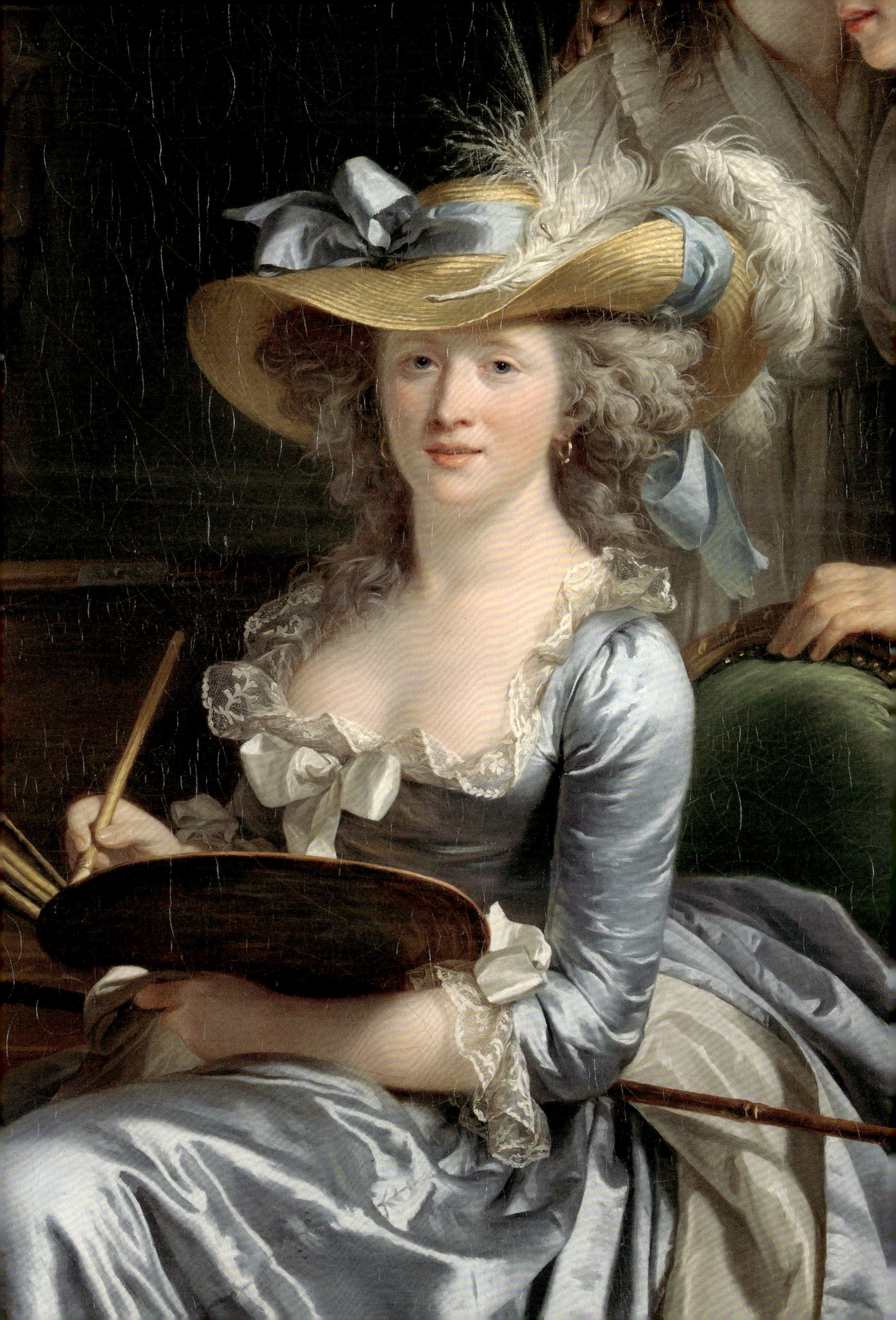

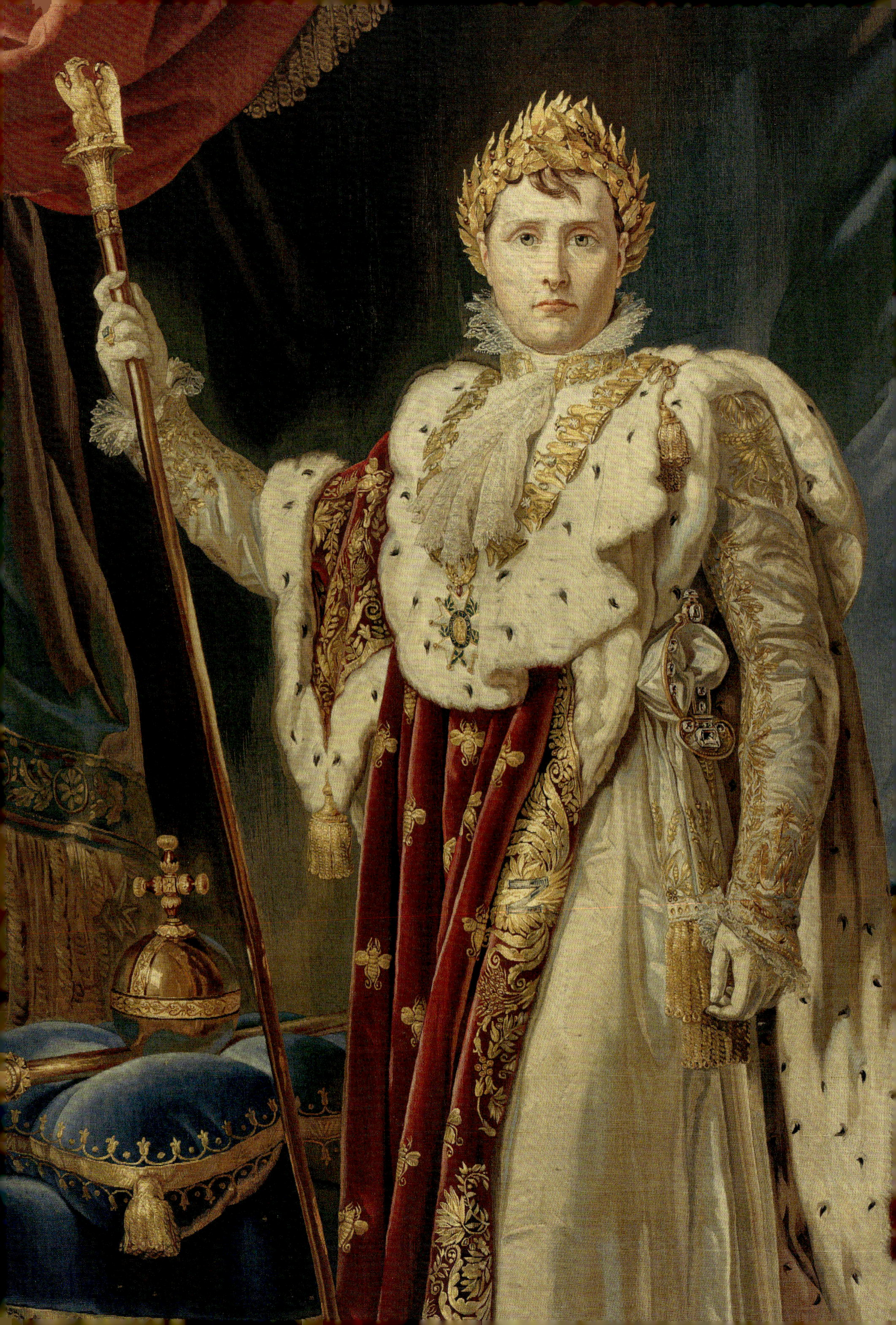

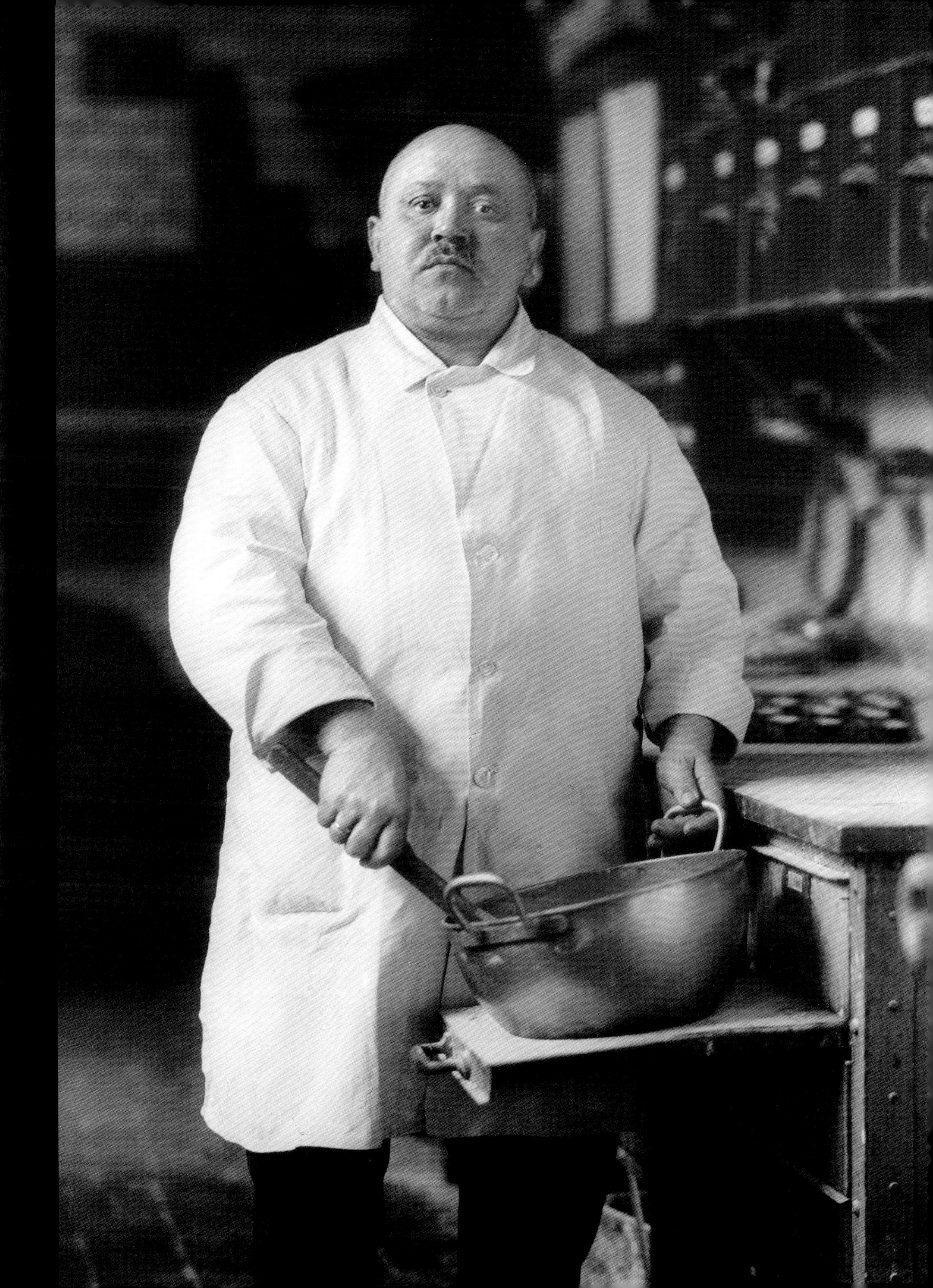

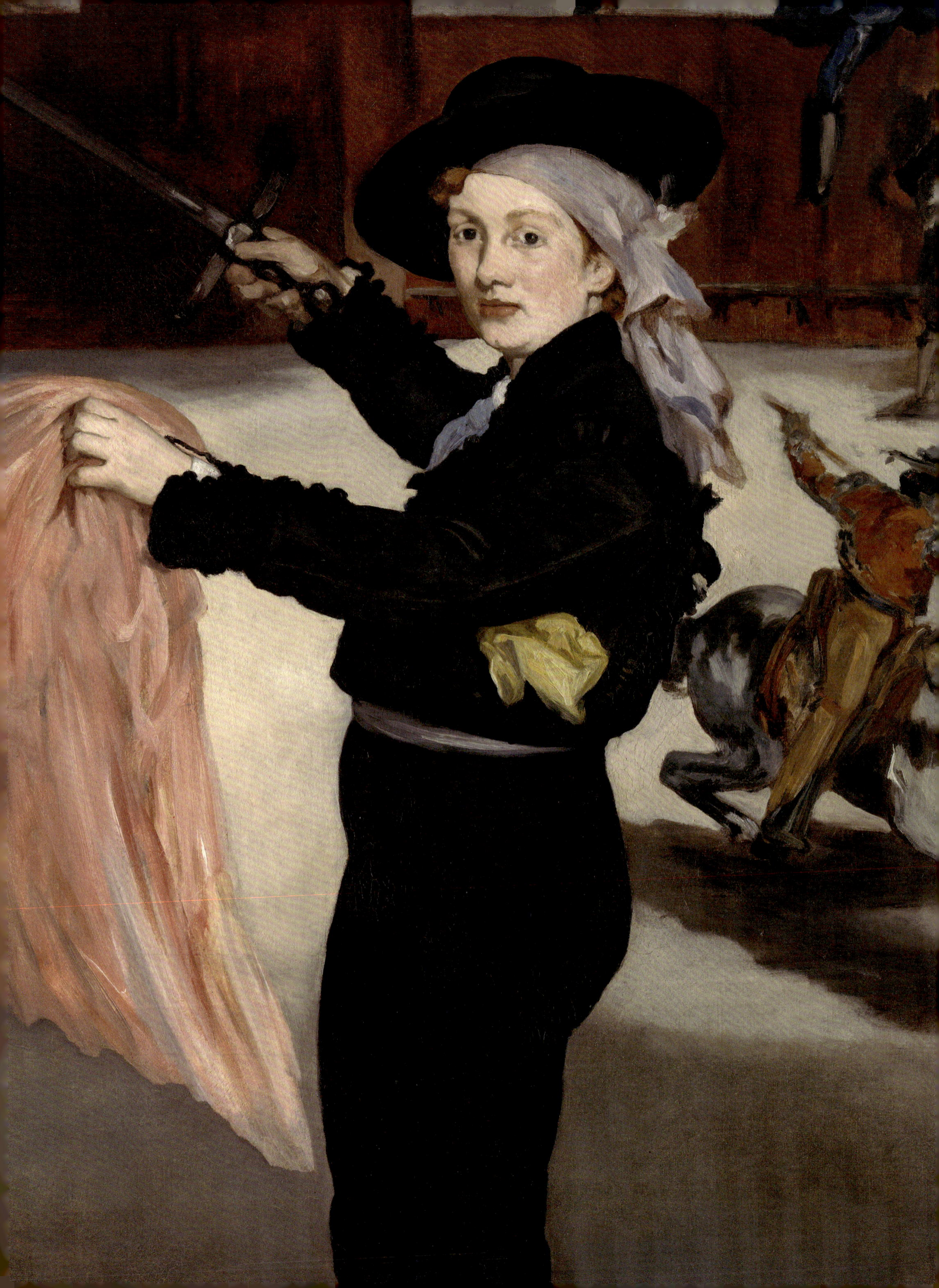

HOW TO READ PORTRAITS

Kathryn Calley Galitz

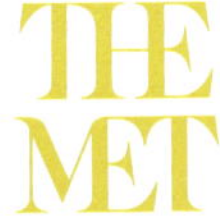

The Metropolitan Museum of Art, New York
Distributed by Yale University Press, New Haven and London

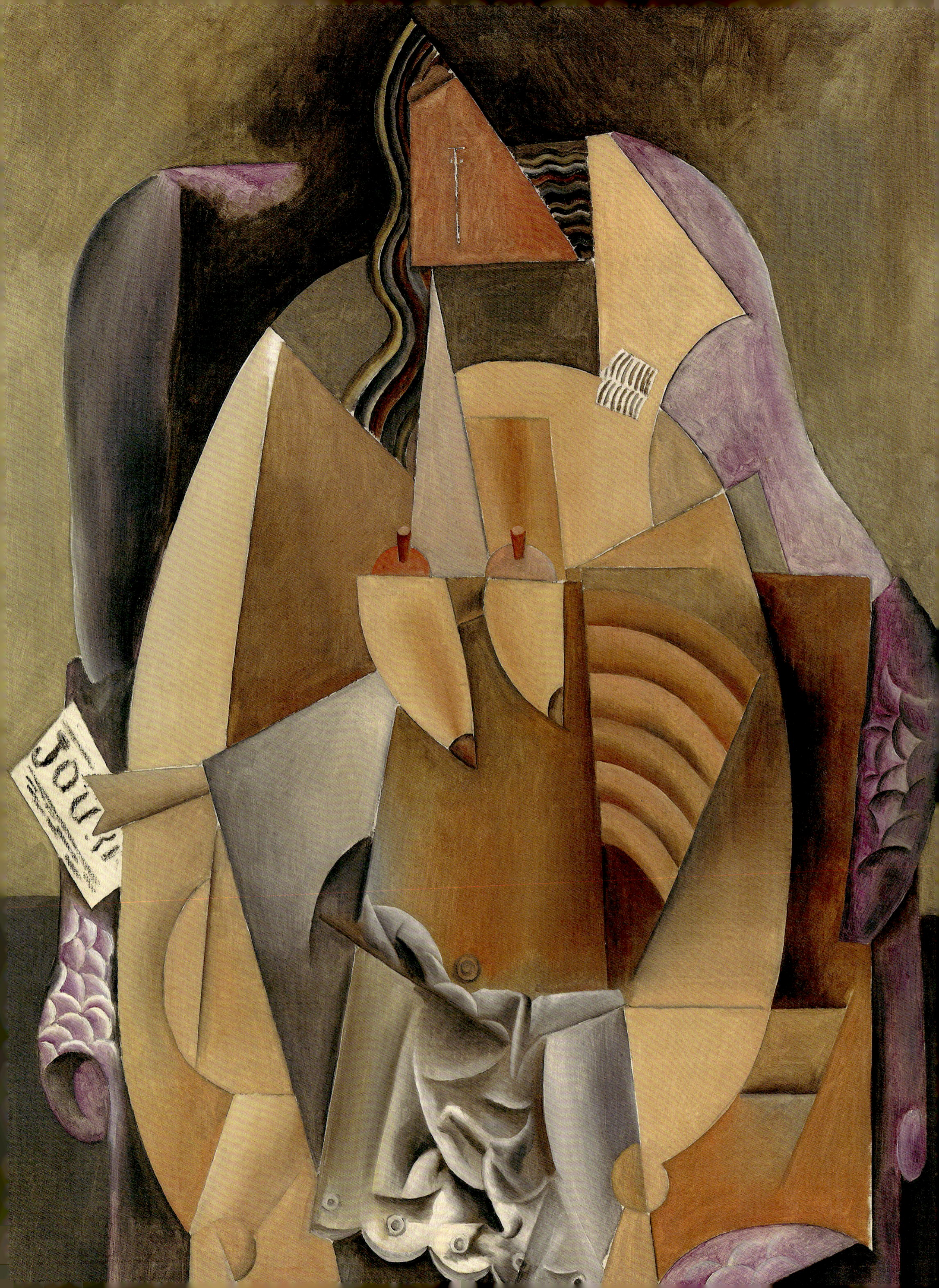
JOUR

CONTENTS

DIRECTOR'S FOREWORD 17

INTRODUCTION 19

BEYOND FACE VALUE 29

THE LANGUAGE OF POWER 49

PUBLIC FACES, PRIVATE LIVES 65

ROLE-PLAYING 85

SUBVERSIONS 99

SUGGESTED READING 114

ACKNOWLEDGMENTS 116

INDEX 117

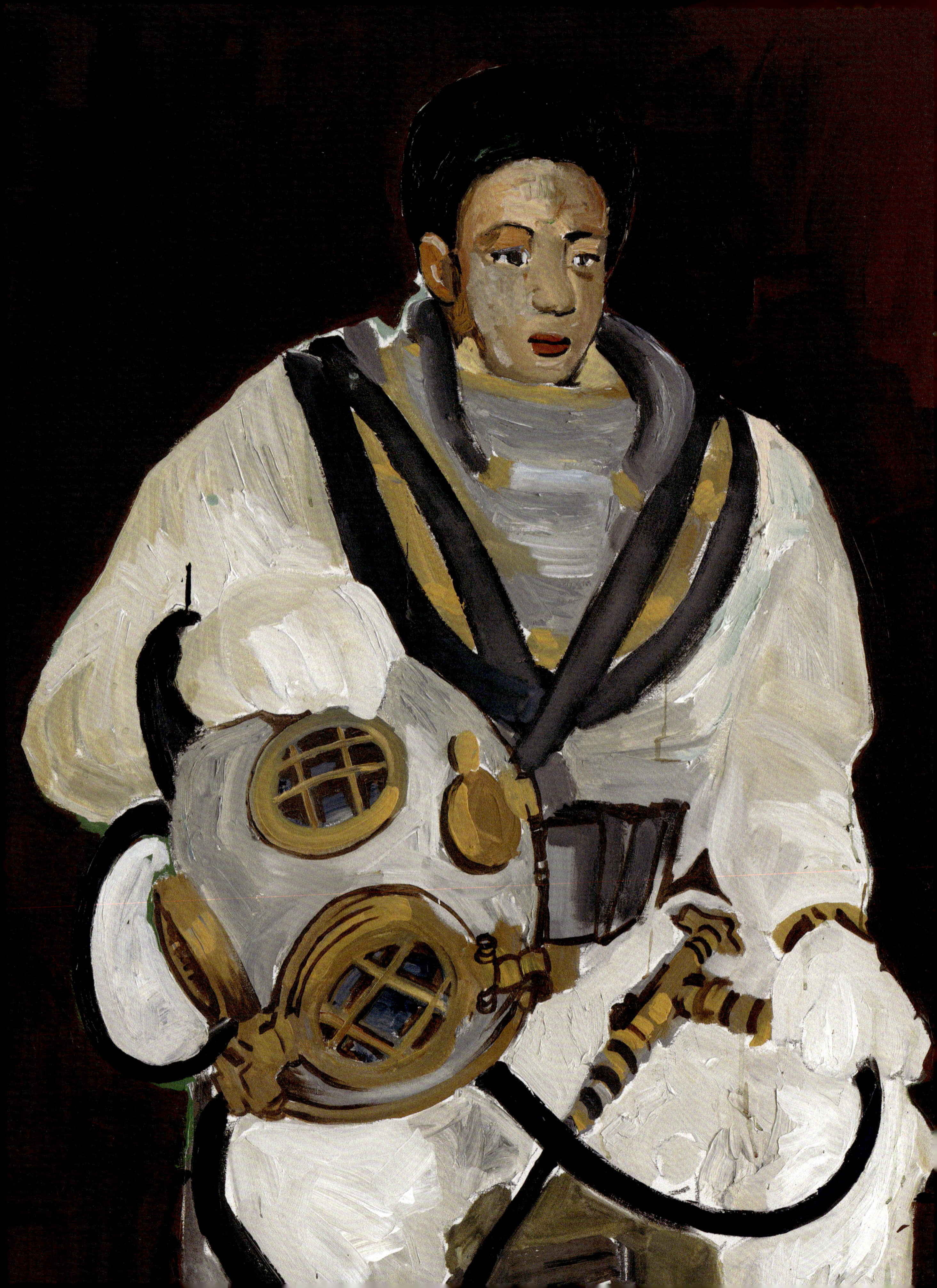

DIRECTOR'S FOREWORD

A visit to The Metropolitan Museum of Art inevitably leads to intimate, face-to-face encounters with fascinating individuals from other eras or places in the form of mesmerizing portraits, whether of a citizen of Roman Egypt, painted on a mummy board, or a modern Japanese family photographed at home. The Met collection, which spans more than five thousand years of art, is rich in portraits encompassing a range of styles and media, from paintings and photographs to likenesses woven into tapestries, sculpted in marble, molded in ceramic, and generated by three-dimensional body scans. Although portraiture was largely the province of the elite for much of its history, it remains resonant and relevant to this day. As an expression of identity, the portrait embodies universal and timeless preoccupations. Indeed, the twenty-first century has witnessed a resurgence of portraiture, with contemporary artists reshaping its very nature by portraying previously marginalized or excluded subjects.

The encyclopedic range of our holdings lends itself to the cross-cultural, thematic consideration of portraiture presented in this work. I can think of no one better suited to write it than Kathryn Calley Galitz, whose publications and teaching exemplify the scholarly breadth of this approach to the subject. The portraits that she has selected from the collection range from the iconic to the unexpected, challenging us to expand our understanding of this deceptively familiar art form.

We are grateful for the support of the Roswell L. Gilpatric Publications Fund, which has made possible the publication of this richly illustrated volume, the twelfth in the Museum's How to Read series. Like the other books in this popular series, it illuminates a vital topic for a wide range of readers through artworks from the unsurpassed Met collection.

Max Hollein

Marina Kellen French Director and CEO
The Metropolitan Museum of Art

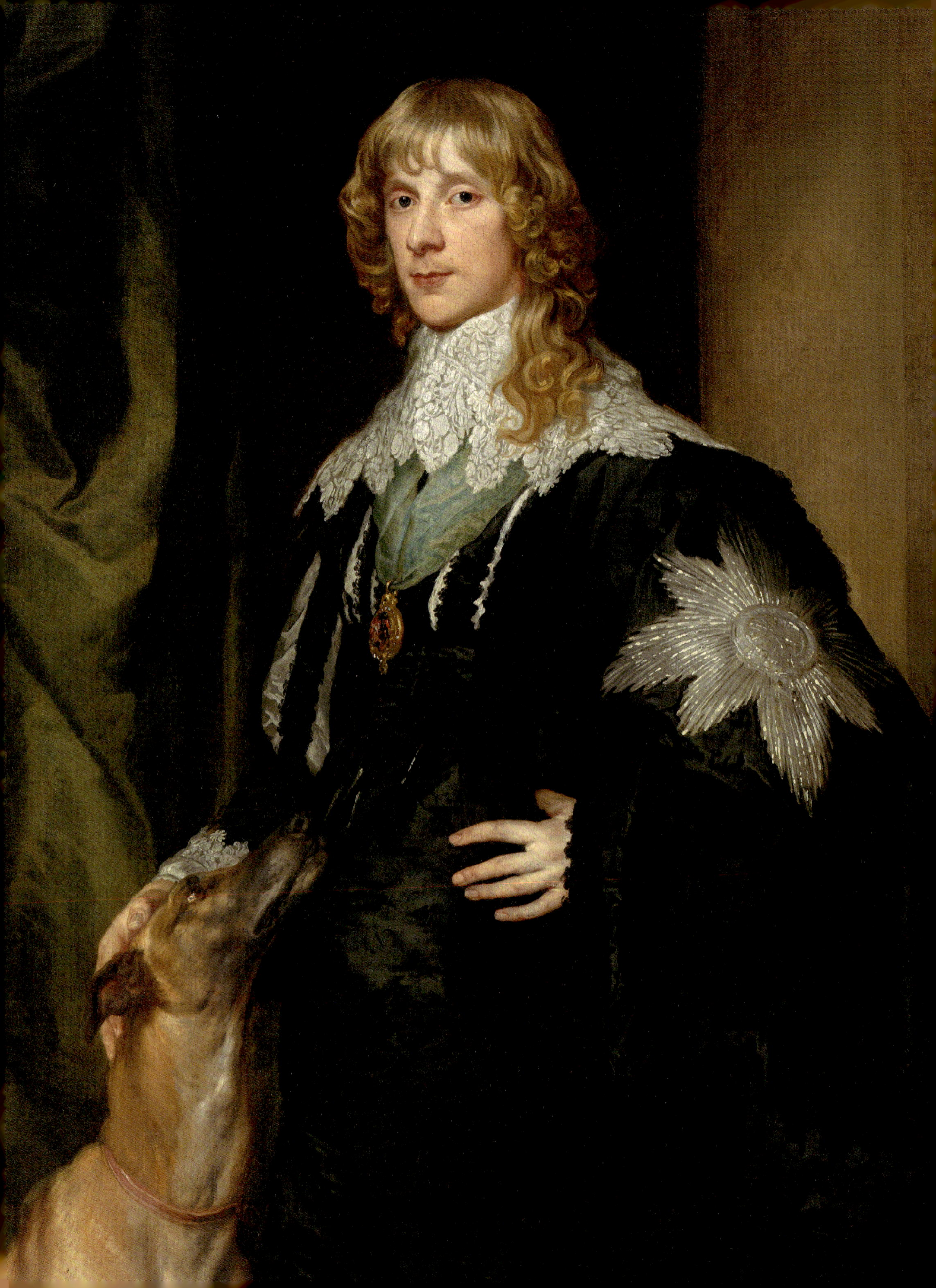

INTRODUCTION

A young man stands with one hand on his hip and the other atop the head of the greyhound nuzzled at his side (fig. 1). His outward gaze meets ours. He is elegantly—even ostentatiously—dressed, clad in luxurious satin, its deep black the perfect foil for the large silver star that adorns his cape. A medal hangs from a blue ribbon around his neck, and a garter edged in gold is partially visible just below his left knee. Man and dog, rendered lifesize, are flanked by drapery and a column that suggest an imposing interior space. As the representation of a specific individual, the work is a portrait, a type of art perhaps never more familiar than today through the ubiquity on social media of its pop-culture incarnation, the "selfie." It depicts James Stuart, Duke of Richmond and Lennox, painted about 1633–35 by Anthony van Dyck, then the most sought-after portraitist in London. At that time the success of a portrait was judged by its resemblance to its subject, or its "likeness," and Van Dyck was acclaimed for his ability to improve upon the actual appearance of his aristocratic and royal clientele—although one of his sitters remarked that she barely recognized herself in her own flattering portrait.

The emphasis on a portrait's likeness in relation to its subject remains a through line in the history of portraiture, albeit with some exceptions. Van Dyck's practice alerts us to the current of idealization that invests portraiture with an inherently deceptive aspect, also seen in classical Greek and Roman sculpture, Benin masks, and portraits of America's Gilded Age elite (see figs. 6, 17, 22). In the hands of other artists and at different moments in time, a portrait's fidelity to observed reality may be further compromised when its subject assumes another identity through role-playing or disguise (see fig. 47) or when its subject verges on the unrecognizable, as in Cubism (see fig. 52). A type of portrait miniature known as "lover's eyes," a token of intimacy popularized in eighteenth-century Europe, challenges expectations of recognizable likeness in portraiture, as the subject of these synecdochal portraits, which depict either an

1. Anthony van Dyck. *James Stuart (1612–1655), Duke of Richmond and Lennox*, ca. 1633–35 (detail of figure 21)

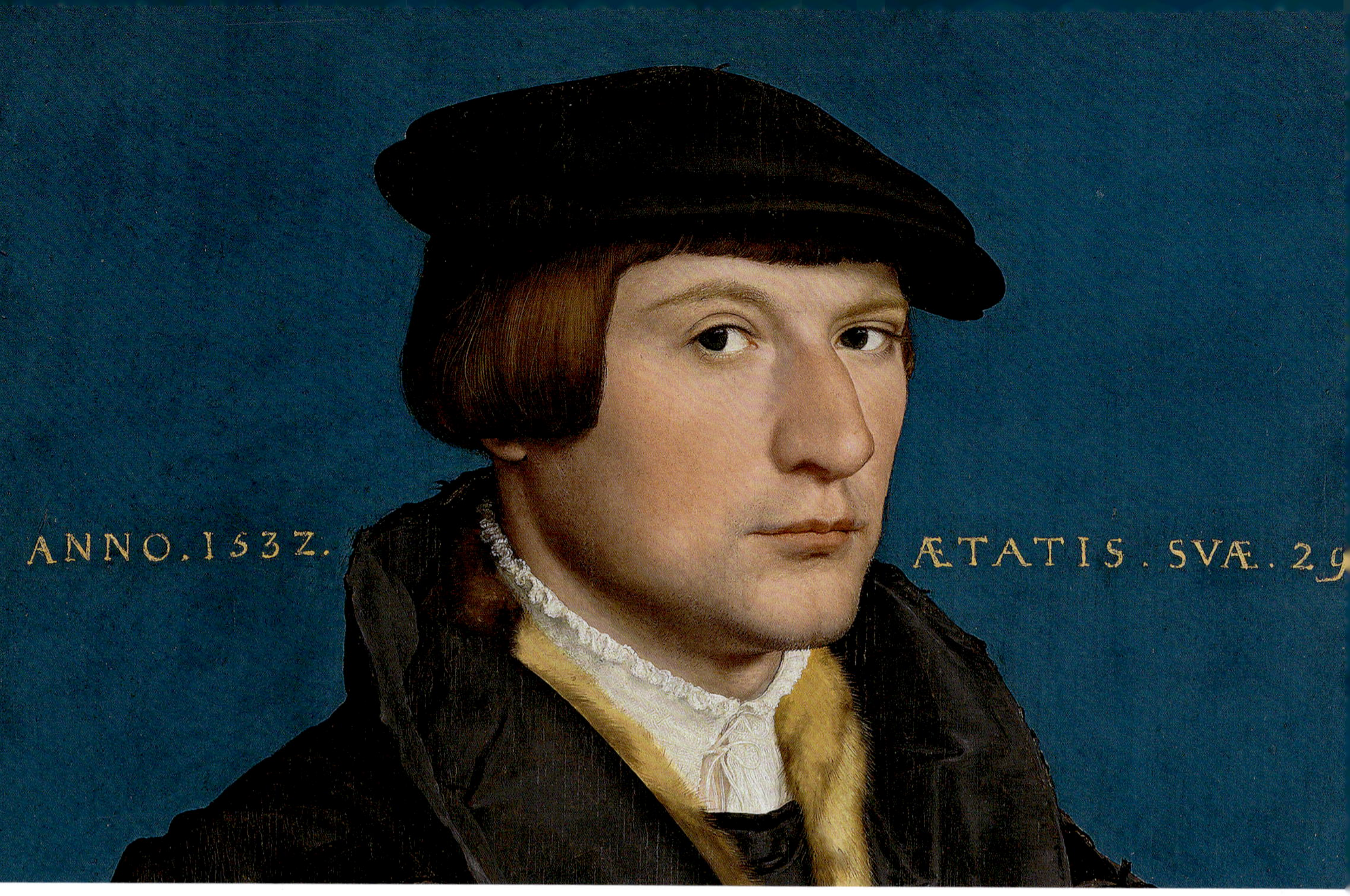

eye or a pair of eyes, was known only to the recipient. The most extreme disruptors to the notion of the portrait as likeness are the works in which symbolically charged objects serve as stand-ins for the subject, as in Marsden Hartley's paintings of Karl von Freyburg (see fig. 53). Even such everyday items as ironing boards and a coffee can filled with paintbrushes have functioned as symbolic portraits (see figs. 54, 55).

That an image of an inanimate object like an ironing board can be presented as a portrait requires a more expansive definition of portraiture, one that goes beyond representational likeness to encompass identity. The origins of portraiture can be traced to a human impulse to record individual identity that manifested as early as the prehistoric era. The handprints stenciled on the walls of caves in present-day Indonesia, France, and Spain synecdochally represent their unknown creators, just as the "lover's eyes" embody their enamored subjects. Similarly, human skulls were plastered and painted in the Middle East some 9,500 years ago to memorialize deceased individuals, signaling a belief in the face as the locus of identity, and funerary or commemorative portraits have been documented in China as early as the late third century BCE. According to classical legend, the first painting was a portrait, made by Dibutades, a young woman in ancient Greece, who outlined the shadow her lover cast upon a wall before he departed, recording his existence for posterity.

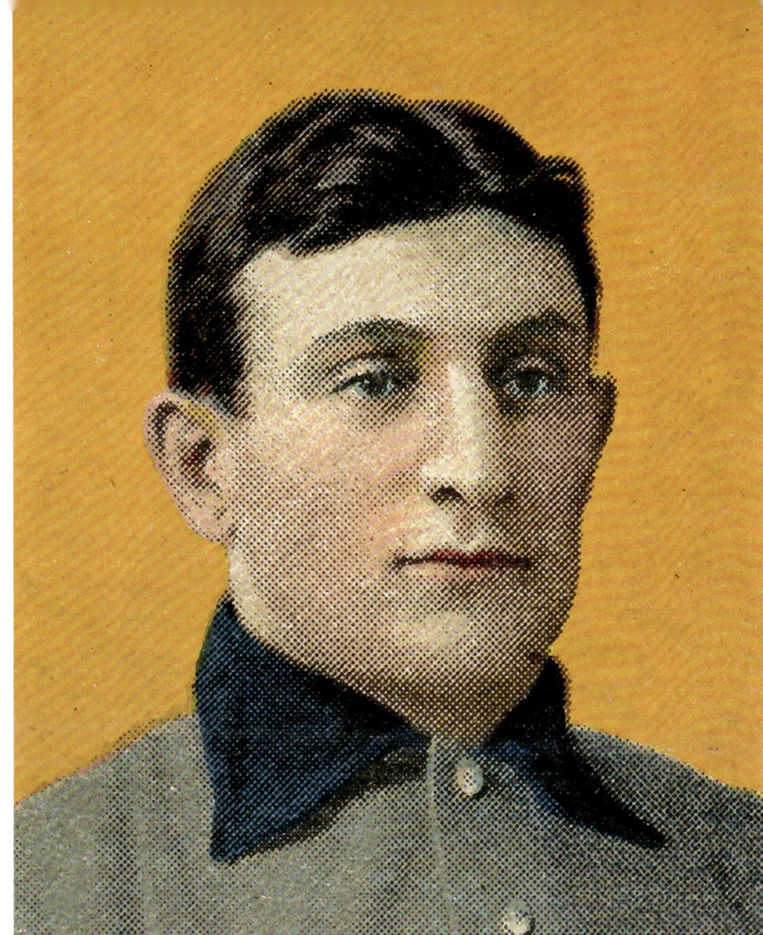

Opposite: 2. Hans Holbein the Younger. *Hermann von Wedigh III (d. 1560)*, 1532 (detail of figure 10)

Right: 3. *Honus Wagner, Pittsburgh, National League, from the White Border Series (T206)I*, 1909–11 (detail of figure 34)

With the reemergence of the portrait as an independent art form in fifteenth-century Europe, the genre became inextricably linked with such aspects of identity as power and social status as well as professional and personal affiliations. European monarchs harnessed the portrait to propagate their authority, expressed through the language of pose and symbolic accoutrements in state portraiture (see fig. 19). Artists in early modern Europe capitalized on a related type, the *portrait d'apparat*, which deploys props and setting to communicate the subject's professional identity (fig. 2; see fig. 10). Similarly, in Van Dyck's portrait of Stuart, the sitter's noble rank and ties to the king of England are conveyed through the full-length format, Stuart's attire, and even the dog's presence, as will be discussed. Collective identity is visualized in the group portrait, which originated in sixteenth-century Holland (the Northern Netherlands). Since then, subjects as varied as Dutch civic-guard companies, eighteenth-century British families, and artists in 1960s New York have been portrayed in this group format (see figs. 36, 32, 35). Celebrity, too, serves as a marker of identity in portraiture, whether the subject is a twentieth-century ballplayer or a seventeenth-century opera singer (fig. 3; see figs. 34, 42).

Over time, the portrait as an expression of identity has been called into question by works that present people not as individuals but as examples of types representing various social classes, professions, and cultures. Social types recur in European art, especially in printed imagery. In the second half of the nineteenth century, the distinction between portrait and type dissolved in portraitlike figure paintings such as Édouard Manet's images of Victorine Meurent playing a range of modern Parisian types (*Young Lady in 1866*, 1867; 89.21.3) and works by Claude Monet for which his wife, Camille, modeled (*Women in the Garden*, ca. 1866, Musée d'Orsay, Paris). In the 1860s inexpensive photographs documenting people from diverse cultures proliferated, reflecting contemporary ethnographic interests as well as European and American colonialist expansion. The subjects, typically shown in traditional dress, are captured in situ or posed in the photographer's studio. These photographs look like standard portraits but were marketed as collectibles featuring a range of "exotic" types, denying the subjects their individuality.

Similarly, beginning in the Weimar Republic August Sander photographed hundreds of his fellow Germans for *People of the 20th Century*, a never-finished project that he described as his "attempt to create a contemporary physiognomy of German humanity." He organized his subjects into seven categories that form a social hierarchy; *Pastrycook* of 1928 belongs to that of "The Skilled Tradesman" (fig. 4). Like most of the photographs in Sander's vast compendium, the subject is identified by occupation rather than by name, underscoring the image's intended function as a representative type rather than a portrait of an individual—or, put another way, as an expression of the universal rather than of the specific. That said, Sander deployed the conventions of portraiture in these works, including the use of props and settings to signify professional or social identity, much like a traditional *portrait d'apparat.* Here the mixing bowl that the sitter authoritatively wields and the bakery with its flour-dusted floor connote "pastry cook." Sander's subject commands the photographic frame through his sheer physical presence and direct, outward gaze; his dominance of the surrounding space signals his social status, a compositional device Sander frequently deployed in these works. The cook's confident bearing and telling details such as the subtle sheen of his pristine leather shoes and wedding band convey the dignity of the individual and his work. We sense in this photograph something of the man himself, going against type to assert his individuality beyond his professional identity—and we sense Sander allowing him to do so. Portraitlike, *Pastrycook* confounds its ostensible function as a type. It embodies Sander's declared intent to realize "simple, natural portraits that show the subjects in an environment corresponding to their own individuality," which challenges an exclusively typological reading of these images. The scholar Graham Clarke summed up the expressive tension between the general and the specific that underlies Sander's approach: "While he seeks 'types,' he celebrates individuals."

4. August Sander (German, 1876–1964). *Pastrycook*, ca. 1928, printed 1976. Gelatin silver print, 11½ × 8½ in. (29.2 × 21.6 cm). Warner Communications Inc. Purchase Fund, 1979 (1979.521.1)

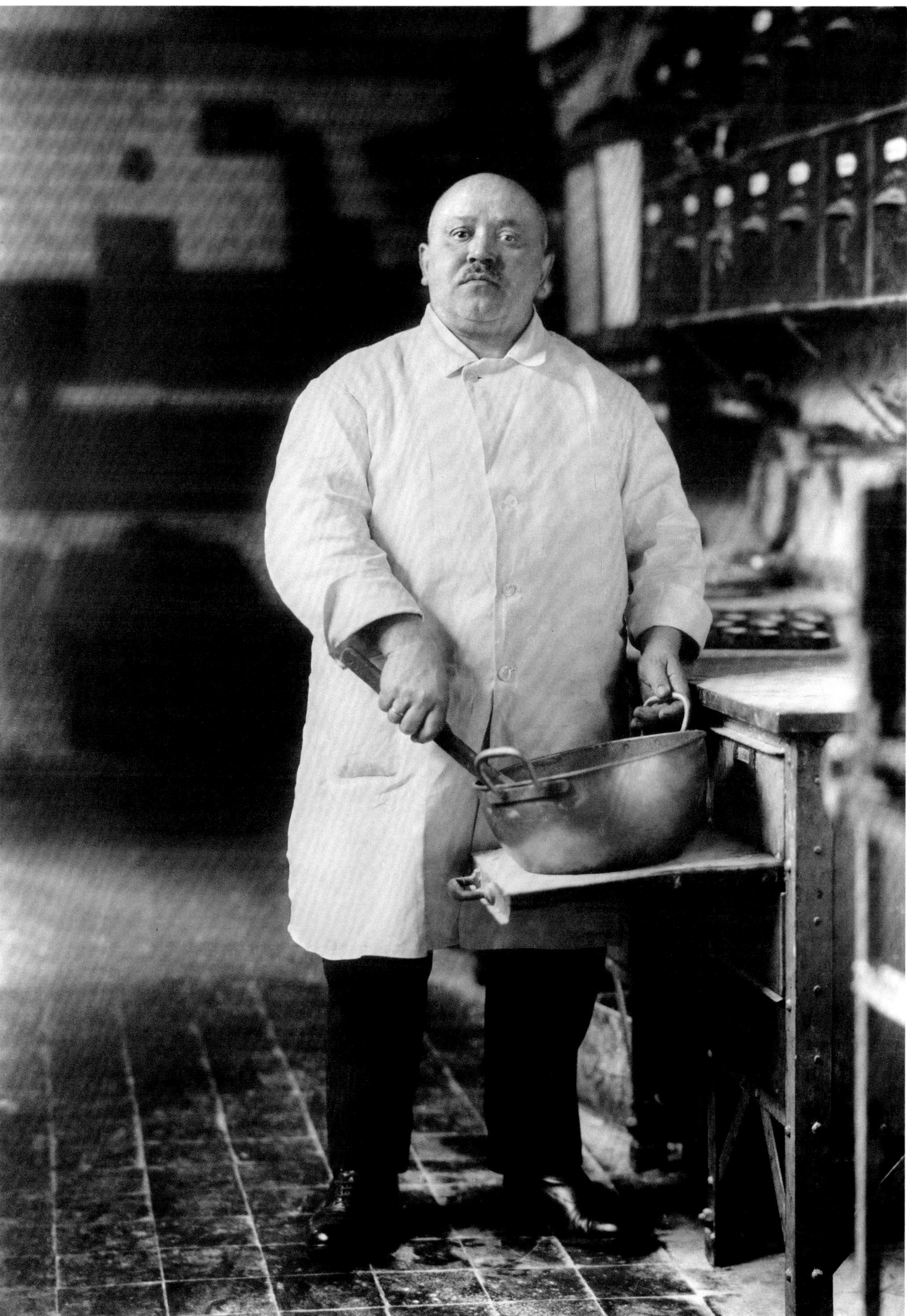

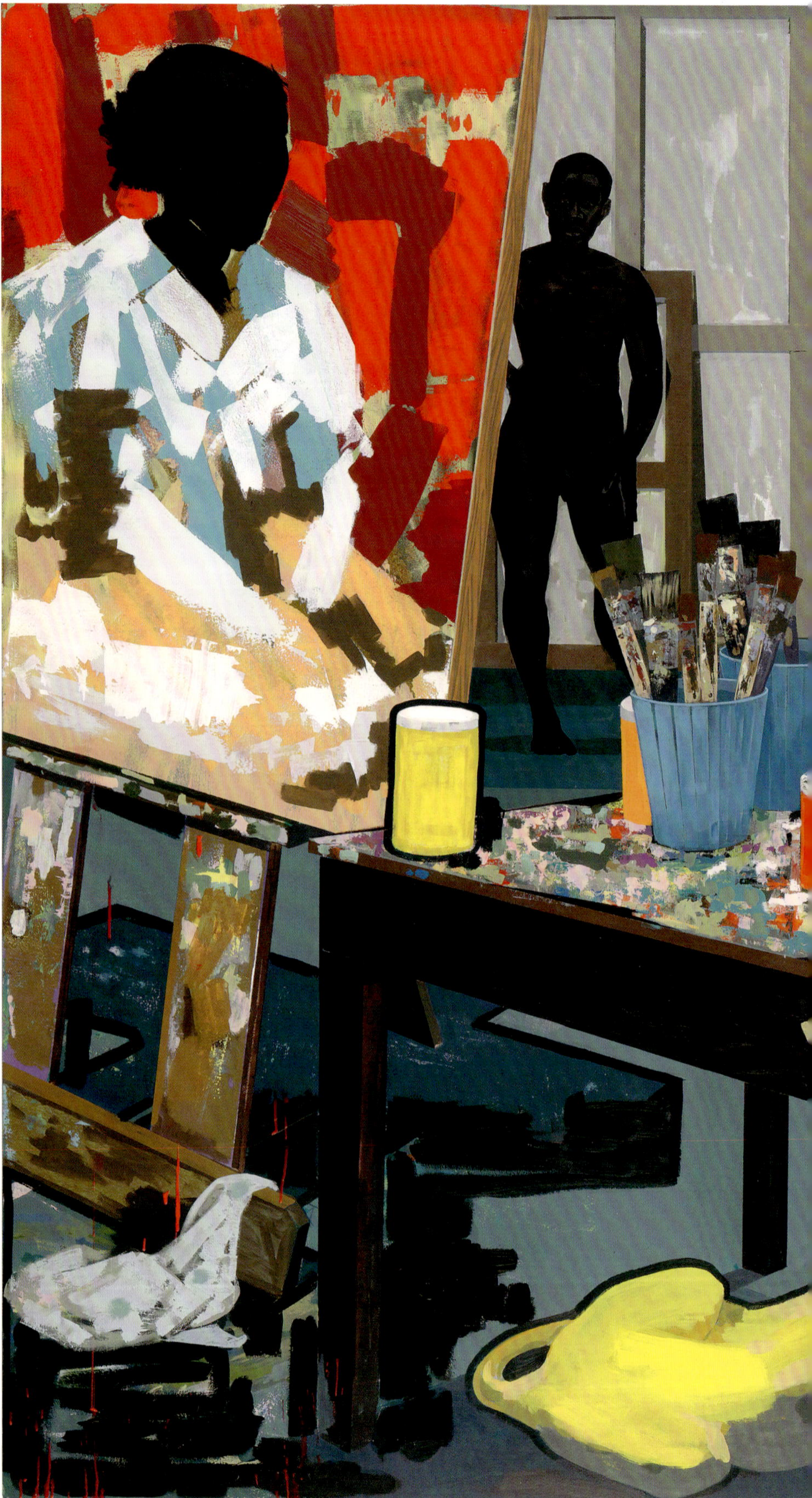

5. Kerry James Marshall (American, b. 1955). *Untitled (Studio)*, 2014. Acrylic on PVC panels, 83⅜ in. × 9 ft. 11¼ in. (211.6 × 302.9 cm). Purchase, The Jacques and Natasha Gelman Foundation Gift, Acquisitions Fund and The Metropolitan Museum of Art Multicultural Audience Development Initiative Gift, 2015 (2015.366)

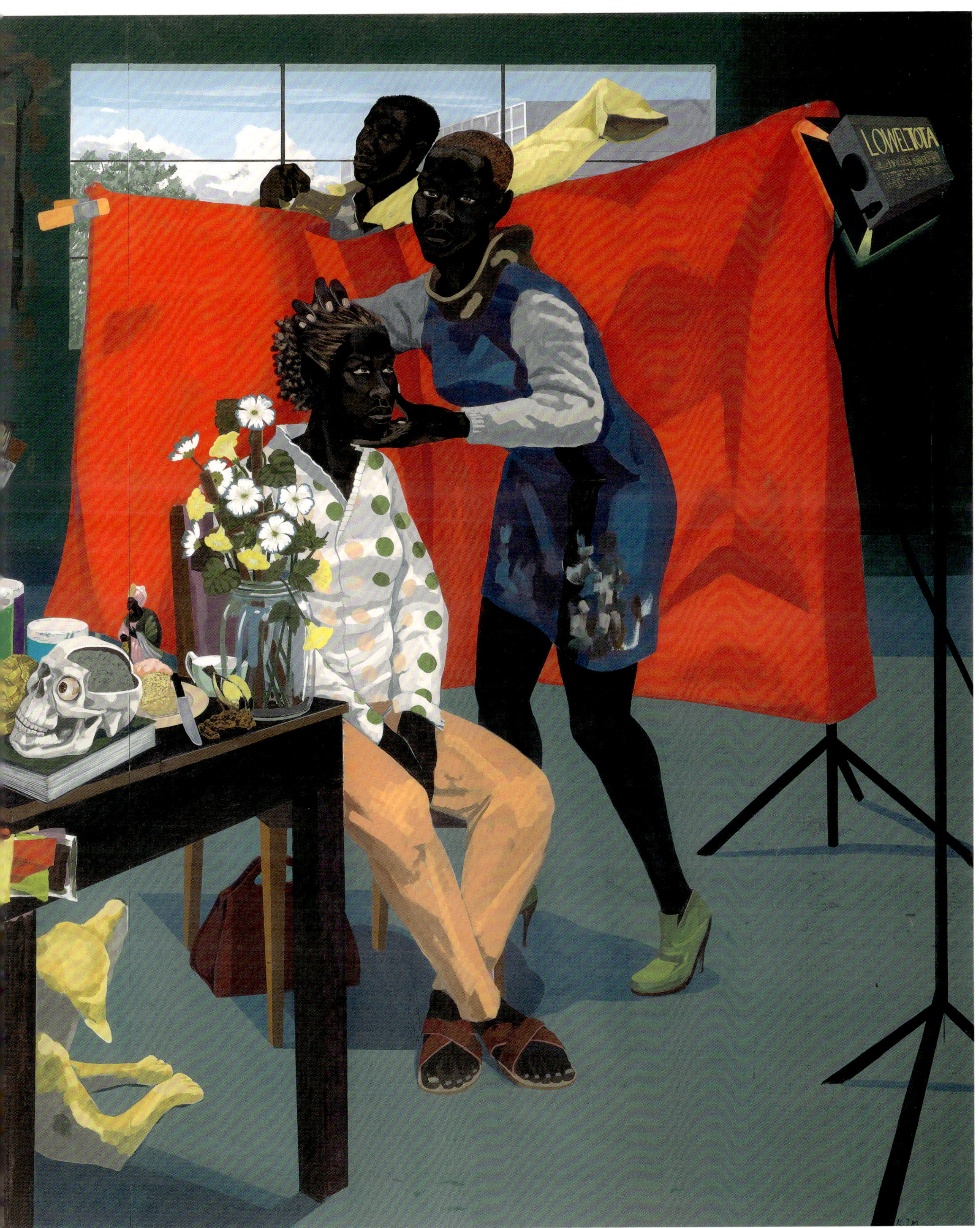
LOWEL TOTA

For the photographer Cindy Sherman, the type has been a vehicle for exploring gender-based stereotypes through portraiture. Since the 1970s Sherman has photographed herself in costume, makeup, wigs, and, occasionally, prosthetics to play an array of mostly female "characters," to use her term. Curator Eva Respini likened Sherman's Untitled Film Stills series to "an August Sander catalogue for the media age" (see fig. 48). The works resist categorization; although the artist dismisses the suggestion that the images of herself in assumed personae are self-portraits, her photographs play on different portrait types, from the celebrity film still and head shot familiar from popular culture to the Old Master *portrait d'apparat* and the self-portrait enshrined in the Western art-historical canon. Sherman's overt role-playing reveals both the artifice and the instability of identity in portraiture.

Sherman's self-portraitlike images are in keeping with the subversive tendencies in portraiture that came to the fore in the aftermath of Manet's Victorine Meurent paintings, whose defiance of clearly defined genres, depiction of modern subjects, and technique scandalized 1860s Paris. As the twentieth century dawned, the portrait increasingly served as a vehicle for artistic experimentation and for the artist's subjective response to the sitter, effectively a shift in focus from the subject to the artist (see figs. 51, 52). A more inclusive repertoire of subjects further altered the terrain of portraiture. Alice Neel's "pictures of people," as she referred to her portraits, challenge the entrenched hierarchy of portraiture by featuring sitters whose race, gender, sexuality, and social class had largely been unrepresented. Neel's work anticipates the emphasis on identity in contemporary portraits. Photographers Deana Lawson and Catherine Opie and painters Amy Sherald and Titus Kaphar have increasingly subverted the Western canon of portraiture as a form of social critique, to remedy its historical exclusion of certain subjects and its focus on Whiteness. Opie's photographs of her friends in Los Angeles's gay and lesbian community evoke the style of sixteenth- and seventeenth-century Old Master portraits, while Sherald paints only people of color, rendering their flesh in shades of gray to underscore their universality.

The subversiveness of Kerry James Marshall manifests itself in his ongoing interrogation of the art-historical canon. Since 1980 he has painted exclusively Black subjects, their skin unequivocally black as, in his words, "a response to the tendency in the culture to privilege lightness." A view of an artist's studio figures among a group of Marshall's paintings that engage with the reciprocal acts of viewing and being viewed that are fundamental to portraiture (fig. 5). Its subject recalls the tradition of portraits of artists at work, from the self-portrait of Diego Velázquez behind his easel in *Las Meninas* (1656, Museo Nacional del Prado, Madrid) to Gustave Courbet's self-aggrandizing portrayal at the center of his atelier (1855, Musée d'Orsay, Paris). Marshall's work is not a portrait, however; it is an imagined studio view, but one in which portraiture takes center stage. At its focal point, an artist adjusts the profile of a seated model under the glare of a Lowell Tota floodlight and gazes outward, as if acknowledging our presence. Is the artist a modern Dibutades, reinventing the art of painting in the twenty-first century? Her subject's unfinished likeness appears not on the wall of a cave but on a paint-splattered easel facing outward for us to see. Marshall playfully embedded references to other types of painting: the objects cluttering the table that evoke still life, the model behind the easel (a male nude—the cornerstone of an artist's academic training), and the landscape glimpsed through the studio window. Even the dog reads as a nod to the faithful canine as an accessory in Old Master portraits, recalling the greyhound in Van Dyck's painting of Stuart. Marshall's wide-ranging vision transcends the imagined studio that is his subject, lending the work the air of a contemporary allegory of painting. That its protagonist is a Black woman artist painting a Black subject redresses historical omissions in the Western canon.

The resurgence of figurative art in the 1980s engendered portraiture's renaissance in all media. The faces we encounter in these more recent works are more diverse, yet the portrait's fundamental emphasis as an expression of identity remains. The cross-cultural reading of portraits that follows underscores the shared preoccupations, bound neither to place nor time, that gave rise to this flourishing and ever-evolving artistic tradition.

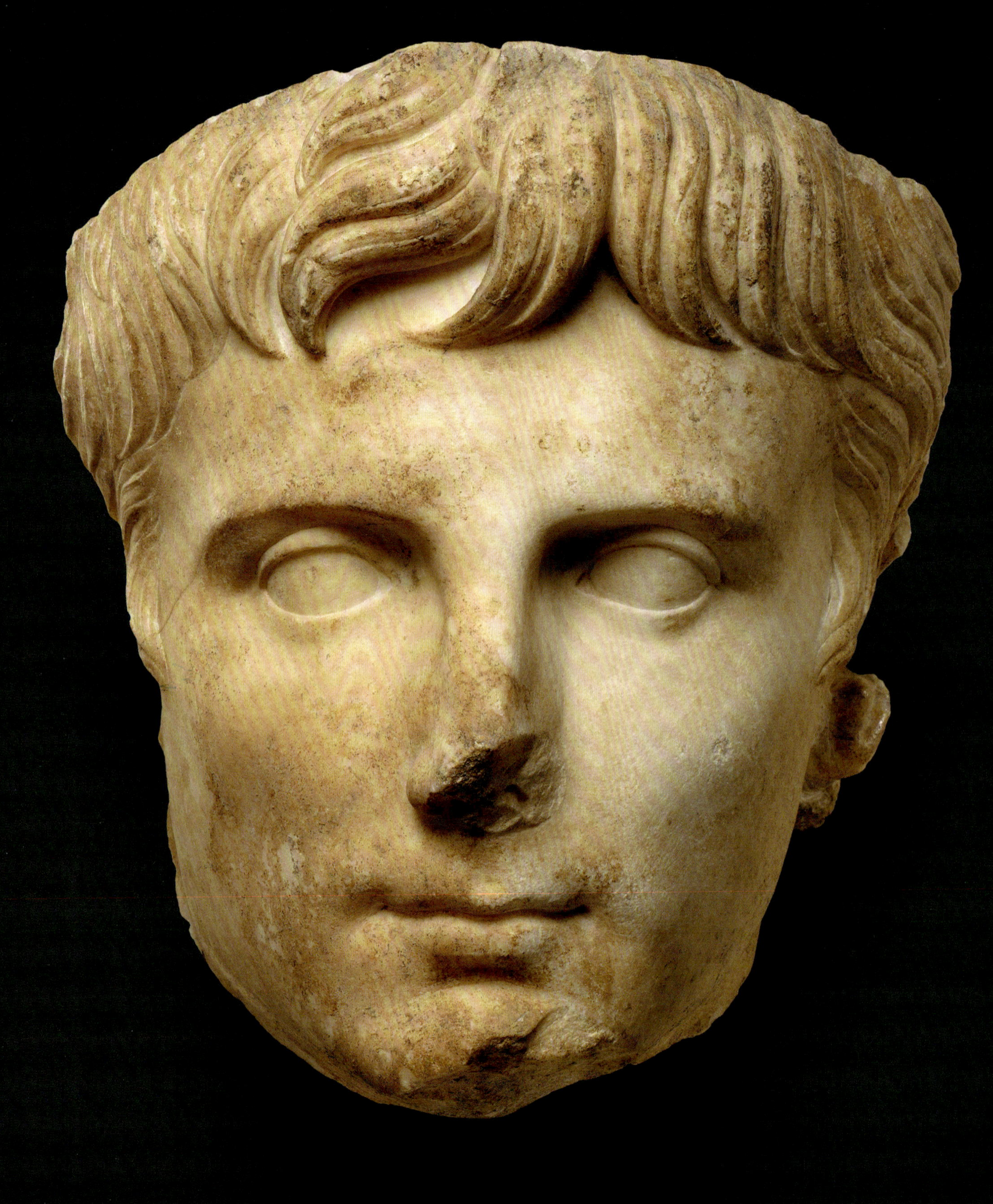

BEYOND FACE VALUE

Throughout its early history, the portrait was fundamentally a record of appearance. The naturalism of Greco-Roman portraiture held sway for centuries, reaching Africa in the first century CE by way of Roman Egypt and informing the portraits that later emerged in Renaissance Europe. Likeness similarly informed Indigenous portrait types in ancient Peru as well as portraiture in Ming-dynasty China. Yet even in these ancient examples, portraits go well beyond face value, whether intended as an expression of power and status or as an exploration of identity.

By the first century CE, when the Roman writer Pliny the Elder composed his mythical account of Dibutades's invention of portraiture, the portrait had become a thriving art form in the West. He wrote in his *Natural History* of "the honor attached to portraits." In his view, a portrait conferred immortality upon its subject and signified "having achieved success in life." Augustus, the first Roman emperor (ruled 27 BCE–14 CE), apparently shared Pliny's belief in the power of portraiture, which he avidly exploited to communicate his imperial authority. His example would be emulated by generations of rulers, from his immediate successors to European monarchs and the self-proclaimed emperor of France, Napoleon I (see fig. 19). With the establishment of the Roman Empire in 27 BCE, Augustus commissioned a likeness, now known as the Primaporta type (named for the Italian town where the work was found), that became the model for his public imagery. A larger-than-lifesize head made after his rule is based on this imperial type, which presents the emperor as "first among equals," as he had reinvented himself (fig. 6). Unlike his earlier portraits, which were more expressive and dynamic, it is devoid of emotion; instead, it projects the calm dignity that the Romans admired in classical Greek sculpture from the fifth century BCE. Augustus was in his mid-thirties when this portrait type was created, yet his likeness is strikingly youthful. His idealized features, rendered in perfect symmetry, bear no trace of wrinkles or furrowed brows to mar the smooth perfection of his face. The large central lock of hair falling on his forehead is also associated with this portrait type. A description of the emperor's appearance recorded later in the century suggests the portrait's divergence from actual likeness. The Roman biographer

6. Emperor Augustus. Roman, ca. 14–37 CE. Marble, H. 12 in. (30.5 cm). Rogers Fund, 1907 (07.286.115)

Suetonius noted that Augustus, while "remarkably handsome," was "negligent of his personal appearance." By his old age, "his left eye had only partial vision. His teeth were small, few, and decayed . . . his eyebrows met above the nose." Nonetheless, Augustus's portrait projected an image of a perpetually handsome and youthful emperor, even into his eighth decade. Its unchanging aspect metaphorically expressed the stability of his regime, which spanned more than forty years.

During Augustus's rule, his image was ubiquitous. It was disseminated across the vast reaches of the Roman Empire on works ranging from everyday objects like buttons and coins (among the earliest vehicles for portraits) to precious cameos and colossal statues, all of which served as forceful visual reminders of his omnipotence. His likeness was perpetuated after his death, and it served as the model for his successors, who sported variations of his distinctive hairstyle in their imperial portraits, signaling both their alignment with his authority and the continuity of the empire. In nineteenth-century France, Napoleon I adopted a similar look, cultivating its imperial associations.

While Augustus established the paradigmatic use of portraiture as a living leader's instrument of power, the portrait was deployed for a different end in Roman Egypt: to serve the dead. Portraits of men, women, and even children, some likely realized while the sitters were still alive, were made to cover the faces of mummified bodies in funerary rituals, providing the deceased a likeness for the afterlife. These portrait busts, produced in the first and second centuries, were painted on thin wood panels with a mixture of beeswax and powdered pigments in the encaustic technique. Known as Faiyum portraits, after the area in Egypt where many of them were discovered in the late nineteenth century, they synthesize Greco-Roman stylistic influences and Egyptian funerary beliefs. Their subjects, shown in contemporary dress, are portrayed in a realistic style that departs from the idealized aspect of earlier Egyptian mummy portraits. The likenesses are individualized, revealing distinct features, hairstyles, facial hair for the men, and even scars. A startlingly lifelike portrait of a teenage boy named Eutyches (his name is inscribed in Greek letters across the

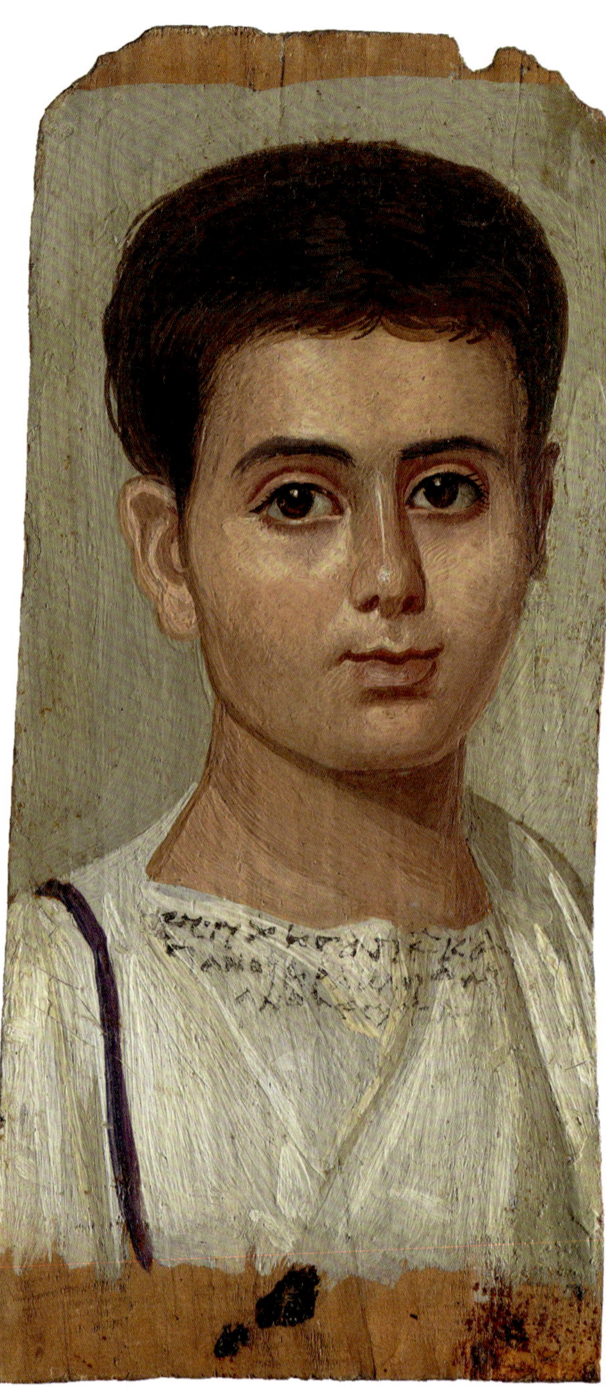

7. Portrait of the Boy Eutyches. Egyptian, Roman period, 100–150 CE. Encaustic on wood, 15 × 7½ in. (38 × 19 cm). Gift of Edward S. Harkness, 1918 (18.9.2)

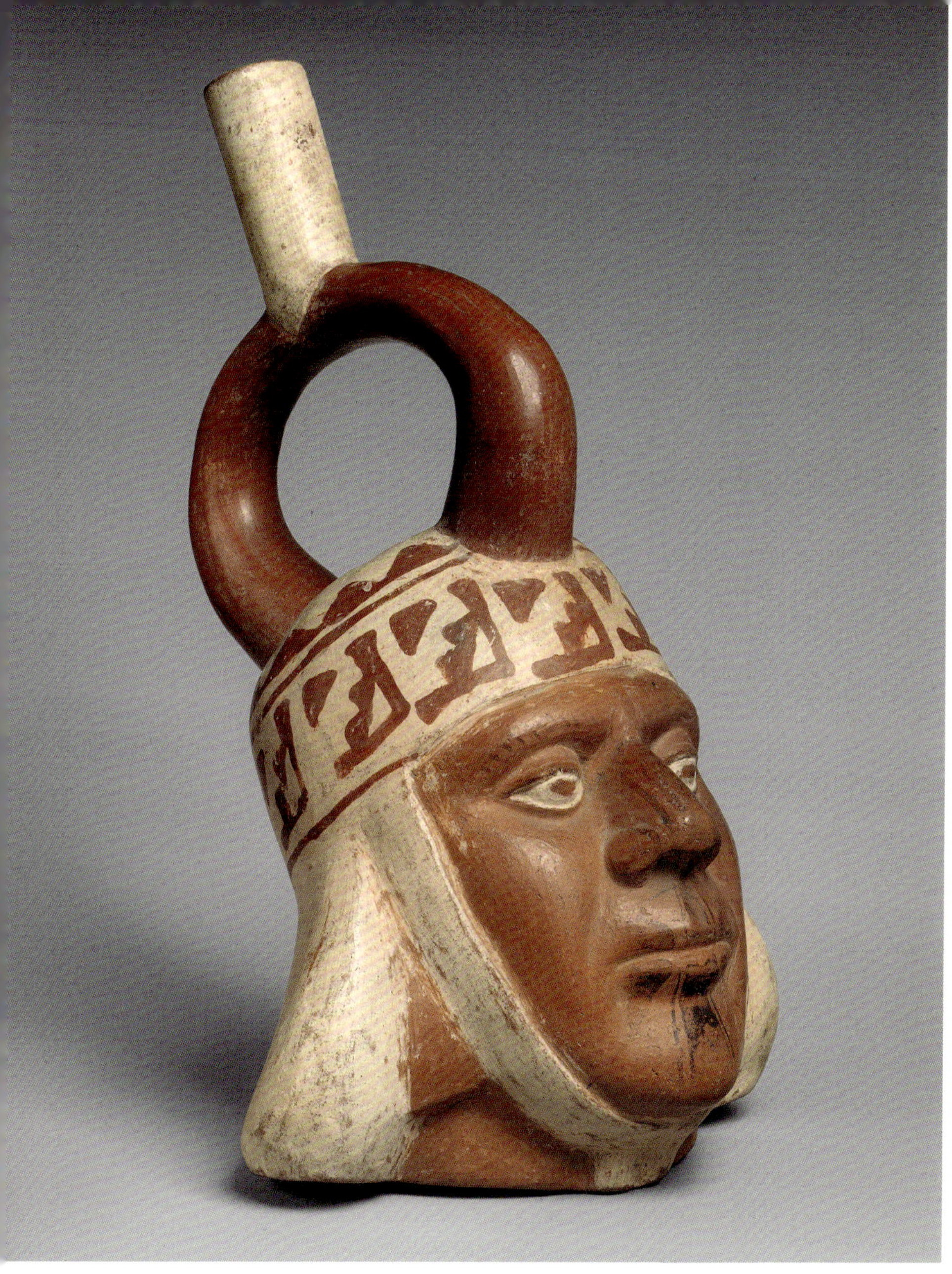

8. Moche artist(s), 500–800 CE. Bottle with portrait head. Peru, North Coast, 500–800 CE. Ceramic, slip, H. 10⅜ × W. 6⅜ × D. 7 in. (26.4 × 16.2 × 17.8 cm). Gift of Henry G. Marquand, 1882 (82.1.28)

neckline of his Roman-style tunic) was realized about a century after Augustus's death, and the teenager's closely cropped curls recall the emperor's imperial portrait type (fig. 7). Following the convention of Faiyum portraits, Eutyches is represented as living: the angled placement of the shoulders and the slight turn of the head suggest both volume and incipient movement; the softly rounded features are modeled through the interplay of light and shadow; and the dark pupils of his larger-than-lifesize eyes reflect points of light. The portrait's naturalism, characteristic of the Faiyum style, conveys the enduring and far-reaching influence of classical Greek painting from the fifth and fourth centuries BCE. Its funerary function, though, is uniquely Egyptian.

The Faiyum portraits attest to the flourishing of portraiture in Roman Egypt early in the first millennium. A tradition of figurative imagery also thrived on the north coast of Peru, where Moche potters produced a distinctive body of ceramics from about 500–800 CE. Known as "portrait heads," these vessels take the form of lifelike, individualized human heads (fig. 8). Nearly all the nine hundred or so known works of this type represent men.

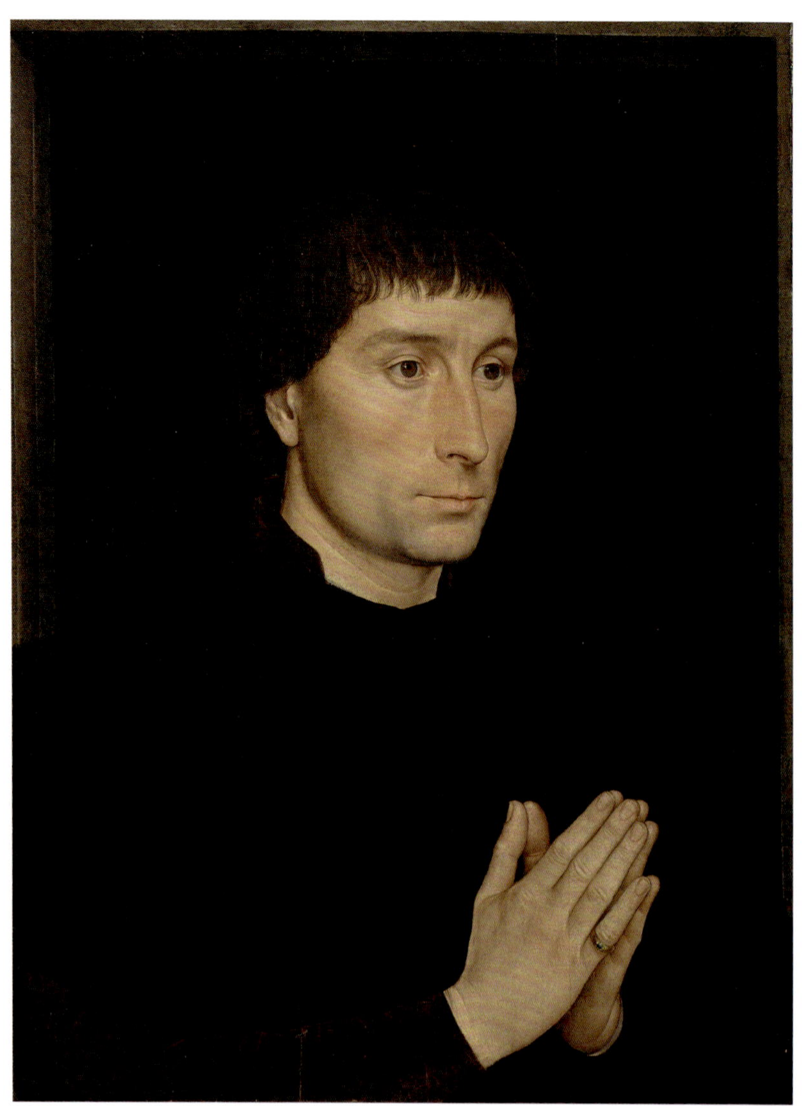

9a. Hans Memling (Netherlandish, act. by 1465–d. 1494). *Tommaso di Folco Portinari (1428–1501)*, ca. 1470. Oil on wood, image 16⅝ × 12½ in. (42.2 × 31.8 cm). Bequest of Benjamin Altman, 1913 (14.40.626)

A stirrup-spout bottle is typical of these portrait heads in its depiction of the subject: with wide-open eyes, as seen in the Faiyum portraits, a tightly closed mouth, and painted details to personalize the likeness. The treatment of the eyes, accented with cream paint, adds an expressive element. As the creation of the Moche portrait heads predates a tradition of writing in South America, both the identities of their subjects and their function remain unknown. It has been posited that the portrait heads represent prominent men in Moche society, venerated ancestors, or the decapitated heads of enemies. For the Moche, the head was a locus of power that contained a life force. Although the vessels were discovered in tombs, evidence of wear on some suggests that they had been used by the living before being buried as part of funerary rituals.

These ceramic heads were formed using two-piece molds (one for the front, the other for the back), which were then painted with slip, or liquid clay, that was mixed with mineral pigments for color. While more than one head could be cast from the same mold, no two are exactly alike: details applied in paint, along with the treatment of other elements, such as ear ornaments and headdresses, individualize the vessels, underscoring their portraitlike aspect. In at least one case, multiple portrait heads were made of the same person at different ages; although his appearance changes over time, he is identifiable by a distinctive scar on the upper lip.

Individualized portraits such as those seen in the Greco-Roman, Faiyum, and Moche traditions waned in Europe during the Middle Ages (from about 500 to

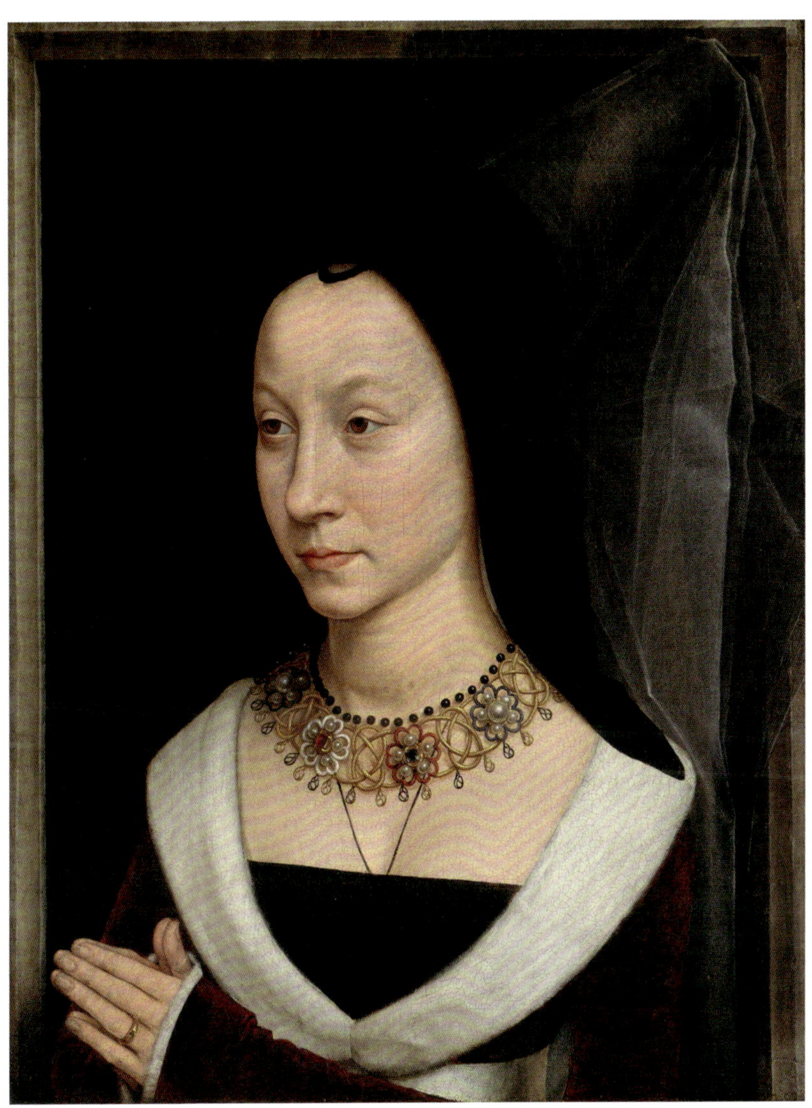

9b. Hans Memling (Netherlandish, act. by 1465–d. 1494). *Maria Portinari (Maria Maddalena Baroncelli, b. 1456)*, ca. 1470. Oil on wood, image 16⅝ × 12⅝ in. (42.2 × 32.1 cm). Bequest of Benjamin Altman, 1913 (14.40.627)

1500 CE), when, under the aegis of the Church, religious subjects dominated the arts. Representations of Christ, saints, and other biblical figures were not intended as portrait likenesses but as timeless embodiments of sacred actors. Such subjects were typically identified in medieval art by attributes, or objects associated with them, rather than by their appearance. Their depictions, imagined by the artist, were informed by artistic convention.

Portraits of living subjects reappeared in fourteenth-century Europe in the form of figures in contemporary dress who populated the margins of illuminated manuscripts, pious witnesses to the biblical narratives unfolding in their presence. They represent the patrons, or donors, of these works of art, who are at times depicted with members of their family. The subjects of donor portraits, as such works are known, are often portrayed in profile and smaller in scale than their sacred counterparts or are painted in a different style, signaling their status as human rather than divine. Although donor portraits represent specific individuals, their primary purpose was to aid their subjects in private devotion, not to record appearance.

Nevertheless, donor portraits evolved in the fifteenth century to convey a more accurate likeness, in keeping with the period's increased emphasis on the individual. One such pair, painted in Bruges, Belgium, in about 1470 by Hans Memling, embodies the new approach (figs. 9a, b). Portraits of the banker Tommaso di Folco Portinari and his wife, Maria Portinari, originally formed separate wings of a three-panel altarpiece, or triptych, facing an image of the Virgin Mary and the Christ

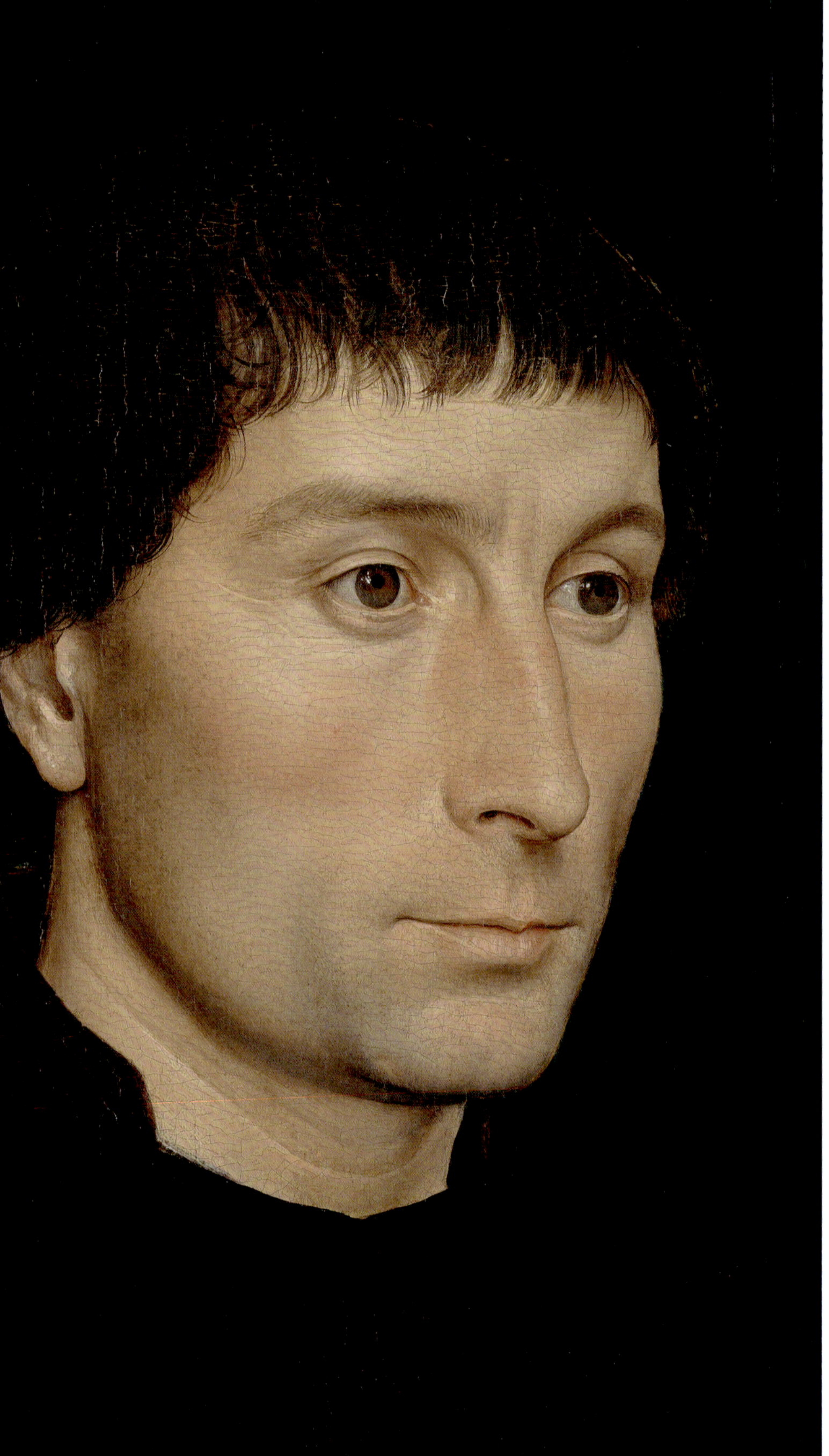

Details of
figures 9a, b

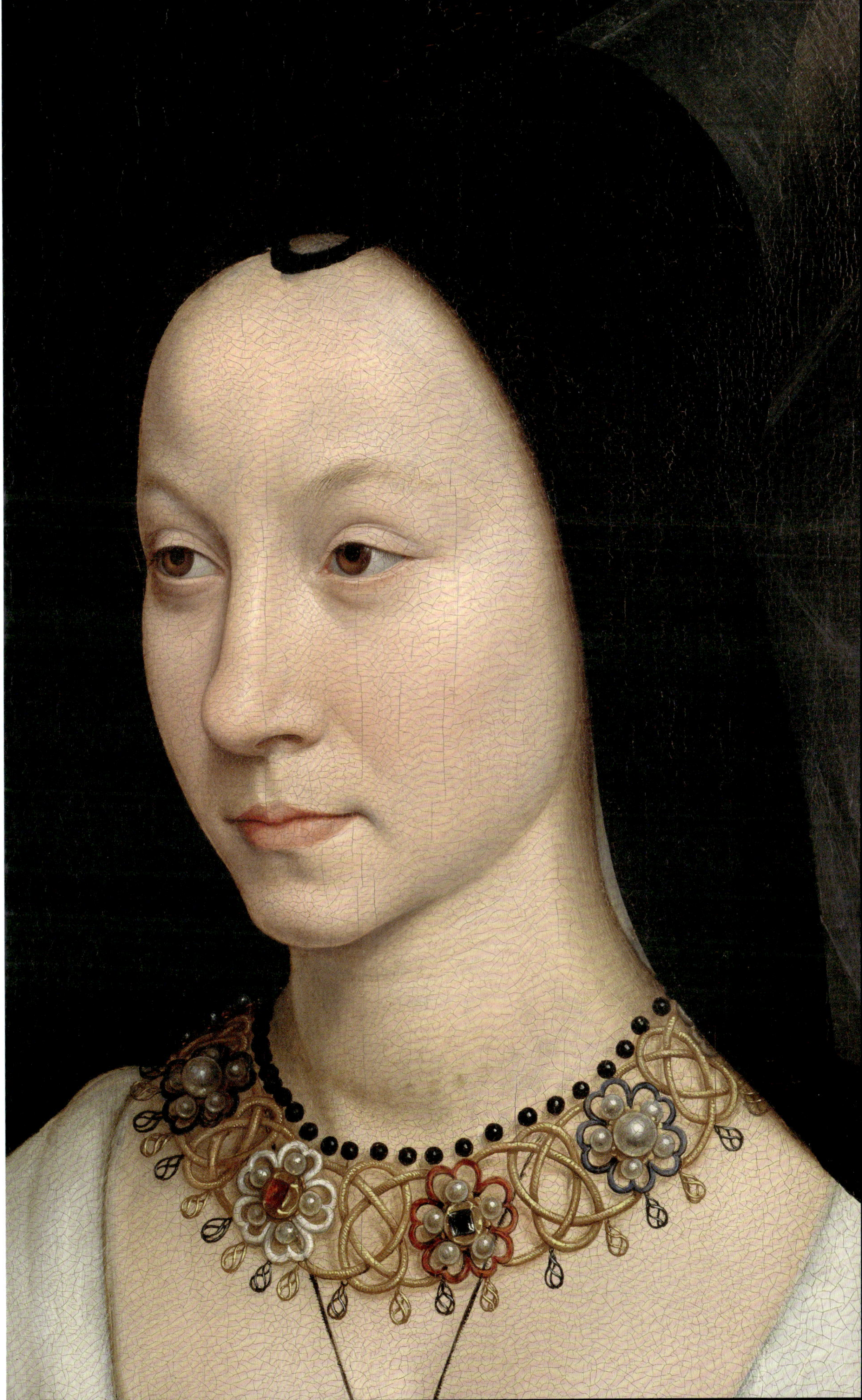

Child. The altarpiece, probably realized in commemoration of their recent marriage, presented the couple as united in their pious devotion. Placed before trompe l'oeil stone frames, husband and wife, each with hands clasped in prayer, seemingly project into real space, an illusionistic effect that heightens the realism of Memling's style. Memling individualized his portrayal of Tommaso, who was then in his early forties, through such details as the scar visible through the trace of stubble on his chin and the crow's-feet at the corners of his eyes. The portrait of Maria, who was only fourteen or fifteen years old, appears more idealized. The smooth perfection of the face, softly rounded and depicted in a flattering three-quarter view, suggests that Memling sought to minimize the teenager's angular features; a nearly contemporaneous portrait by Hugo van der Goes depicts her sharp cheekbones and prominent nose (*The Portinari Triptych*, 1478, Uffizi Gallery, Florence). Memling's fusion of idealization and naturalism in his portraits ensured that his services were in high demand among the elite of Bruges in the closing decades of the fifteenth century.

Beyond recording likeness, Memling's portraits signified the sitters' social status (although the works were probably painted for their personal use), which he conveyed through their clothing and jewelry. The sheer neckline of Maria's dress highlights her elaborate jeweled and enameled necklace. Its resemblance to one that had recently been worn by Margaret of York at her marriage to the Duke of Burgundy has been read as a sign of the Portinaris' close ties to the Burgundian court. The couple is dressed in the latest style, with Tommaso clad in a sleeveless jacket, or jerkin, and Maria wearing an expensive hennin, or headdress, that reveals her fashionably shaved hairline. Later that decade Maria would again don both the necklace and the headdress for her portrait by Van der Goes, suggesting intentionality in her self-presentation in a work destined for public display on the high altar of a church in Florence, Italy.

While Memling made the paintings of the Portinaris to frame a devotional image, portraiture decisively reemerged in fifteenth-century Europe as an independent genre, freed from religious imagery. Portraits were exchanged among nobles as diplomatic gifts and given as tokens of friendship among the elite. In the first modern treatise on the theory of painting, published in Florence in 1435, Leon Battista Alberti memorably conjured the power of the painted likeness: it can both "make the absent present" and transmit individuals' visages to future generations "so that they can be recognized with great pleasure and with great admiration for the artist." The resemblance of a portrait to its subject became the standard by which the genre was judged over the next several centuries; as the critic Roger de Piles wrote in 1708, "the greatest perfection of a portrait is extreme likeness." European rulers relied on portraits to determine the suitability of potential spouses, and a poor or inaccurate likeness was seen as potentially damaging to the reputation of its royal subject.

The popular expectation of likeness in portraiture was perfectly met by the verisimilitude of Northern Renaissance painting such as Memling's and, the following century, Hans Holbein the Younger's. Holbein, who first made a name for himself in Basel, Switzerland, in the 1520s, settled in London in 1532, where he reigned as the leading portraitist in Tudor England. He was renowned for his ability to transcend physical resemblance, imbuing his subjects with a sense of inner life. In one portrait of a young man, Holbein imparted the sitter's commanding presence through his penetrating, alert gaze and imposing form, emphasized by the voluminous cloak in which he is swathed, its satin and velvet almost palpable (fig. 10). The sitter was a German merchant in the Hanseatic League, whose London office was not far from Holbein's studio. It is one of seven known portraits by Holbein of members of this commercial trading group. Significantly, only one explicitly references the sitter's professional identity through props and setting, the *Portrait of Georg Gisze* (1532, Staatliche Museen zu Berlin, Gemäldegalerie). In the others, Holbein communicated the sitters' identities and aspects of their character

10. Hans Holbein the Younger (German, 1497/98–1543). *Hermann von Wedigh III (d. 1560)*, 1532. Oil and gold on oak, 16⅝ × 12¾ in. (42.2 × 32.4 cm), with added strip of ½ in. (1.3 cm) at bottom. Bequest of Edward S. Harkness, 1940 (50.135.4)

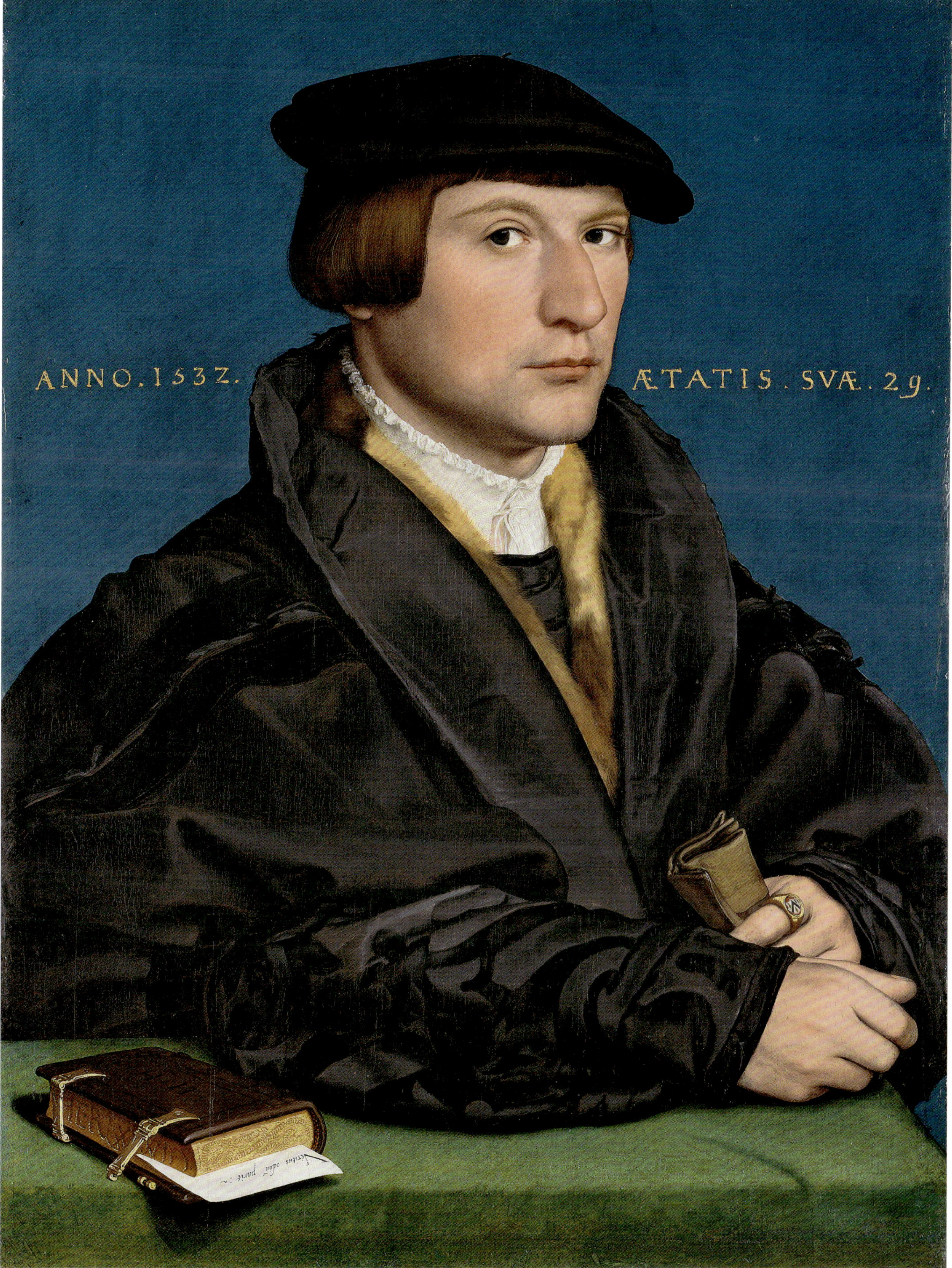
ANNO.1532.
ÆTATIS.SVÆ.29.
Veritas odiū parit :~

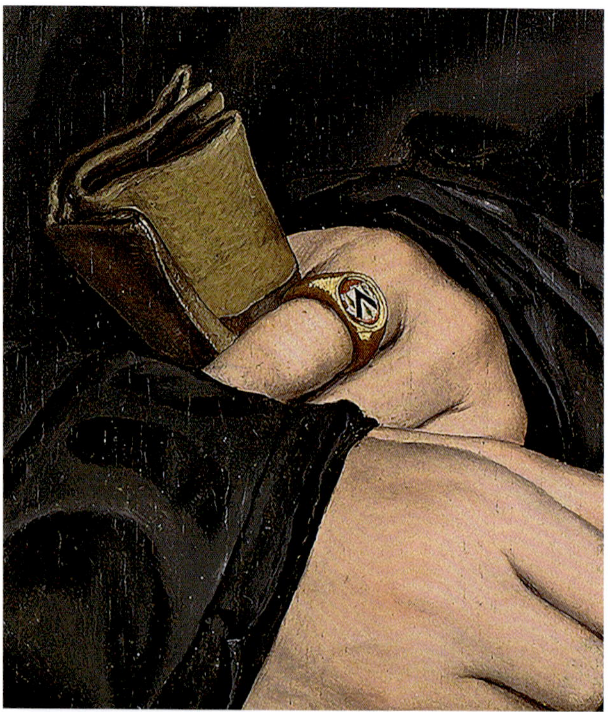

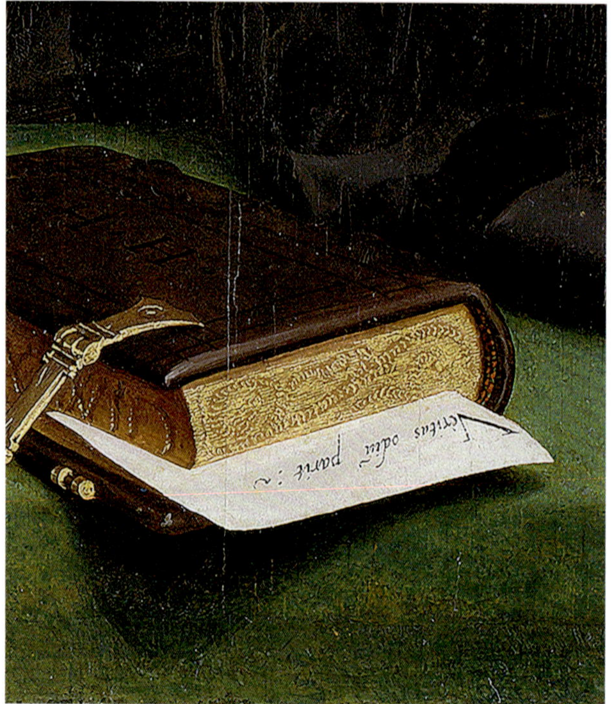

Above: Details of figure 10

through text and accessories. Here, the gilded inscription in Latin that frames the sitter's head tells us the date of the work—1532—and his age, twenty-nine, and marks Holbein's first use of this form of direct address in his portraits. These inscriptions, seemingly suspended in pictorial space, betray the portraits' inherent artifice, despite their lifelike aspect.

The sitter's signet ring, unmissable on his left index finger, bears a coat of arms that identifies him as belonging to the Wedigh family of Cologne. He is probably Hermann von Wedigh III, whose relative, displaying a signet ring emblazoned with the same familial arms, appears among Holbein's Hanseatic League portraits (*A Member of the Wedigh Family*, 1533, Staatliche Museen zu Berlin, Gemäldegalerie). Holbein's sitters—both men and women—often sport such eloquent accessories, including hat badges and jewels that are emblematic of identity and social status. Wedigh also proffers what is likely his motto, written on the sheet of parchment visible between the pages of a leather-bound book. It reads, in Latin, "Truth breeds hatred," a quote from the Roman playwright Terence, whose works were prized in sixteenth-century humanist circles. In Holbein's portraits, such mottoes reflect both their subjects' classical erudition and their personal values.

The verisimilitude typical of Holbein's work resonated in the aftermath of World War I in a German movement known as *Neue Sachlichkeit*, or New Objectivity. Its hard-edged, descriptive realism was both a deliberate homage to the pictorial style of the Northern Renaissance masters and an emphatic rejection of the emotions on display in more recent expressionistic art. Otto Dix's 1922 portrait of the Dresden businessman Max Roesberg, which the sitter commissioned, conjures the German merchants Holbein portrayed nearly four hundred years earlier (fig. 11). Its detailed setting and palette of predominantly green, blue, and brown appear directly descended from Holbein's precedents. Dix also seemed to nod to Holbein's portrait of Gisze, from the shadow the figure casts to the signaling of his subject's profession, as the

11. Otto Dix (German, 1891–1969). *The Businessman Max Roesberg, Dresden*, 1922. Oil on canvas, 37⅛ × 25⅛ in. (94.3 × 63.8 cm). Purchase, Lila Acheson Wallace Gift, 1992 (1992.146)

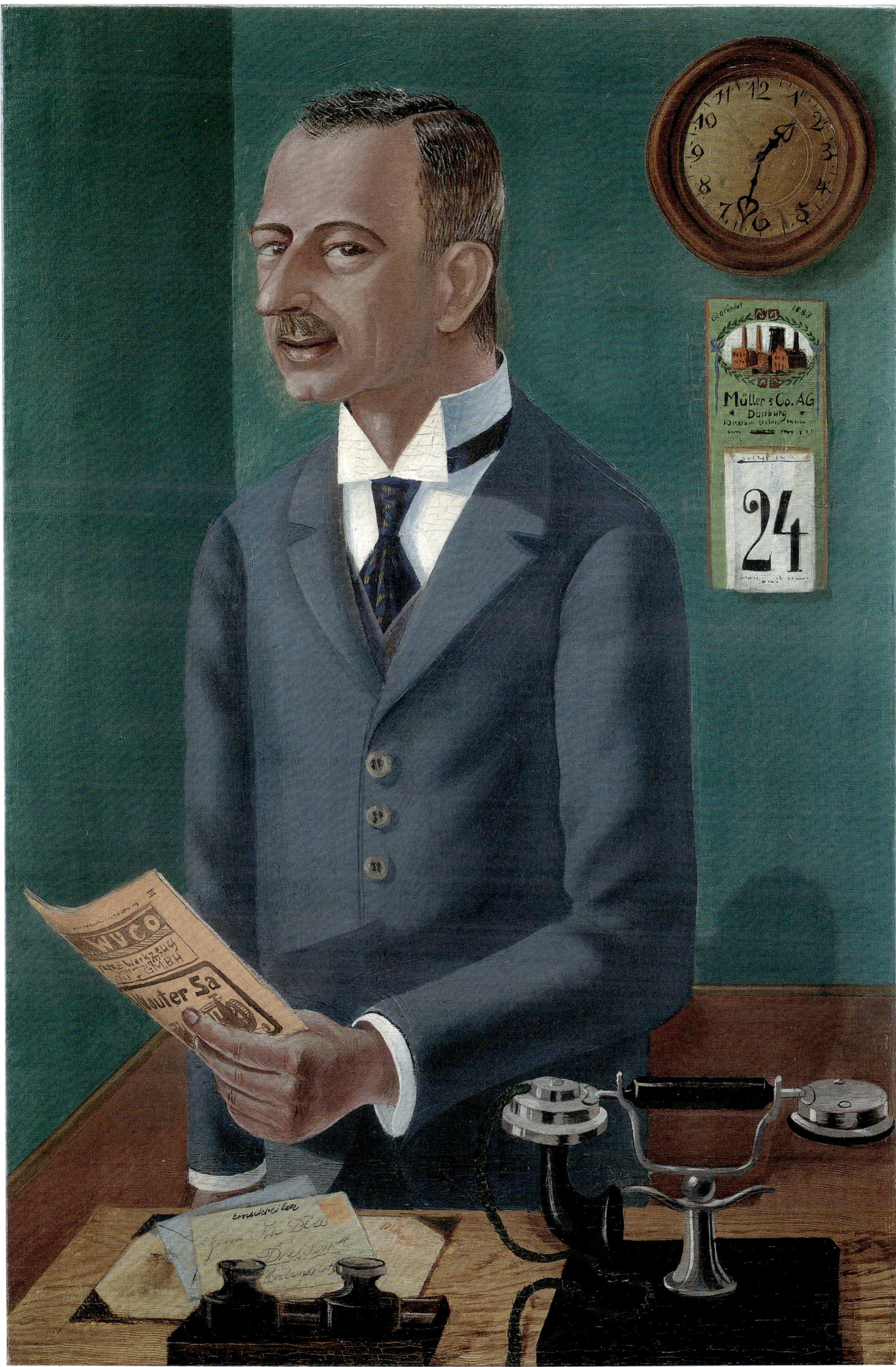

Gegründet 1883
Müller & Co. AG
Duisburg
24

co-owner of a metal foundry, through the objects that surround him in his office. Here the high-status coats of arms and jeweled emblems that signify identity in Holbein's portraits give way to the mundane, from the catalogue of machine parts in Roesberg's hand to a cheap wall calendar advertising a factory, all signs of industrialized Germany between the wars. Prominently displayed in the foreground is the latest-model telephone; conspicuous in its modernity, it nearly upstages the sitter himself, whose pose is as rigid as his starched collar. The clock, which precisely marks the hour at 1:32, might be a nod to its symbolic function in Renaissance art as a marker of the passage of time and, by extension, of mortality.

Notwithstanding the verism of Dix's style, he deliberately departed from rendering the likeness accurately: amplifying the size of the forehead, playing up the angularity of Roesberg's features, and depicting him as noticeably older than his thirty-seven years, in keeping with his practice of aging his male sitters. Such exaggerations are characteristic of the "ugliness" Dix defiantly espoused in his art as an aspect of reality not represented in traditional portraits; they also read as social critique. (That Dix spared Roesberg from a harsher portrayal likely reflects the fact that he was one of the artist's patrons.) His unflattering, satirical approach to his subjects is antithetical to the idealized likenesses that were the specialty of fifteenth-century artists such as Memling (see figs. 9a, b) and the seventeenth-century Flemish painter Anthony van Dyck (see fig. 21). "The essence of every human being is expressed in *their external appearance*," Dix later said of portraiture.

Dix's focus on "external appearance" as a sign of character and August Sander's contemporaneous compilation of a collective photographic portrait of German society (see fig. 4) both reflect the Weimar Republic's broader cultural engagement with physiognomic theory, the belief that facial features were indicative of inner character. The theory had gained currency in Europe through the Renaissance rediscovery of classical texts on physiognomy and remained influential into the twentieth century. In 1920s Germany it infused art and literature and, most insidiously, fueled the racial theories espoused by the rising Nazi movement.

Physiognomy is also deeply rooted in Chinese cultural history, as evidenced by a popular fortune-telling tradition as well as by portraiture. "Whoever paints a portrait must be thoroughly familiar with the rules of physiognomy," according to the fourteenth-century *Secrets of Portrait Painting*. In the sixteenth century physiognomy informed an interest in portraits of ordinary individuals, a departure from the Chinese convention of portraits of emperors, which related to the state cult of ancestor worship and were typically painted posthumously.

A nearly lifesize portrait by the artist Ruan Zude of his great-granduncle, painted from life, represents the newer type of private portrait (fig. 12). It was made in either 1561 or 1621 to mark the uncle's eighty-fifth birthday, according to the inscription along its upper left side. The portrait belongs to a subgenre of Chinese art known as birthday painting; such works were customarily given to commemorate an elder's auspicious anniversary. Ruan rendered the sitter's features in the linear style characteristic of Chinese painting before its assimilation of Western modeling techniques in the mid-seventeenth century. His detailed depiction of his uncle's wizened face—notably the deep furrows of the cheeks, the lifelike expression of the eyes, and the slightly upturned lips—markedly contrasts with the simpler treatment of the man's robe, emphasizing the subject's alert, inquisitive nature.

The birthday painting's imagery appropriately references the sitter's long life. The octogenarian subject wears an inner garment, visible beneath the robe's folded left sleeve, whose decorative pattern fuses swastikas and interlocking *H*'s, symbols of longevity. Recent scholarship suggests that the deep blue robe in which Ruan portrayed his uncle emulates the costly leisure attire, known as *zhong jing fu*, worn by government officials of the Ming

12. Ruan Zude (Chinese, 16th or early 17th century). *Portrait of the Artist's Great-Granduncle Yizhai at the Age of Eighty-Five.* Chinese, Ming dynasty (1368–1644), 1561 or 1621. Hanging scroll; ink and color on silk, image 61¾ × 37⅞ in. (156.8 × 96.2 cm). Seymour Fund, 1959 (59.49.1)

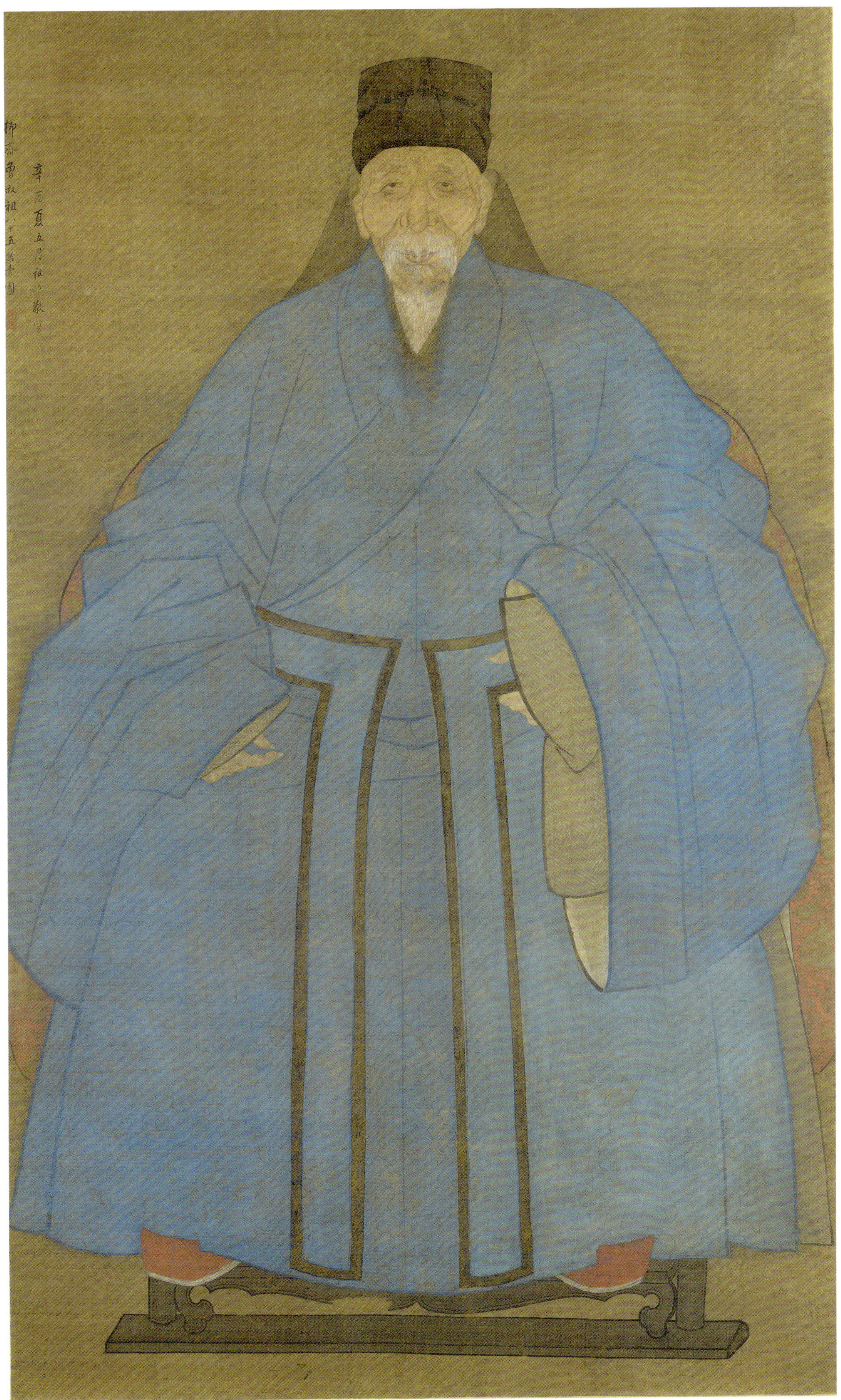
柳齋曾叔祖八十五歲壽圖

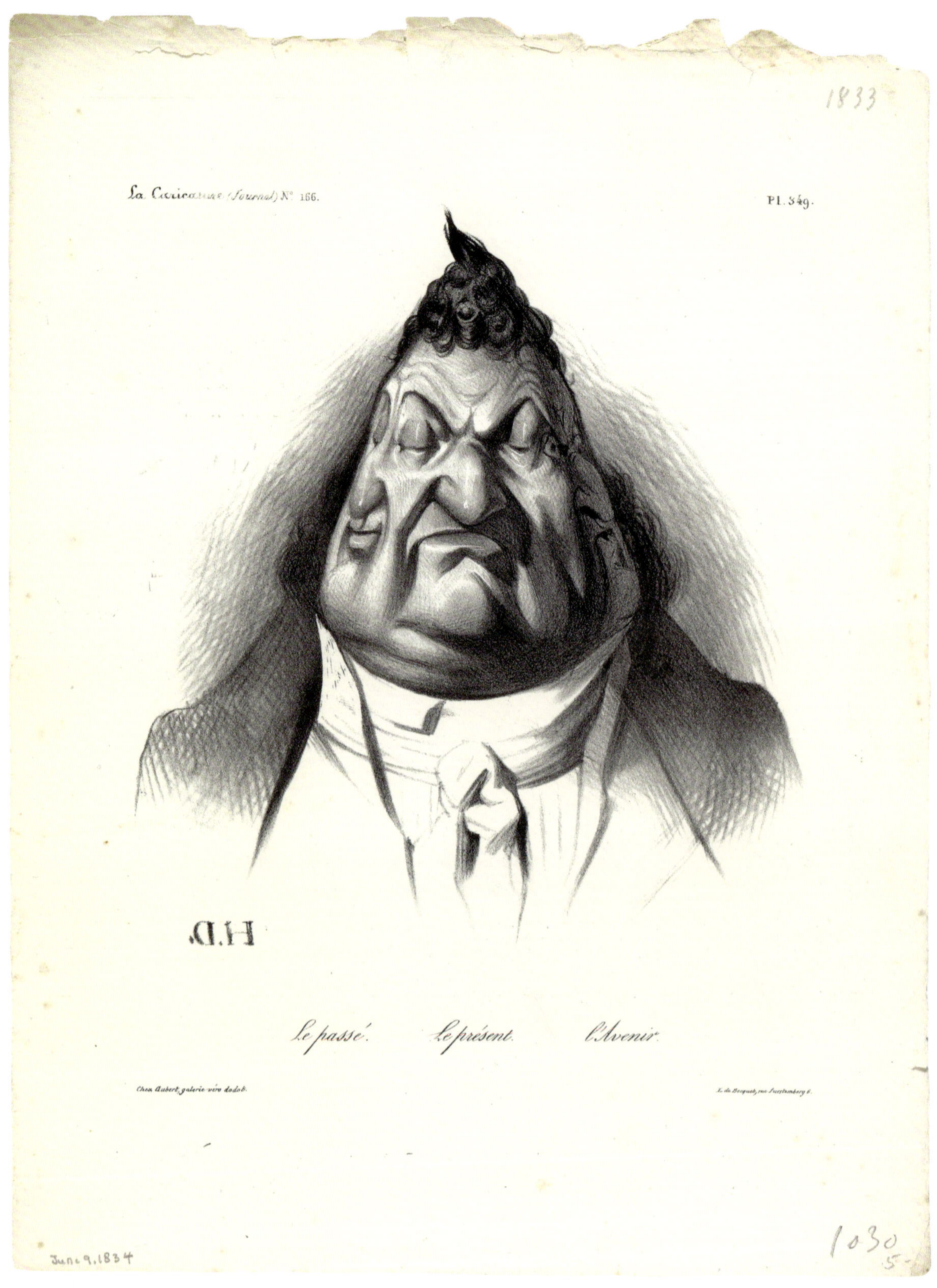

13. Honoré Daumier (French, 1808–1879). *The Past, the Present, and the Future*, published in *La Caricature*, no. 166, Jan. 9, 1834. Lithograph, sheet 13¾ × 10⅝ in. (35 × 27 cm). Harris Brisbane Dick Fund, 1941 (41.16.1)

dynasty. By the late sixteenth century, it had become fashionable for ordinary citizens to wear similar robes as a sign of wealth and status. It is possible that the luxurious robe was a birthday gift, like the painting itself, or the artist may have chosen to paint an idealized image of his uncle wearing such a garment for posterity. Whether real or imagined, the sitter's dress recalls the use of jewelry and clothing as status symbols in Renaissance portraiture.

Physiognomy is also closely aligned with another Western portrait type, the caricature. An exaggerated likeness realized for humorous or satirical ends, not unlike Dix's portraits, caricature came to prominence in eighteenth-century Europe, although its origins date to antiquity. Its resurgence was fueled by the publication, between 1775 and 1778, of a series of influential essays by the Swiss minister Johann Kaspar Lavater, whose assessment of physiognomic classifications and their attendant personality traits informed contemporary readings of appearance as a key to character. Its rise also coincided with an increased interest in the lives of public figures, stimulated by the growth of the popular press. Even the likes of the Prince of Wales and Napoleon Bonaparte were not spared from caricature's comic exaggerations and biting distortions.

In nineteenth-century France King Louis-Philippe was widely caricatured as the embodiment of a corrupt and increasingly oppressive regime known as the July Monarchy (1830–48). His distinctive head, flanked by heavy, bewhiskered jowls and topped by a toupee, was first caricatured in the form of a pear—a fruit quick to spoil, a metaphor for his rotting regime—in 1831; the imagery soon became ubiquitous. The French word for pear, *poire*, a colloquialism for "fathead," also invited wordplay at the king's expense. Honoré Daumier capitalized on this potent motif in a group of political caricatures, including a scathing image of a three-faced king, which was published in the liberal journal *La Caricature* in 1834 (fig. 13). The past, present, and future of the work's title are reflected in Louis-Philippe's changing visage: according to the accompanying description, his face evolves from "fresh and plump" to "pale, thinner, and worried" and finally becomes "glum and decrepit." Over time the pear was so closely associated with the king that its image served as a stand-in for him. The subversive power of this and other caricatures was not lost on the government of Louis-Philippe, which reinstated censorship laws in 1835, the year after Daumier's lithograph was published, effectively suppressing subsequent images of "the pear of France."

However exaggerated the likeness may be, caricature can be understood as portraiture in that its success is contingent upon the recognizability of its intended target. As an expression of character or personality trait, caricature also accords with the idea of the portrait as a reflection of the inner self that emerged in early modern Europe; it aligns with Holbein's use of symbolic accessories and personal mottoes to express his sitters' character.

An increasing interest in exploring individual character can be seen in the advent in the fifteenth century of the literary genre of autobiography, exemplified by such works as *The Book of Margery Kempe*, from about 1438. During the Renaissance, artists' biographies, notably Giorgio Vasari's influential *Lives of the Artists*, published in 1550, stimulated the public's fascination with artists. Both of these trends coincided with the emergence of the self-portrait as a distinct subgenre of portraiture.

Rembrandt was a leading practitioner of the form, devoting more than forty years of his career in the seventeenth century to an investigation of his own likeness. He produced some forty painted self-portraits, as well as etched and drawn ones—an undertaking with few parallels in the history of European art. His self-portraits run the gamut from early, experimental studies of light effects and facial expressions to bravura showcases of his imagination and technical prowess; his etched self-portraits in particular contributed to his fame in his lifetime. Rembrandt's intentions in realizing his self-portraits are far from clear. Scholars have variously suggested that he was engaged in an artistic rivalry with his peers and with past masters such as Raphael and Peter Paul Rubens; that he painted them for a growing market of collectors; and that he was searching for his own identity as an artist. The multiple personae he assumed in his works, donning the guises of real and imagined historical figures as well as that of a virtuoso court artist, wearing a beret and a gold chain, evoke modern constructs of identity as fluid.

Rembrandt began painting himself as a working artist in the early 1650s. Breaking with tradition in self-portraiture and rejecting the prevailing ideal of the gentleman artist, he donned studio garb rather than fashionable clothes. In a self-portrait of 1660, the year he turned fifty-four, Rembrandt, attired in his work clothes, captured his reflection in a mirror (fig. 14). The result is notable for its unfiltered realism, from the wrinkles and furrows of his face to the bags under his eyes, almost tangible in their painterly rendering, to his uneven complexion and sagging jawline. The artist's weathered visage, presented with naked candor, suggests the turmoil Rembrandt had endured in both his personal and professional lives for the better part of the previous two decades, including his 1656 declaration of bankruptcy. Its unsparing approach is characteristic of the self-portraits that chronicle his last ten years, works in which he ultimately forged a new professional identity, according to the scholar H. Perry Chapman. Rembrandt's vacillation in this period as to his projected image—craftsman or virtuoso—is suggested by changes he made as he painted. The present canvas is one of two self-portraits in which he replaced the plain linen cap he wore while working with a beret, like those worn by earlier artists in their self-portraits; in two others, he transformed the painter's cap into fanciful headwear. It was not until the 1660s that he showed himself at work, painter's tools in hand, as in his last self-portrait of about 1665 (Kenwood House, London, The Iveagh Bequest). Chapman contends that in these late self-portraits Rembrandt fashioned a new professional identity, that of the independent artist as craftsman, upending tradition.

Rembrandt's self-portraits profoundly influenced subsequent generations of artists, including Vincent van Gogh (see fig. 39) and Francis Bacon, both of whose repeated forays into self-portraiture recall Rembrandt's practice. Bacon painted his first self-portrait in 1956 at the age of thirty-seven and would paint fifty-two more works specified as self-portraits over the next three decades. The self-portrait had acquired a new conceptual framework since Rembrandt's time, however, notably Freudian psychoanalysis, which encouraged explorations of the inner life that ventured beyond the "profound sensibility" Bacon admired in Rembrandt. For example, in fin-de-siècle Vienna, Egon Schiele plumbed the depths of extreme emotional and physical states in some hundred self-portraits before his untimely death in 1918. Bacon claimed, however, that he was driven by "expediency" to paint self-portraits rather than by the desire to explore his psyche. "I've done a lot of self-portraits," he said in 1975, "really because people have been dying around me like flies and I've had nobody else left to paint but myself." His many and deeply felt losses included the death four years earlier of his lover and frequent subject George Dyer.

Eschewing Rembrandt's realism, Bacon described his own approach as "a kind of tightrope walk between what is called figurative painting and abstraction." A 1979 self-portrait takes the form of a triptych, a format the artist favored in his portrait "studies," as he typically titled such works, as if to imply that they were unresolved (fig. 15). The format calls to mind Renaissance altarpieces that served as vehicles for early portraits, such as Memling's paintings of the Portinaris. Bacon himself likened this presentation to police mug shots, in which the subject is shown head-on and in profile. "I see images in series," he explained, and the triptych allowed him to capture multiple facets of a single subject. In this triptych of his own face, the two side panels mirror one another and seemingly coalesce into a more fully resolved likeness in the center panel. The darkness that obscures his features and appears to deform his head conjures Rembrandt's expressive use of chiaroscuro. To that point, Bacon's description of Rembrandt's "great late self-portraits" applies equally well to his own work: "The whole contour of the face changes time after time; it's a totally different face . . . and by this difference it involves you in different areas of feeling."

Bacon's characteristic formal distortions recall the exaggerated forms of caricature. And, like caricature, the

14. Rembrandt (Rembrandt van Rijn) (Dutch, 1606–1669). *Self-Portrait*, 1660. Oil on canvas, 31⅝ × 26½ in. (80.3 × 67.3 cm). Bequest of Benjamin Altman, 1913 (14.40.618)

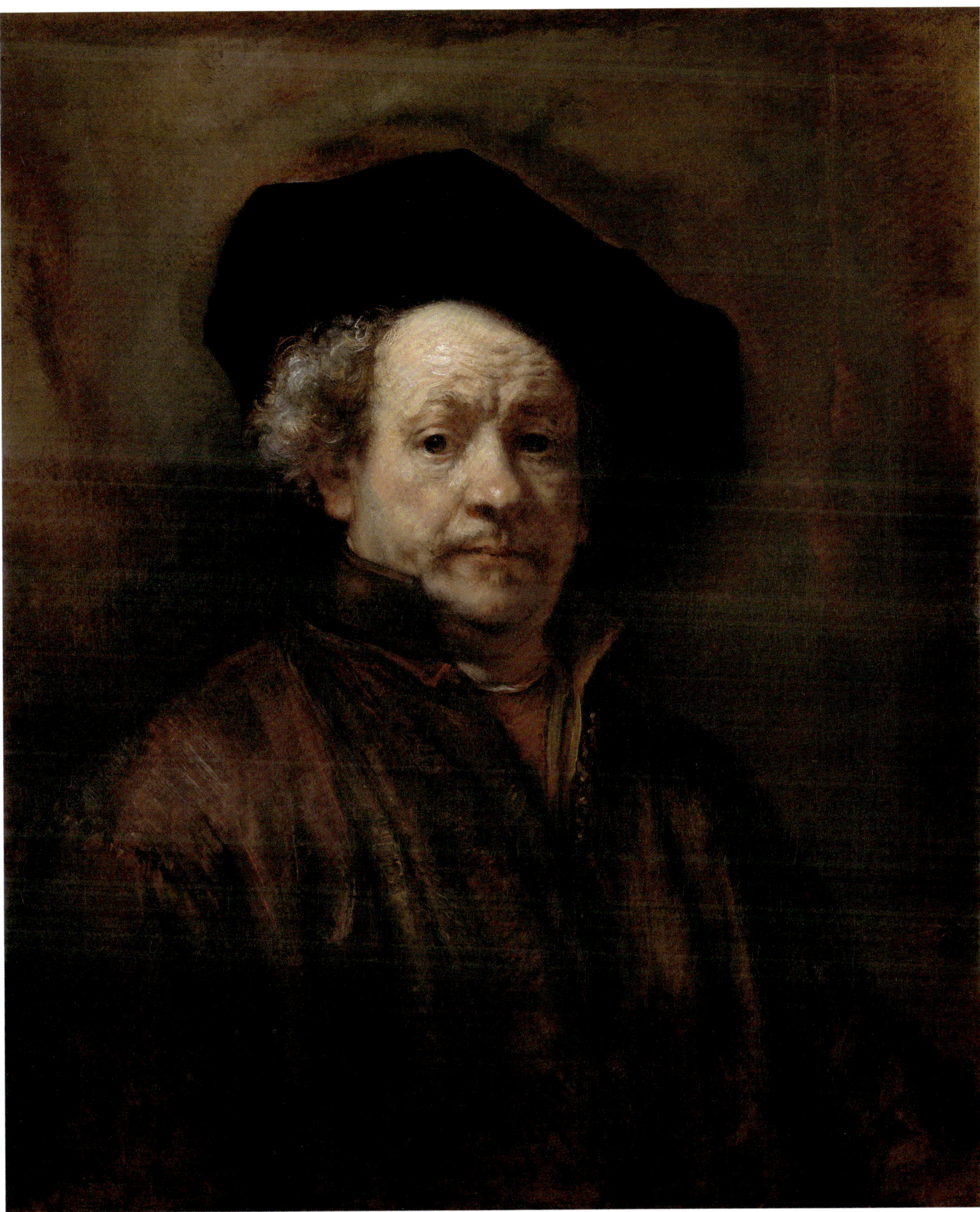

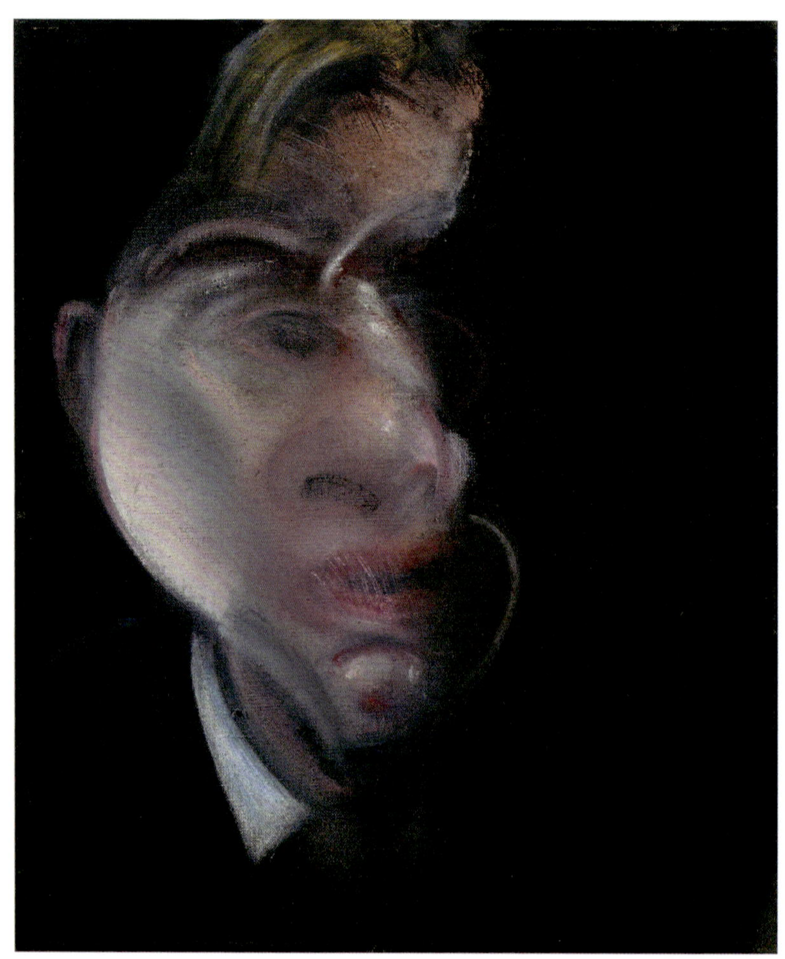

15. Francis Bacon (British, b. Ireland, 1909–1992). *Three Studies for Self-Portrait*, 1979. Oil on canvas, each 14¾ × 12½ in. (37.5 × 31.8 cm). Jacques and Natasha Gelman Collection, 1998 (1999.363.1a–c)

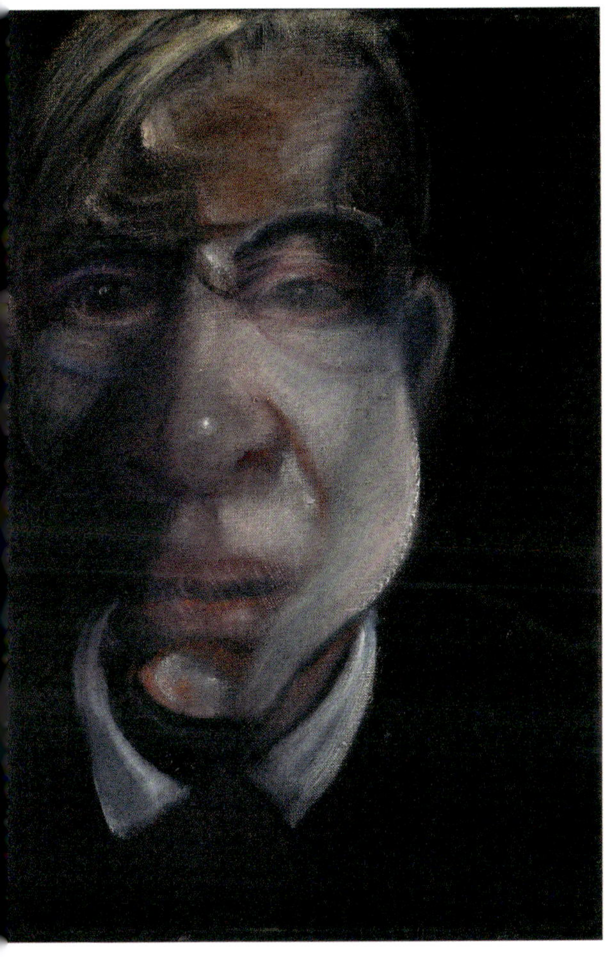

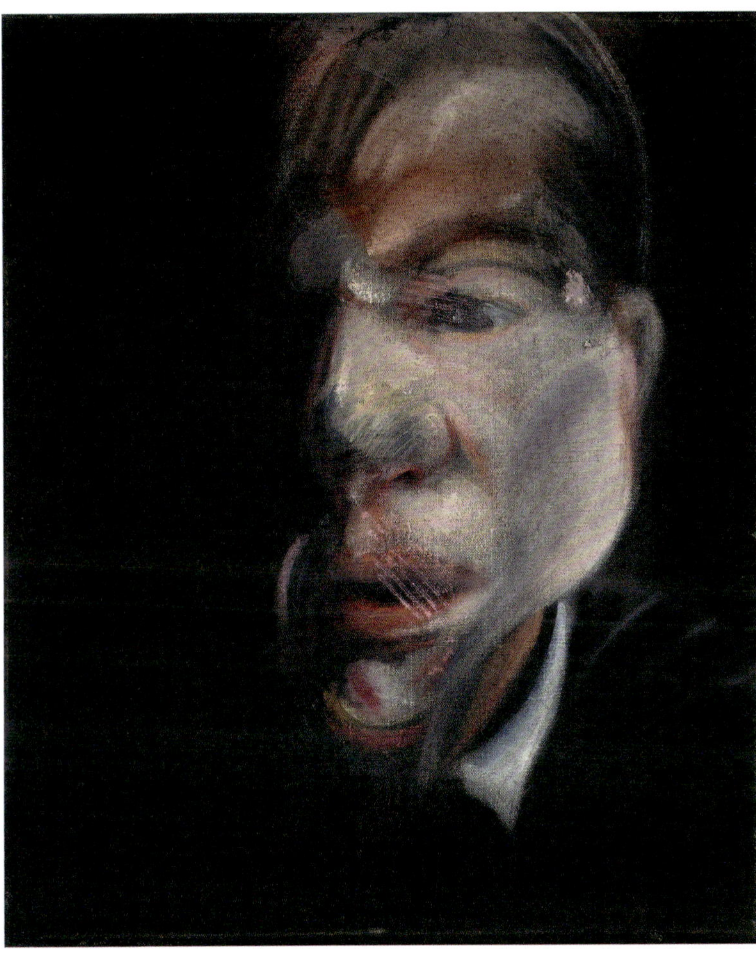

artist's work is firmly grounded in recognizable likeness. "One wants a thing to be as factual as possible and at the same time as deeply suggestive or deeply unlocking of areas of sensation," he explained. Despite the distortions, the trio of faces in his triptych—all gazing outward with slightly parted lips, as if speaking—are infused with a lifelike immediacy, as in Rembrandt's self-portrait. But while his predecessor achieved that effect with uncompromising realism, Bacon transcended likeness, believing that a portrait was truer to reality if went beyond what he called "simple illustration." Nonetheless, his search for artistic truth attests to the endurance of likeness as the foundation of portraiture—whether as a goal or as a point of departure.

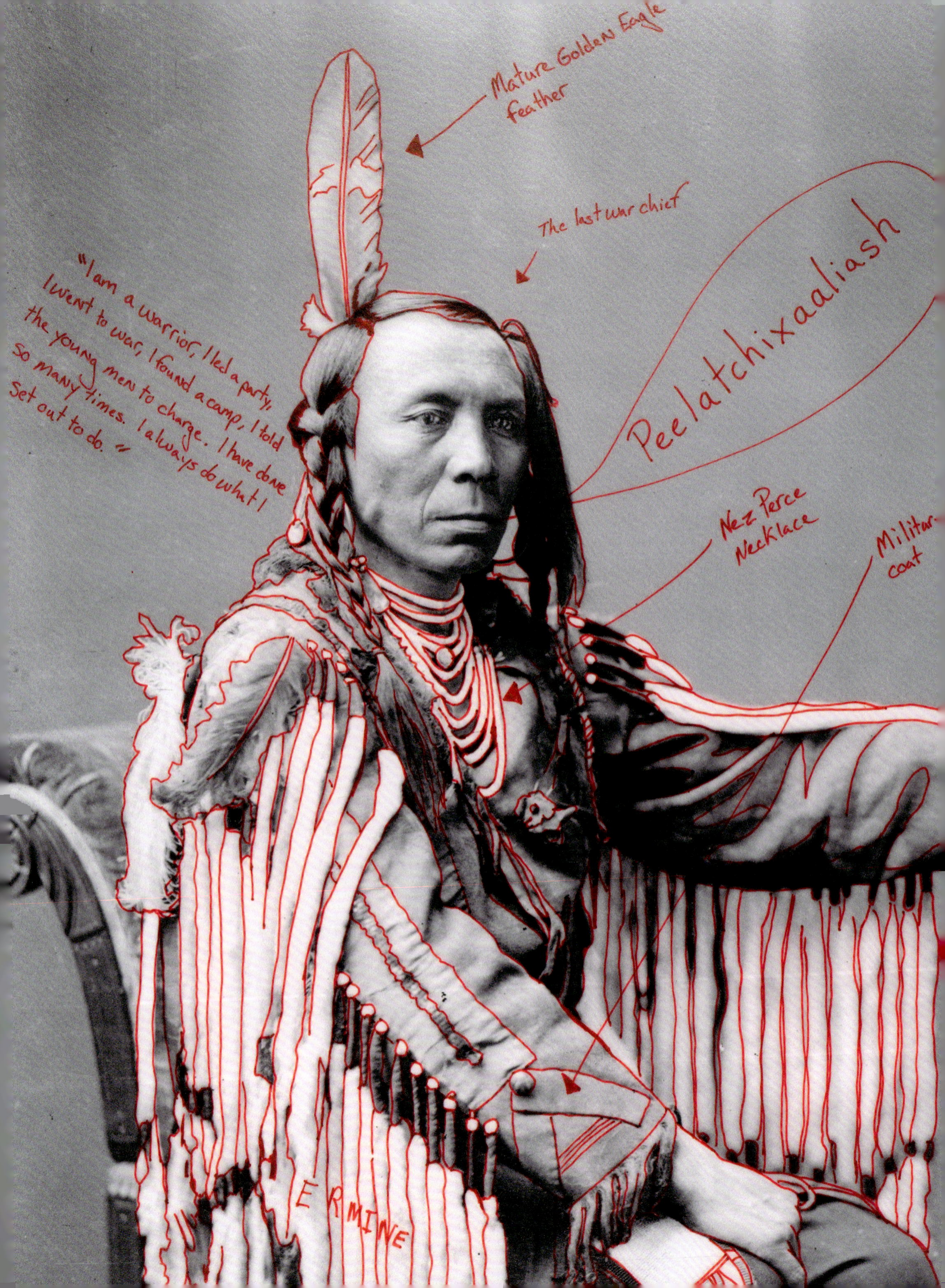
Mature Golden Eagle feather
The last war chief
Peelatchixaaliash
"I am a warrior, I led a party, I went to war, I found a camp, I told the young men to charge. I have done so many times. I always do what I set out to do."
Nez Perce Necklace
Militar coat
ERMINE

THE LANGUAGE OF POWER

Portraiture soared to prominence in sixteenth-century Europe as elites capitalized on their painted likenesses' capacity to convey their power and social status. Monarchs including Elizabeth I, queen of England, and Charles V, Holy Roman emperor and king of Spain, deployed the portrait as an embodiment of their absolute authority. Some contemporary commentators advocated that the genre be reserved for subjects who were worthy, by royal birthright or individual accomplishment, of the honor of being portrayed. However, affluent members of the professional class, from the Medici banker Tommaso Portinari in Bruges to the merchants of the Hanseatic League in London, also sought to have their portraits painted as a mark of their standing in society (see figs. 9a, 10). Not incidentally, these wealthy patrons were often portrayed by the same artists as royal and aristocratic sitters, elevating their status by association. In response to the burgeoning demand for portraits as representations of authority and prestige, artists developed a language of pose and gesture, often enhanced by the expressive use of props and setting, that became synonymous with power. Many of the artistic conventions that took hold in the sixteenth century endure to this day, even as the range of people portrayed has expanded across class, race, and gender in response to evolving social mores and shifting dynamics of power.

An influential precedent for the portrait as a projection of power dates to the dawn of the first millennium, when the Roman emperor Augustus utilized his sculpted, idealized image to assert imperial authority (see fig. 6); his model resonated for centuries in Europe and beyond, as seen in two early sixteenth-century dynastic portraits, one from the kingdom of Benin (now southern Nigeria) and the other from the Florentine Republic (figs. 17, 18). Although a tradition of idealized portraits of rulers had been established in Benin during the fifteenth century, images of women rarely figured in its royal imagery. An ivory pendant mask has been identified as a portrait of Idia, the queen mother, or *iyoba*; she was the first woman in the Oranmiyan dynasty to hold this honorific title, which was created by her son, Oba (King) Esigie, and still exists. Its form reflects the symbolic importance of the head for the Edo peoples of Benin as the source of thought and character and, by extension, one's destiny. In keeping with the portrait's commemorative function, its subject has been idealized, as reflected by the serene expression

16. Wendy Red Star. *Peelatchixaaliash/Old Crow (Raven)*, 2014 (detail of figure 26)

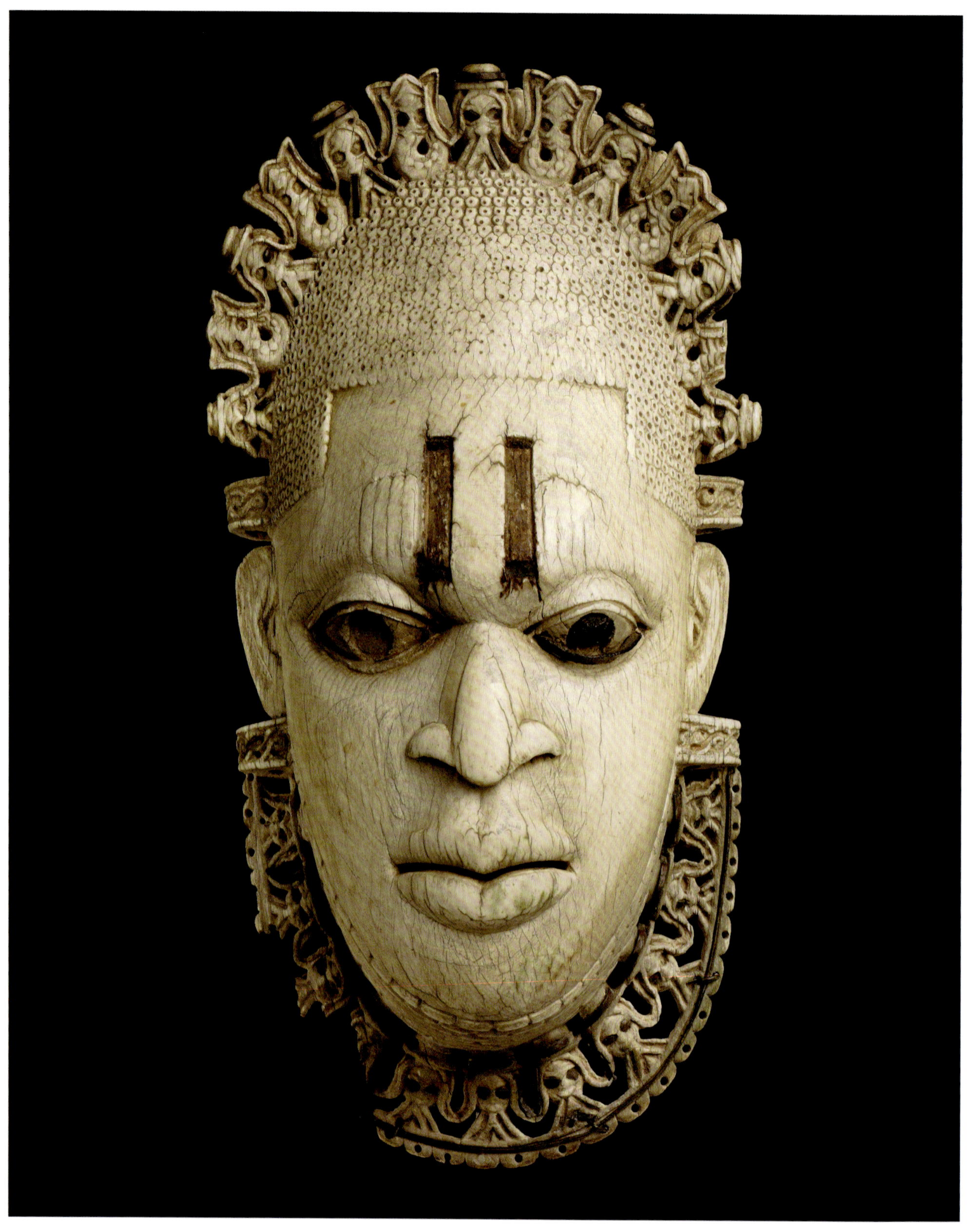

17. Edo artist. *Queen Mother Pendant Mask: Iyoba.* Nigeria, Igun-Eronmwen guild, Court of Benin, 16th century. Ivory, iron, copper (?), H. 9 3/8 × W. 5 × D. 2 1/2 in. (23.8 × 12.7 × 6.4 cm). The Michael C. Rockefeller Memorial Collection, Gift of Nelson A. Rockefeller, 1972 (1978.412.323)

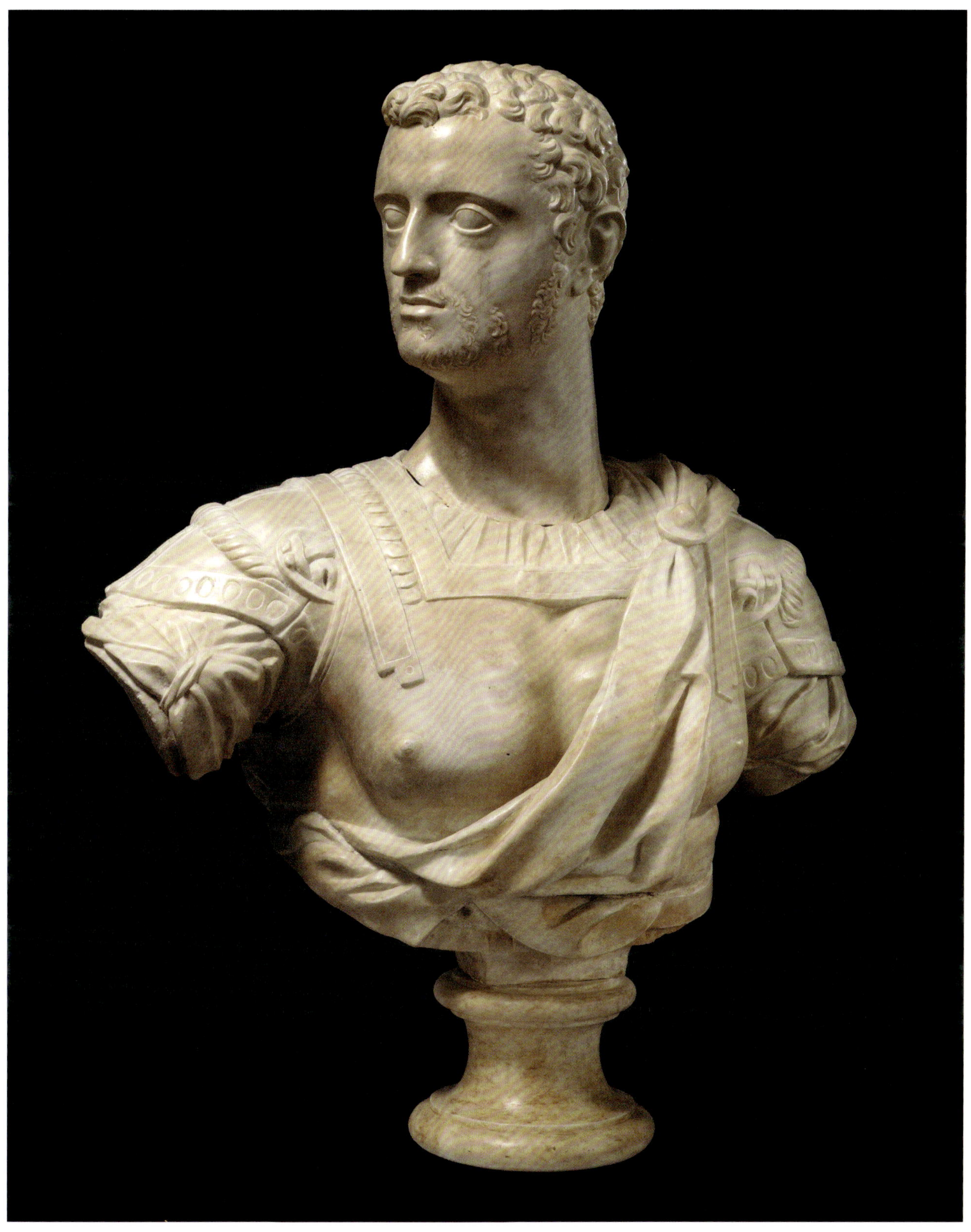

18. Baccio Bandinelli (Italian, 1493–1560). *Cosimo I de' Medici (1519–1574), Duke of Florence*, 1539–40. Marble, H. 31½ × W. 30⅞ × D. 12 in. (80 × 78.4 × 30.5 cm); with socle: H. 37¾ in. (95.9 cm). Wrightsman Fund, 1987 (1987.280)

and the perfect symmetry of the features. The portrait was likely realized while Idia was alive or soon after her death. Her image recalls earlier representations of Benin rulers, underscoring both her royal status and the continuation of the dynasty—much the way the idealized portraits of Augustus's successors did during the Roman Empire, as the African art scholar Alisa LaGamma has noted. At the same time, the queen mother's likeness is individualized to the point that it is recognizable in another, nearly identical ivory mask (The British Museum, London).

The portrait's potency is reinforced both by the material of which it is made and by the imagery that appears in the queen mother's crown and collar, attributes of royalty. In Benin culture, the white of the ivory evokes the god of the sea, Olokun, who is the king's spiritual counterpart. The abundance of ivory in the region attracted Portuguese traders, who brought wealth to the kingdom; they appear as symbols of the king's power in the bearded faces that are carved into the crown and collar. In the crown, their stylized visages alternate with carved mudfish, which can survive in both the sea and on land by burrowing in the mud, an allusion to the king's dual nature as human and divine. The portrait mask is hollow, suggesting that it functioned as an amulet, worn by the king during rituals, attesting to the power of both the portrait and its subject.

The Benin mask's affinity with antique prototypes such as the Roman imperial portrait demonstrates a shared artistic vocabulary for representing power in the African and European artistic canons. Similarly, the Florentine duke Cosimo I de' Medici, who came to rule through a military coup in 1537, at the age of seventeen, adopted the classicizing language of authority from Roman imperial prototypes to legitimize his power.

In the early years of his reign as duke of Florence, Cosimo favored portraits of himself in armor to assert his military might. A marble bust by Baccio Bandinelli, made in the decade after Cosimo came to power, depicts the duke *all'antica*, or "in antique fashion" (see fig. 18). He sports a form-fitting armor in the style of an ancient Roman type known as a lorica and a cloak, typically worn by Roman military commanders, called a *paludamentum*, which is draped over the armor and fastened at his left shoulder. Roman emperors were often portrayed wearing such a cloak in their portrait statuary and on coinage as a symbol of their military authority. Here, the diagonal placement of its drapery accentuates the dynamism of Cosimo's pose, marked by a sharp turn of the head. Presented as a side view, his image recalls the profile busts of Roman emperors on coins and cameos. Cosimo's eyes were carved without pupils, recalling the unincised eyes characteristic of sculpted busts of Augustus. In fact, Cosimo consciously modeled himself after the Roman emperor, whom he venerated; his art collection included a bust as well as cameo portraits of Augustus. While Cosimo's features are idealized, in keeping with the Augustan model, the portrait is also individualized, like that of Idia, the Benin queen mother. In a departure from Roman imperial prototypes, Cosimo's likeness includes the beard with which he then styled himself, as seen in contemporaneous portraits. Subsequent *all'antica* portrait busts of the duke from the 1540s attest to their political efficacy when Cosimo was consolidating his power. Through his public image, Cosimo astutely aligned himself with Augustus and his imperial lineage, reinforcing his own claim to rule. Nearly three hundred years later, Napoleon Bonaparte would do the same in France.

Bonaparte, who also rose to power in a coup d'état, declared himself emperor of France in 1804. And, like Cosimo, Emperor Napoleon I marshaled art to assert his legitimacy as a ruler. An 1805 portrait by François Gérard shows him swathed in the ermine-lined velvet mantle that he wore for his coronation and draws upon images of both imperial and royal authority. Signaling its success as an official portrait, multiple copies were made for distribution throughout the empire and, upon the order of Napoleon himself, it was reproduced as a tapestry, woven between 1808 and 1811 at Gobelins, the imperial tapestry works (fig. 19). Gérard's painting is likely based on an

19. Manufacture Nationale des Gobelins (French, est. 1662), after an 1805 painting by baron François Gérard (French, 1770–1837). *Portrait of Napoleon I*, woven 1808–11. Wool, silk, silver-gilt thread, 87½ × 57½ in. (222.3 × 146.1 cm). Purchase, Joseph Pulitzer Bequest, 1943 (43.99)

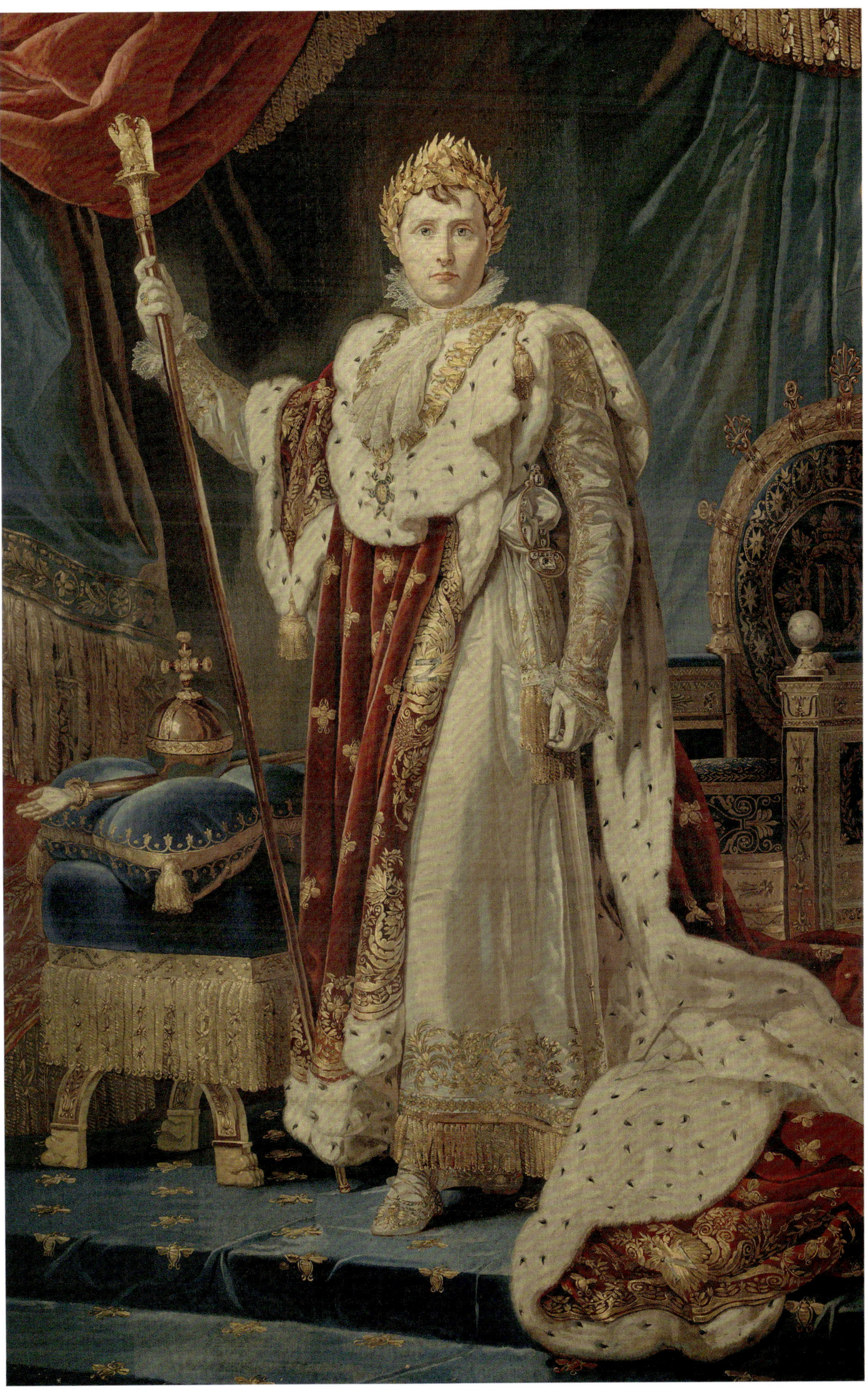

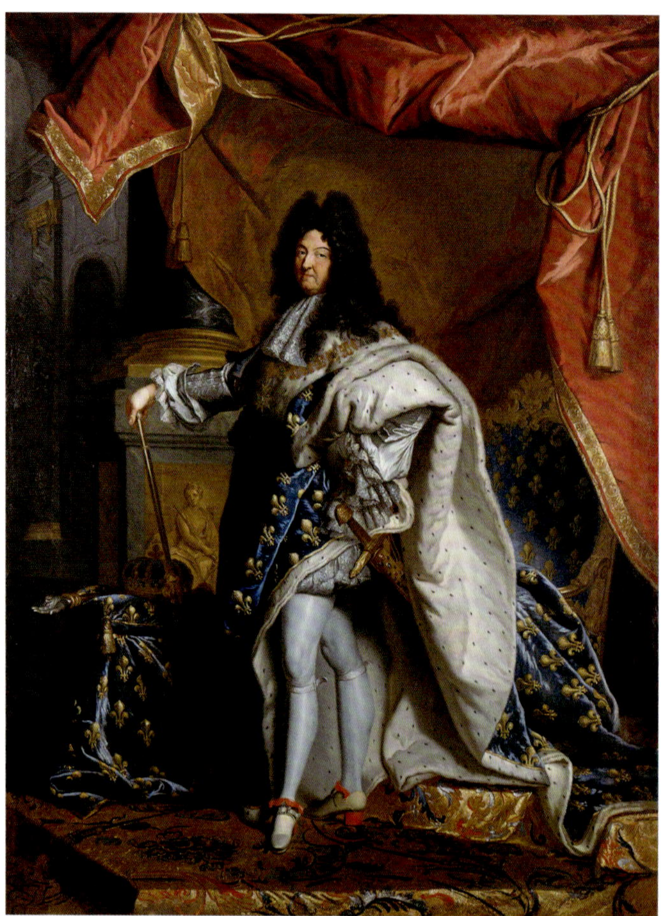

20. Hyacinthe Rigaud (French, 1659–1743). *Louis XIV (1638–1715), King of France*, 1701. Oil on canvas, 9 ft. 1 in. × 76⅜ in. (277 × 194 cm). Musée du Louvre, Paris

earlier portrait that the artist made from life—one of the few that are known, as Napoleon only reluctantly sat for artists, having allegedly declared, "No one knows if portraits of great men are likenesses; it suffices that genius lives." The idealized facial features and the prominence of the central locks of hair beneath the crown of gold laurels directly borrow from Augustus's imperial imagery to promote Napoleon's own power. Napoleon also modeled himself after another emperor, Charlemagne (ruled 768–814), whose iconography looms large in Gérard's portrait, from the imperial bees (a nineteenth-century misreading of cicadas, considered the oldest emblem of French kings) that are embroidered on Napoleon's robe and woven into the carpet covering the dais, to the ivory Hand of Justice, a replica of Charlemagne's (the original was destroyed during the French Revolution) that Napoleon adopted as an element of his own regalia to denote judicial power.

Gérard's Napoleon belongs to the tradition of state portraiture, that is, official images of rulers, typically portrayed with the symbolic trappings of their authority. Faced with the iconographic challenge of creating Napoleon's public image, Gérard and other artists in the service of the emperor drew from artistic precedent. The presentation of Napoleon, in the Throne Room of the Tuileries Palace, mirrors that of King Louis XIV in a 1701 portrait by Hyacinthe Rigaud, which became the prototype for state portraits of the Bourbon kings of France (fig. 20). The portrait of Louis XIV embodied his absolute authority at a time when it was widely believed that monarchs ruled by divine right, or the authority of God; accordingly, rulers were portrayed in full-length poses, often frontally, evoking the hieratic depictions of God and the saints in religious painting. While the composition of Gérard's portrait is indebted to Rigaud's prototype, Gérard updated his portrayal with emblems of the nascent Napoleonic dynasty: the imperial bee took the place of the fleur-de-lys, the stylized lily symbolic of the Bourbon kings; a gold orb, a representation of earthly domination, displaced the royal crown shown in Rigaud's portrait. Finally, Napoleon wears a chain of gold eagles displaying the cross of the Legion of Honor, a national order of merit he established in 1802, which remains the highest French decoration.

State portraiture also informed the work of Antwerp-born Anthony van Dyck, who established himself as the most sought-after portraitist in London during the reign of King Charles I (1625–49). The artist's seventeenth-century biographer observed that "apart from the likeness, he gave a certain nobility to the heads and grace to the poses." The portrait of the king's cousin James Stuart, fourth Duke of Lennox (and later first Duke of Richmond), exemplifies Van Dyck's celebrated abilities to flatter his royal and aristocratic sitters and to convey grandeur and authority through scale as well as setting (fig. 21). Lennox is portrayed with his beloved greyhound in an imposing interior, theatrically framed by drapery and a pillar in a composition recalling Titian's 1533 portrait of Emperor Charles V with a dog, which Van Dyck could have seen in the king's collection (Museo Nacional del Prado, Madrid). Lennox's hand-on-hip stance, another nod to Titian's precedent, thrusts into prominence the badge of the Order of the Garter, England's most prestigious chivalric order, which is lavishly embroidered in silver thread on his cloak. A second, smaller badge of the order hangs from a pale blue satin ribbon around his neck, and a blue-and-gold garter can be seen below his left knee. Charles I nominated Lennox to the Order of the Garter to mark the duke's twenty-first birthday in 1633, and Van Dyck's magisterial portrait, made at about the same date, likely commemorates his installation as a Knight of the Garter. By borrowing the language of state portraiture, Van Dyck implicitly elevated the status of the young duke. The portrait is replete with other signs of his social standing. Lennox is stylishly dressed in a silk satin suit in keeping with men's fashion in the court of Charles I in the early 1630s. (Such a suit could easily have cost its owner nearly twice the price of a standard full-length portrait by Van Dyck.) The greyhound by his side further signals his status through its association with hunting, then a privileged pastime of the nobility. Dogs are also symbols of fidelity, and Lennox's greyhound can be seen as representing the duke's unfailing loyalty to the king.

It is the hand-on-hip pose, though, that most eloquently telegraphs the sitter's aristocratic status. Although widely condemned as a sign of arrogance and even insincerity in the guides to courtly behavior popular among Van Dyck's aristocratic clientele, the pose gained currency as an expression of masculine authority in seventeenth-century Dutch portraiture, as Joaneath Spicer documented in her study of what she dubbed "the Renaissance elbow." It appears in many of Van Dyck's portraits from the 1630s, including *Charles I at the Hunt* (Musée du Louvre, Paris), which may well have informed Rigaud's 1701 painting of Louis XIV, who assumes an ostentatious variation of the stance.

While Van Dyck favored the hand-on-hip pose in his portraits of aristocrats, his Dutch contemporary Frans Hals deployed it as a signifier of status across a range of sitters: members of civic guard companies pose with hands on hips in an expression of group pride; wealthy merchants and brewers convey a brash self-confidence with jutting elbows. Subsequent generations of artists adopted the hand-on-hip pose as a marker of status. It became emblematic of eighteenth-century Britain's "Grand Style" portraiture—idealized, often full-length portraits that showcase their subjects' wealth and position in the tradition of Van Dyck—as exemplified by the work of Sir Joshua Reynolds and Thomas Gainsborough. At the end of the nineteenth century, the London-based American expatriate artist John Singer Sargent again revived this pictorial tradition, earning the nickname "the Van Dyck of our times" from his contemporary the French sculptor Auguste Rodin. Sargent's style found favor with both America's Gilded Age elite and the British aristocracy, who were eager to be portrayed by his flattering brush.

An innovative double portrait of Mr. and Mrs. Isaac Newton Phelps Stokes, commissioned in 1897 as a wedding present for the American couple, reveals Sargent's modern vision (fig. 22). His portrayal of Edith Minturn Stokes, one hand casually propped on her hip, subverts the traditional male gendering of the hand-on-hip pose, which originated in sixteenth-century images of military subjects and other male authority figures. Women had rarely been depicted in this pose, which would have been seen as contravening the modest behavior expected of them, as the French art critic Roger de Piles emphasized in his 1708 treatise on painting. Opining on poses in portraiture as expressions of the sitter's identity, the critic noted that "in women, they ought to have a noble simplicity, and modest cheerfulness; for modesty ought to be the character of women." No wonder, then, that Gainsborough caused a stir with his portrait of the accomplished musician Ann Ford, shown seated with one leg provocatively crossed above her knee in an informal pose that violated contemporary rules of feminine decorum and even connoted masculinity (*Ann Ford [later Mrs. Philip Thicknesse]*, 1760, Cincinnati Art Museum). The painting prompted one scandalized visitor to the artist's studio to declare, "I should be sorry to have any one I loved set forth in such a manner." More than one hundred years later, Sargent's portrayals of Edith Stokes and other

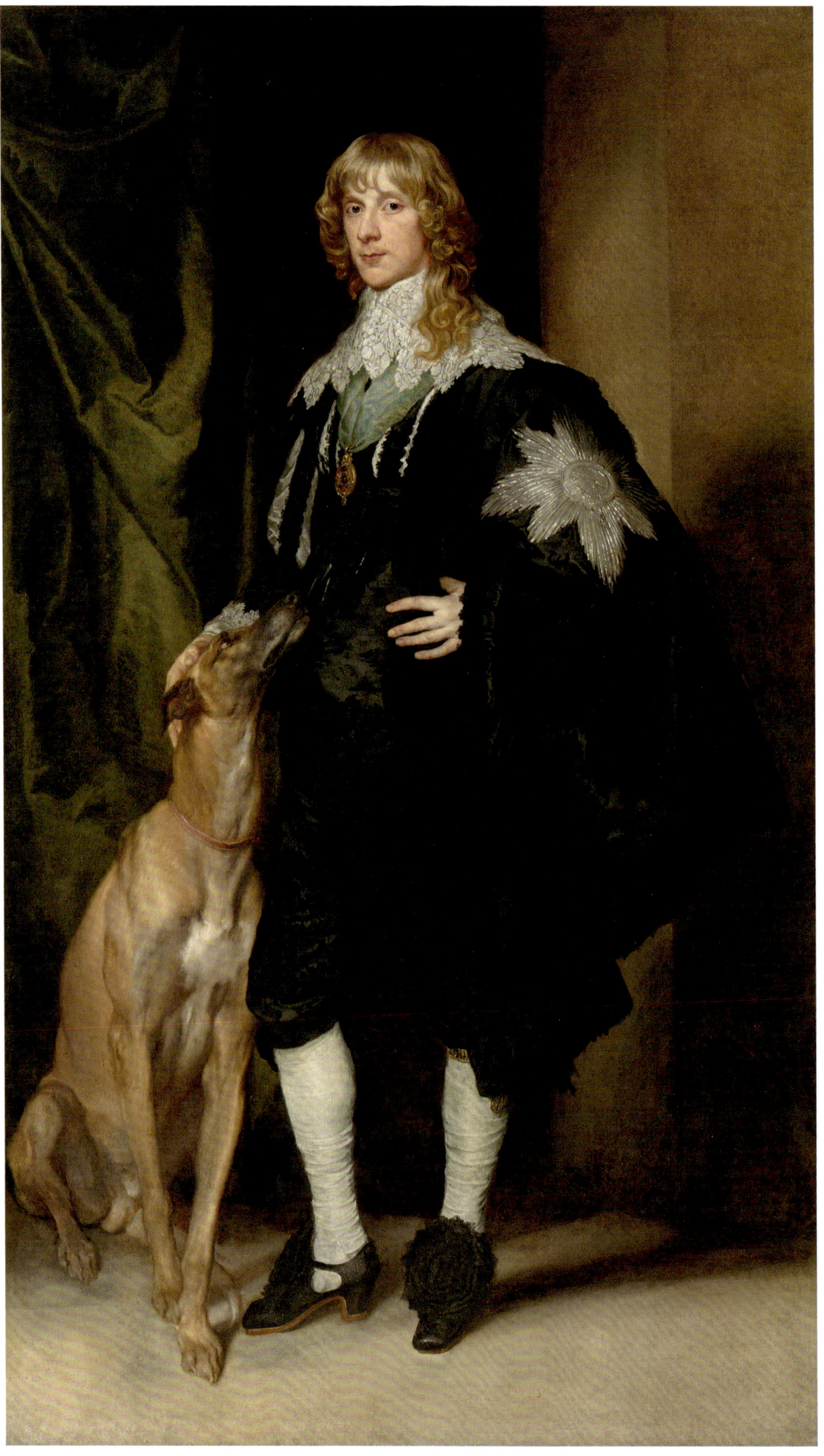

Opposite: 21. Anthony van Dyck (Flemish, 1599–1641). *James Stuart (1612–1655), Duke of Richmond and Lennox*, ca. 1633–35. Oil on canvas, 85 × 50¼ in. (215.9 × 127.6 cm). Marquand Collection, Gift of Henry G. Marquand, 1889 (89.15.16)

Right: 22. John Singer Sargent (American, 1856–1925). *Mr. and Mrs. I. N. Phelps Stokes*, 1897. Oil on canvas, 84¼ × 39¾ in. (214 × 101 cm). Bequest of Edith Minturn Phelps Stokes (Mrs. I. N.), 1938 (38.104)

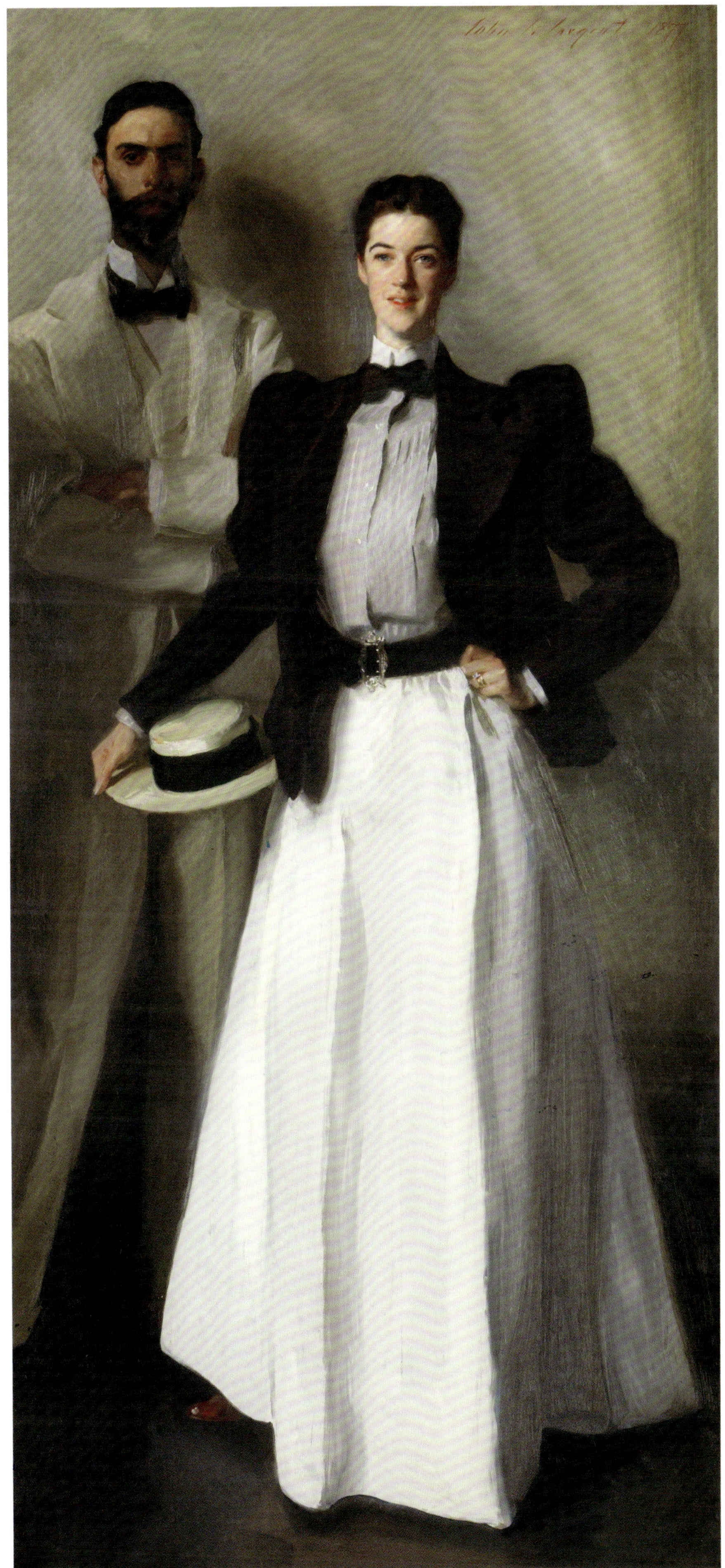

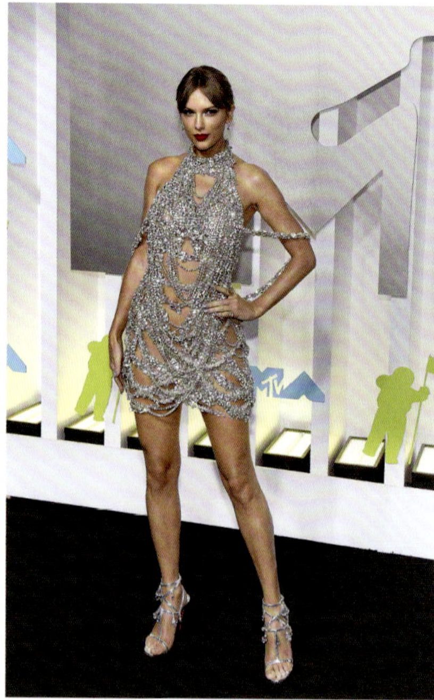

23. Taylor Swift at an awards show, 2022

women in variations of the hand-on-hip pose challenged centuries of the masculine claim to the assertive elbow and its attendant language of power, capturing the period's changing mores.

In a reversal of the traditional power dynamic in portraits of married couples, Edith Stokes dominates the composition, standing front and center and gazing outward; her husband appears in the background as if an afterthought, his partially cropped figure relegated to the shadows. In fact, as he told it, Isaac Stokes was a late addition to the portrait, replacing a Great Dane by Edith's side in a composition that would have mirrored Van Dyck's portrait of Lennox and his greyhound. Sargent's portrayal of Edith, informally dressed in a piqué skirt and serge jacket, has been likened to the ideal emerging at the dawn of the twentieth century of the "New Woman," one who enjoyed greater independence than her Victorian counterpart and played an increasingly public role.

Having shed its original association with masculine power, the hand-on-hip stance has transcended the realm of art, infiltrating everyday life as a projection of self-assurance. Today a pose once exclusive to royal and aristocratic portraiture is ubiquitous. Female stars like Taylor Swift adopt the confident stance when posing on red carpets for photographs that are instantaneously disseminated on the internet to their millions of followers (fig. 23); fans emulate the posture in images they post on social media, thereby proclaiming their own power.

That appropriation of the visual language of power attests to the democratization of the portrait in response to a new social order. Portraiture had almost exclusively focused on the rarefied world of wealth and privilege through the dawn of the twentieth century, when Sargent was still chronicling elite society. That began to change with the urban and industrial growth of the ensuing decades, when Robert Henri and other artists in what became known as New York's Ashcan School gave face to members of the working class and the urban poor. In the 1930s Alice Neel continued to upend portraiture's elite traditions by portraying the bohemian and left-leaning denizens of New York's Greenwich Village, where she lived and worked. Building on the foundation of the Ashcan School artists, Neel capitalized on the power that representation in portraiture implicitly confers upon its subjects. Her "pictures of people," the term she preferred to "portraits," include images of friends, lovers, journalists, and poets. One such painting, made in 1936, early in Neel's career, is of a woman identified only by her first name, Elenka (fig. 24). The up-close, cropped frontal pose and the unflinching directness of the sitter's gaze capture her strong psychological presence. Neel did not pose her sitters, as she once explained: "They unconsciously assume their most characteristic pose, which in a way involves all their character and social standing." A half-open blind behind the sitter reveals a nocturnal darkness, suggesting a degree of intimacy between Neel and her sitter.

Over the next fifty years, Neel's roster of sitters broadened to include her neighbors in Spanish Harlem, where she moved in 1938, her expanding family, and such art-world figures as Andy Warhol and the feminist art historian Linda Nochlin. Neel did not hesitate to depict poverty and suffering, and she challenged portraiture's historical exclusivity by expanding its canon to include those who had been marginalized or excluded; she depicted immigrants, gay couples, unnamed children, and people of color. The humanity she conveyed in her

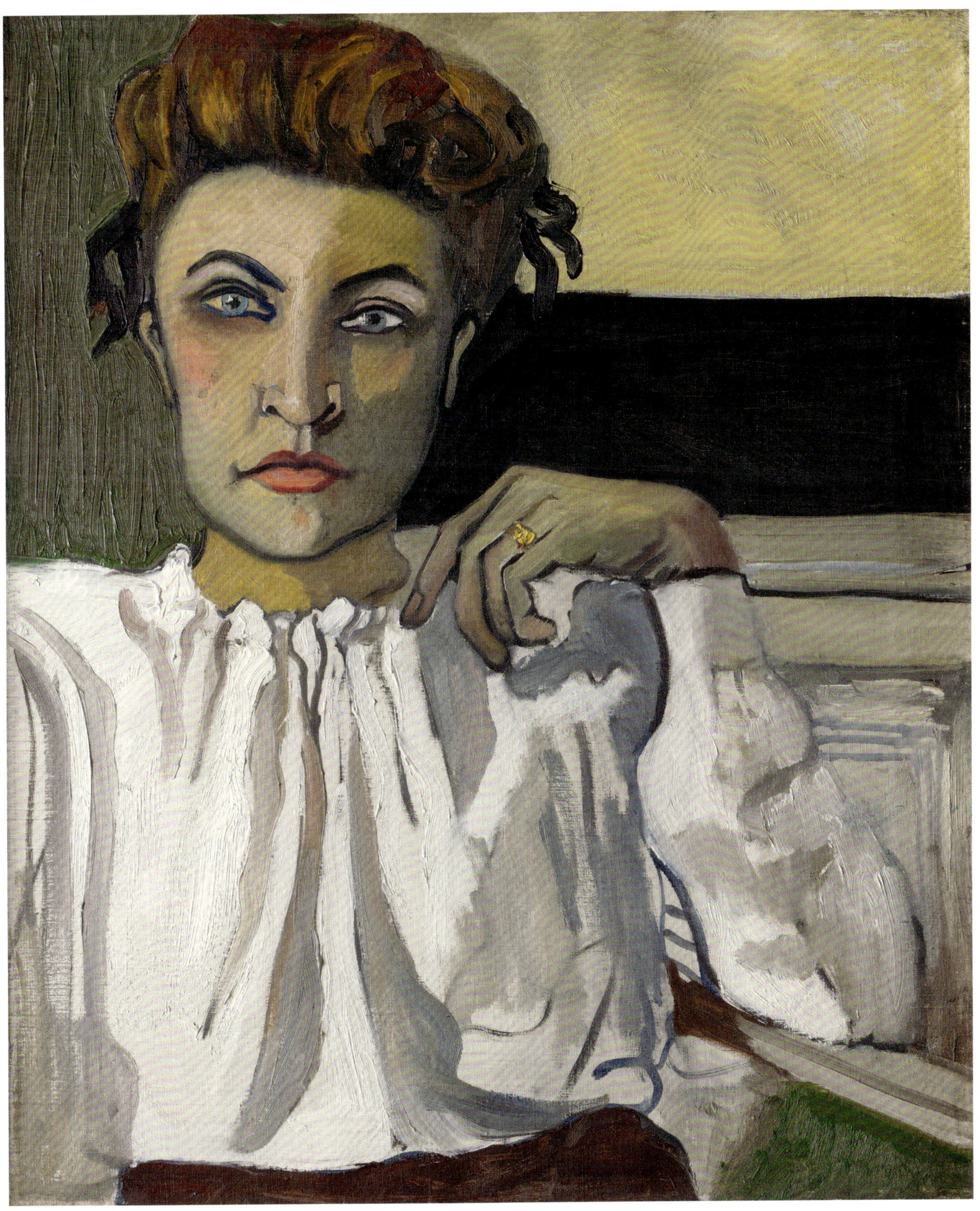

24. Alice Neel (American, 1900–1984). *Elenka*, 1936. Oil on canvas, 24 × 20 in. (61 × 50.8 cm). Gift of Richard Neel and Hartley S. Neel, 1987 (1987.376)

art resonates today in the work of painters such as Henry Taylor and Jordan Casteel (see figs. 27, 59) and the photographer Dawoud Bey.

Neel's contemporary the photographer Seydou Keïta similarly democratized the portrait at a time of rapid modernization and political change in the West African nation of Mali. Between 1948 and 1962 thousands of clients flocked to Keïta's studio in the capital city of Bamako to sit for a black-and-white photograph the size of a postcard. In these private works, intended to be displayed in the home and shared with friends and family (many were mailed to their recipients), the sitters asserted their status in Malian society. In collaboration with the photographer, they constructed identity through symbols of abundance; the resulting images collectively project cosmopolitanism and wealth. The identity of the woman in a photograph from 1956–57 is unknown, as is the case for most of Keïta's portraits from this period (fig. 25). The closely cropped photograph, a format Keïta favored, is dominated by the figure of the young woman, whose direct gaze into the camera's lens recalls that of Elenka in Neel's portrait. She straddles the chair, contravening gendered conventions in European portraiture, as did the hand-on-hip stance in Sargent's portraits of women from the 1890s; variants of her pose recur in Keïta's portraits of women. Her bejeweled wool headdress and puff sleeves were fashionable among Senegalese women living in Bamako from 1945 to 1965. The profusion of jewelry and other adornments conveys affluence, even excess. While some of the accessories might be props from the artist's studio, they are markers of the sitter's social status, whether actual or aspirational. In other portraits by Keïta, such symbols of modernity as radios and cars serve the same function. Here, the young woman's jewelry draws attention to her elegantly arranged hands; elongated fingers were considered a mark of feminine beauty in Malian culture. The contrasting pattern of the African textile that serves as a backdrop, a convention in West African portrait photography, contributes to the portrait's richness, an effect later conveyed by the patterned backgrounds that are similarly a hallmark of Kehinde Wiley's painted portraits (see fig. 46).

For Keïta's subjects, sitting for a portrait was a form of empowerment; Keïta recalled that being photographed was itself a "great event" for his sitters. The late nineteenth-century photographic portraits of Apsáalooke/Crow leaders that the government of the United States commissioned from Charles Milton Bell effectively denied their sitters such agency. These portraits, taken in Bell's Washington, D.C., studio, were occasioned by the Crow Peace Delegations that traveled from Montana to the nation's capital for territorial negotiations, which began in 1873 and ultimately led to the forced ceding of tribal lands to the U.S. government. Bell's photographs are formulaic studio portraits, intended as ethnographic records of what was then believed to be a dying race; consequently, many of the sitters were not identified. Within a decade the portraits had been appropriated as generic representations of Native Americans in popular culture. The use, more than a century later, of Bell's photo of Chief Medicine Crow on packaging for a line of herbal tea led the artist Wendy Red Star, herself Crow, to a project intended to restore to the sitters their humanity and their personal histories. Red Star's series 1880 Crow Peace Delegation (2014) transforms ten of Bell's photographs into powerful expressions of Crow identity (fig. 26). Working with digital reproductions of Bell's original photographs, Red Star used red ink to outline elements of the formal attire that signal the sitters' high rank in Crow society; she also individualized their portraits with annotated commentary that drew from archival biographical research as well as from her own experience growing up on a Crow reservation. She likened her artistic interventions to "marking on history."

By the simple but radical act of naming the sitters, Red Star reclaimed their identities. In the portrait of Peelatchixaaliash, or Old Crow (Raven), the sitter's Crow name appears within a bubble, as if said aloud, a device familiar from comics. Red ink underscores details such as the golden eagle feather Peelatchixaaliash wears as a headdress and the ermine fringes hanging from his shirtsleeves; attesting to his accomplishments in battle, these symbolize his power just as Napoleon's imperial regalia does in Gérard's portrait. The artist's detailed annotations range from the purely descriptive (identifying the "Nez Perce Necklace" and elements of clothing) to the biographical ("the last war chief") to more subjective commentary

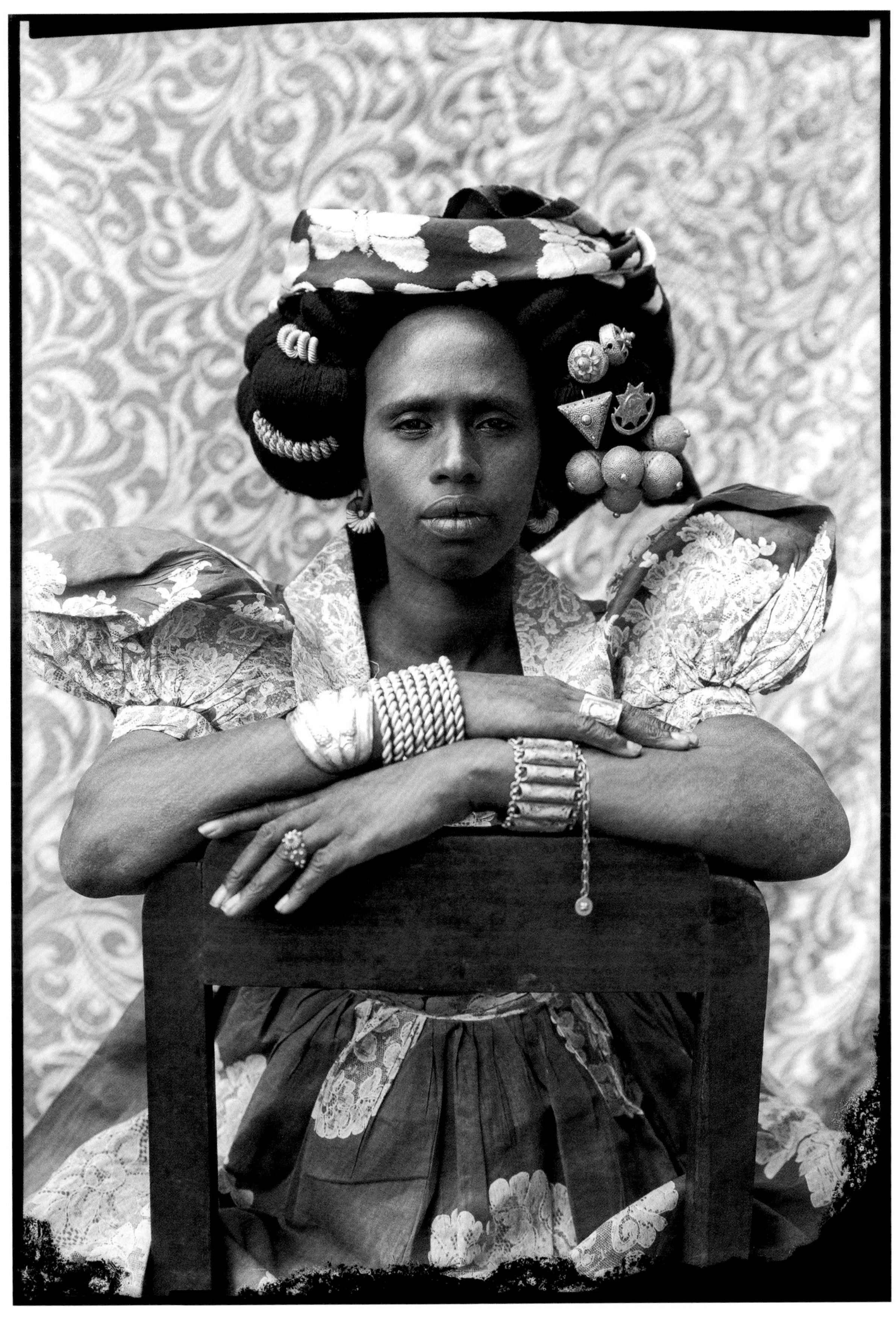

25. Seydou Keïta (Malian, ca. 1921–2001). *Untitled, #313 (Woman Seated on Chair)*, 1956–57. Gelatin silver print, 2001, image 22 × 15½ in. (55.9 × 39.4 cm). Purchase, Joseph and Ceil Mazer Foundation Inc. Gift, 2002 (2002.217)

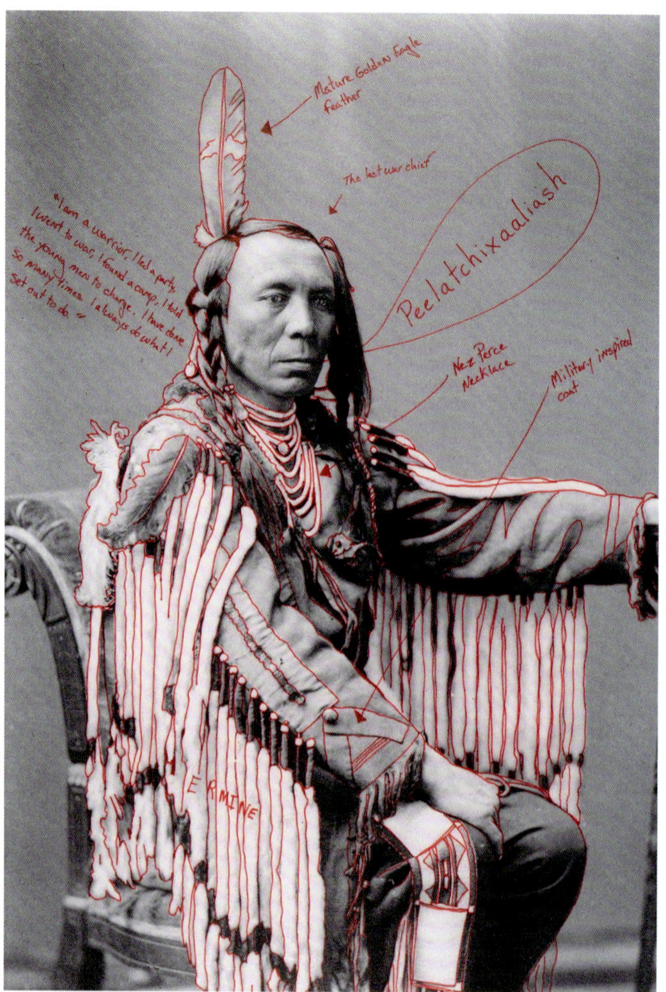

26. Wendy Red Star (Apsáalooke/Crow, b. 1981). *Peelatchixaaliash/Old Crow (Raven)* from 1880 Crow Peace Delegation, 2014. Inkjet print of artist-manipulated digitally reproduced photograph, sheet 24 × 16½ in. (61 × 41.8 cm). Purchase, Nancy Dunn Revocable Trust Gift and John B. Turner Fund, in memory of Loren G. Lipson M.D., 2019 (2019.328)

(such as "I always do what I set out to do," in which the artist assumes the subject's voice). Her interventions in 1880 Crow Peace Delegation invest Bell's portraits of Crow leaders with the power that had been denied to them since their creation in the nineteenth century.

Like Neel and Red Star, the Los Angeles–based artist Henry Taylor expands the canon of portraiture and its attendant language of power by depicting subjects the genre has historically excluded, an artistic approach mirroring broader cultural trends. The subjects of Taylor's portraits, who are mostly Black, run the gamut: strangers the artist has encountered in his daily life; friends and members of his family; and celebrities, including movie stars, athletes, and rappers. Although he also paints from direct observation and memory, his 2017 portrait of Andrea Motley Crabtree, the first Black female deep-sea diver in the entire United States military and the U.S. Army's first woman deep-sea diver, is based on a 1982 photograph (fig. 27). The artist eliminated the background detail in his photographic source, presenting Crabtree, clad in U.S. Army diving dress, in a neutral setting that lends the work a timeless aspect. The work recalls the European tradition of professional portraits, from Hans Holbein's paintings of Hanseatic League merchants to Otto Dix's somewhat satirical depiction of Max Roesberg (see figs. 10, 11). Here Crabtree's diving gear announces her professional identity, just as the office setting identifies Roesberg as a businessman. Her pose on a makeshift seat echoes a convention in European state portraits, in which male leaders such as popes, monarchs, and government officials are shown seated as a sign of their authority. Such allusions to art-historical precedent infuse Taylor's oeuvre.

Taylor titled the portrait *Andrea Motley Crabtree, the first*, the last two words underscoring the significance of her accomplishments. The work belongs among Taylor's portraits commemorating Black athletes and other public figures from earlier generations, including the baseball player Jackie Robinson, the track stars Carl Lewis and Alice Coachman, and Huey P. Newton, the leader of the Black Panther Party. Curator Bennett Simpson has suggested that Taylor painted these retrospective portraits "for reasons both acknowledging and aspirational." That is, by reclaiming the histories of those who have been marginalized or forgotten, Taylor simultaneously honors their successes and offers a more inclusive and inspiring vision of achievement and power.

27. Henry Taylor (American, b. 1958). *Andrea Motley Crabtree, the first*, 2017. Acrylic on canvas, 83⅞ × 59⅞ in. (213 × 152.1 cm). Purchase, Bequest of Gioconda King, by exchange, 2018 (2018.4)

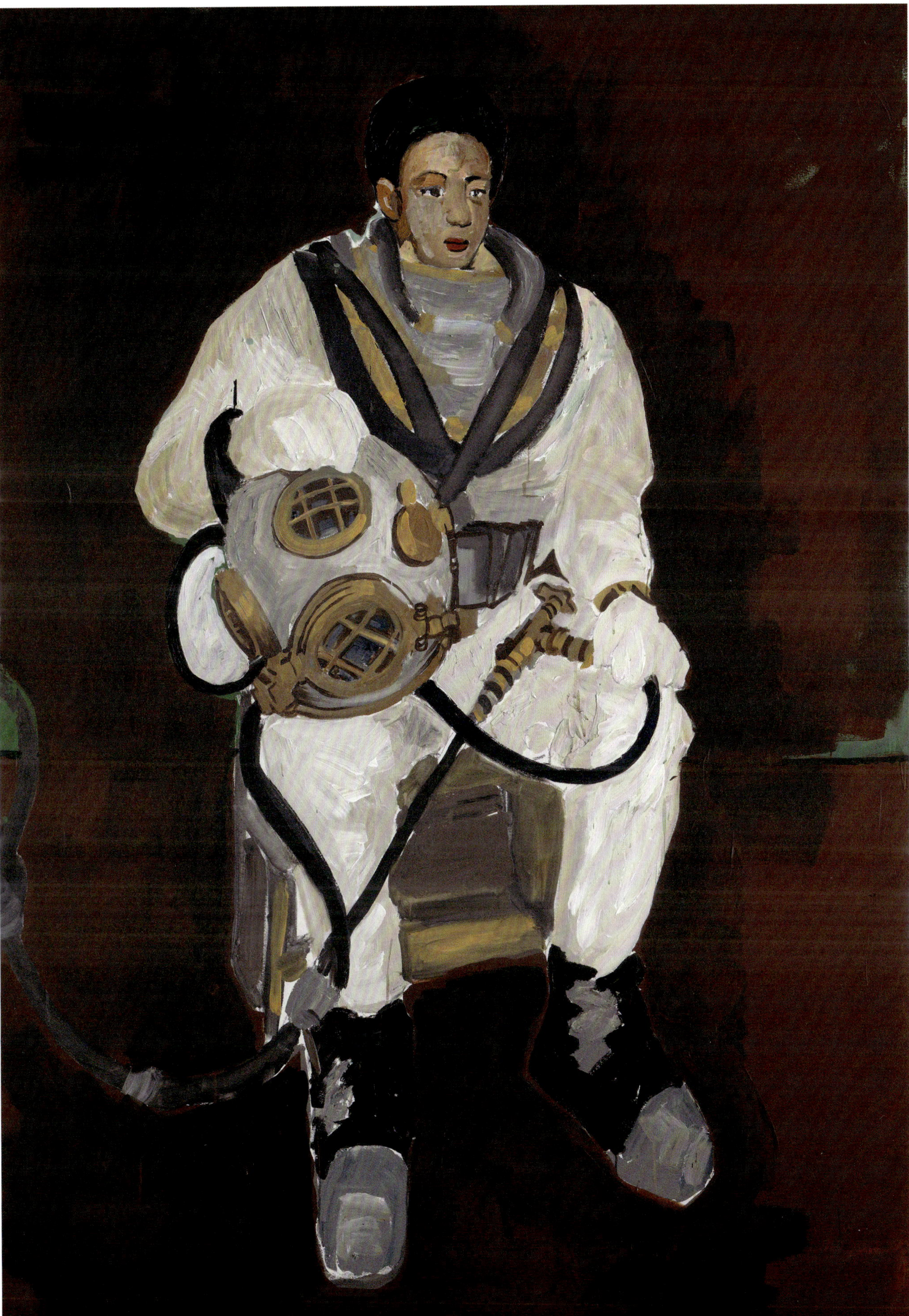

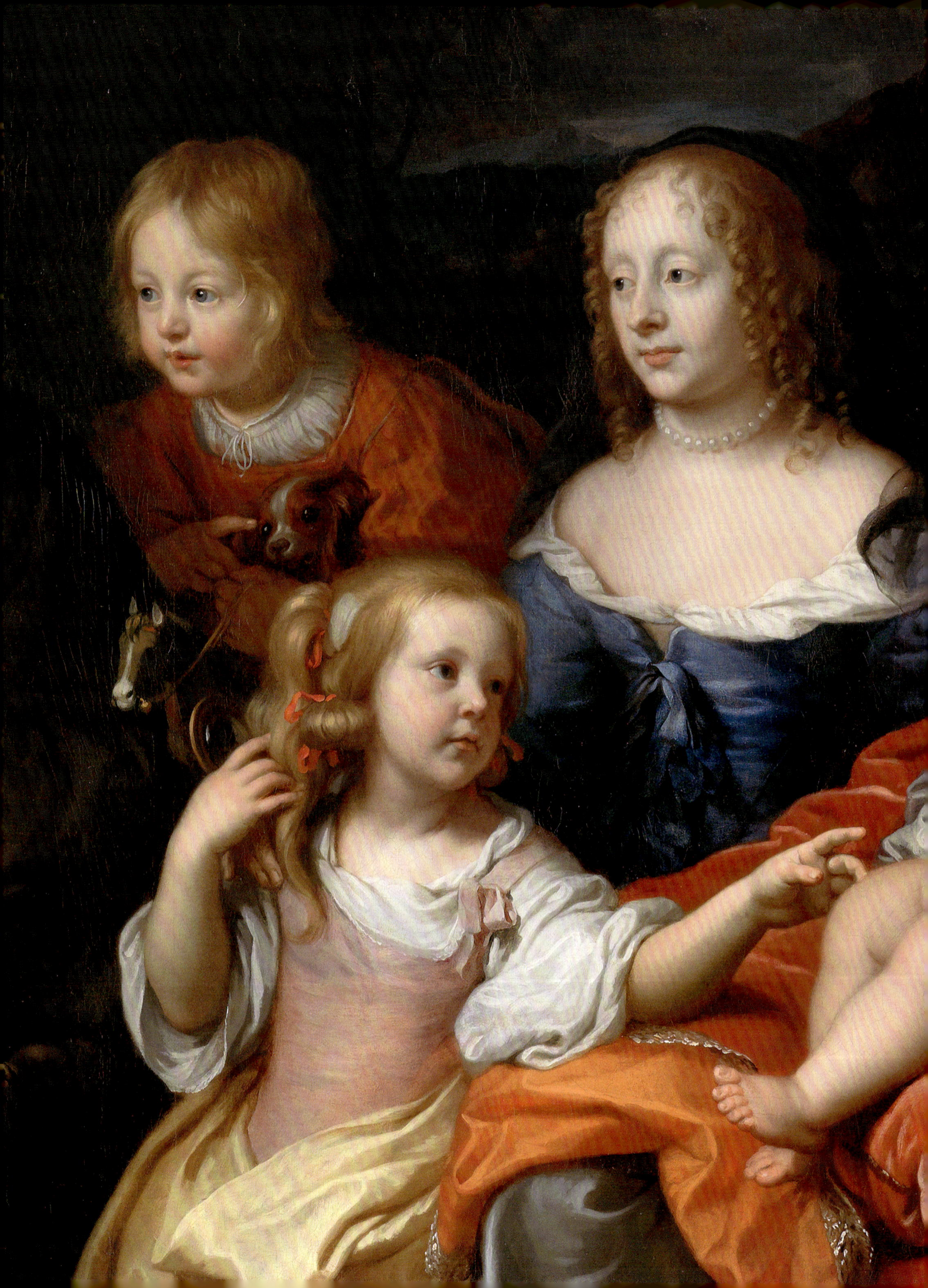

PUBLIC FACES, PRIVATE LIVES

In early modern Europe the portrait responded to changing social mores, notably the increasing separation of private from public life: the rise of individualism spurred private pursuits such as reading and personal devotion, and domestic interiors were reconfigured into smaller rooms with distinct functions. In addition, the eighteenth-century cult of sensibility, or sentiment, promoted emotional expression. The family portrait, rooted in the tradition of dynastic portraiture, began to resonate as a display of affection and intimacy. At the same time, a flourishing newspaper culture stimulated popular interest in the private lives of public figures, a nascent cult of celebrity that prompted a fascination with portraiture and, in turn, fueled its use by celebrities to shape their public image. Audiences flocked to view the portraits of politicians, performers, and other notables exhibited at venues like the Royal Academy in London (founded in 1768), and many of these works were subsequently disseminated in the form of reproductive prints, for which there was a thriving market.

Portraiture has both a public and a private side. The portrait as an expression of status and power is inextricably linked to its public aspect; such portraits are made to be seen widely. Other portraits serve strictly private ends, such as those exchanged by artists as tokens of friendship, the miniatures given to lovers as keepsakes, or the self-portraits that were artists' vehicles for experimentation. Public and private also converge in portraits that make public such private matters as family, relationships, and sexuality.

As a type, the family portrait embodies this duality, as the family unit is at once a social institution and the locus of private life. Its emergence coincided with the flourishing of group portraiture in seventeenth-century Dutch painting. Charles Le Brun's magisterial portrait of the banker and art collector Everhard Jabach and his family, painted about 1660, masterfully balances the two aspects of this mode of portraiture (fig. 29). Its interior setting evokes the Hôtel Jabach, the family's opulent Parisian town house, where the painting first hung. Le Brun portrayed the family as if gathered in one of its many rooms adorned with the landscape paintings that Jabach collected. However, Le Brun's domestic tableau was staged for an audience, as implied by the drapery in the upper left corner, drawn like a theater curtain to present the family. The inclusion in the scene of Le Brun

28. Charles Le Brun. *The Jabach Family*, ca. 1660 (detail of figure 29)

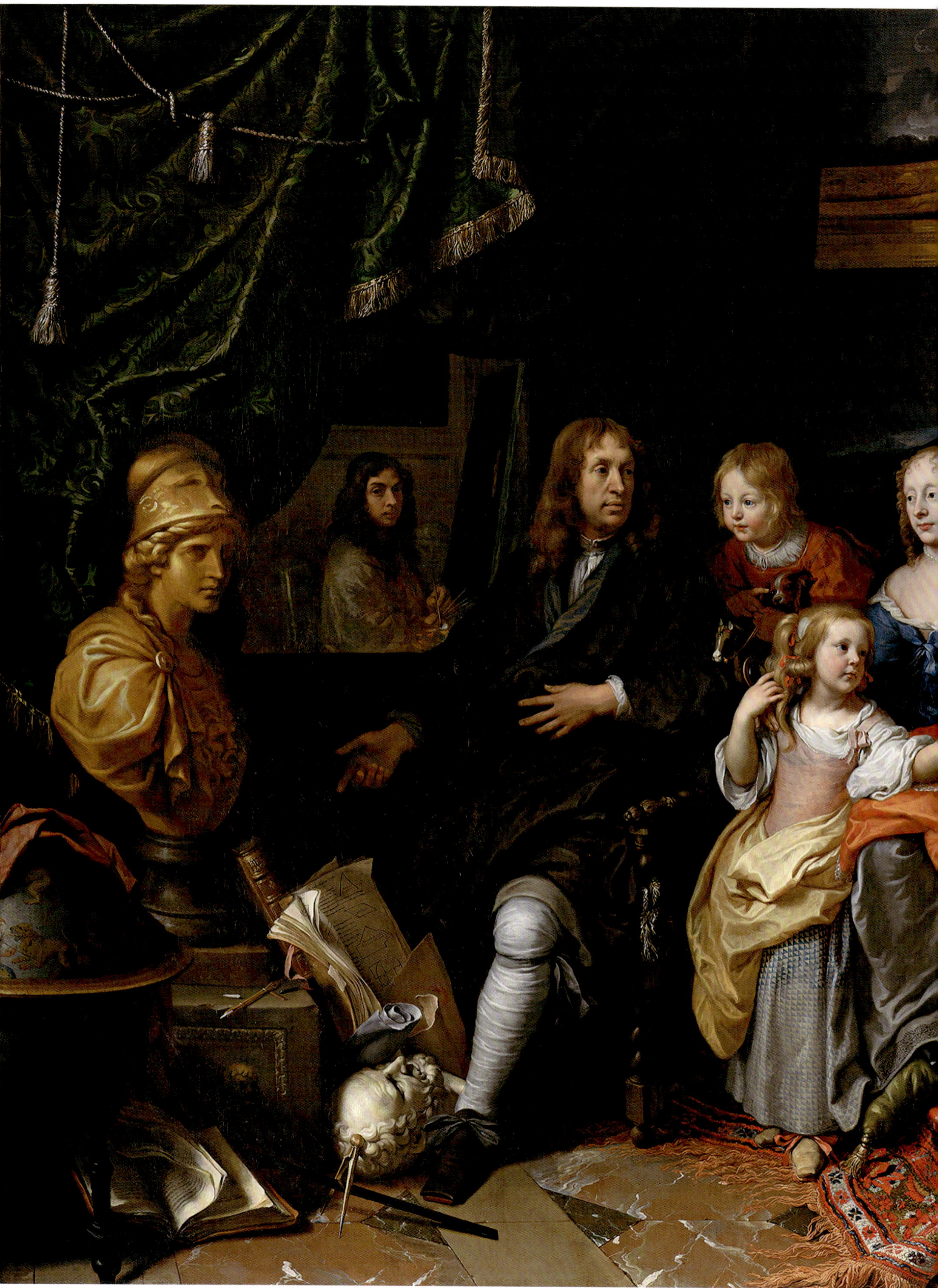

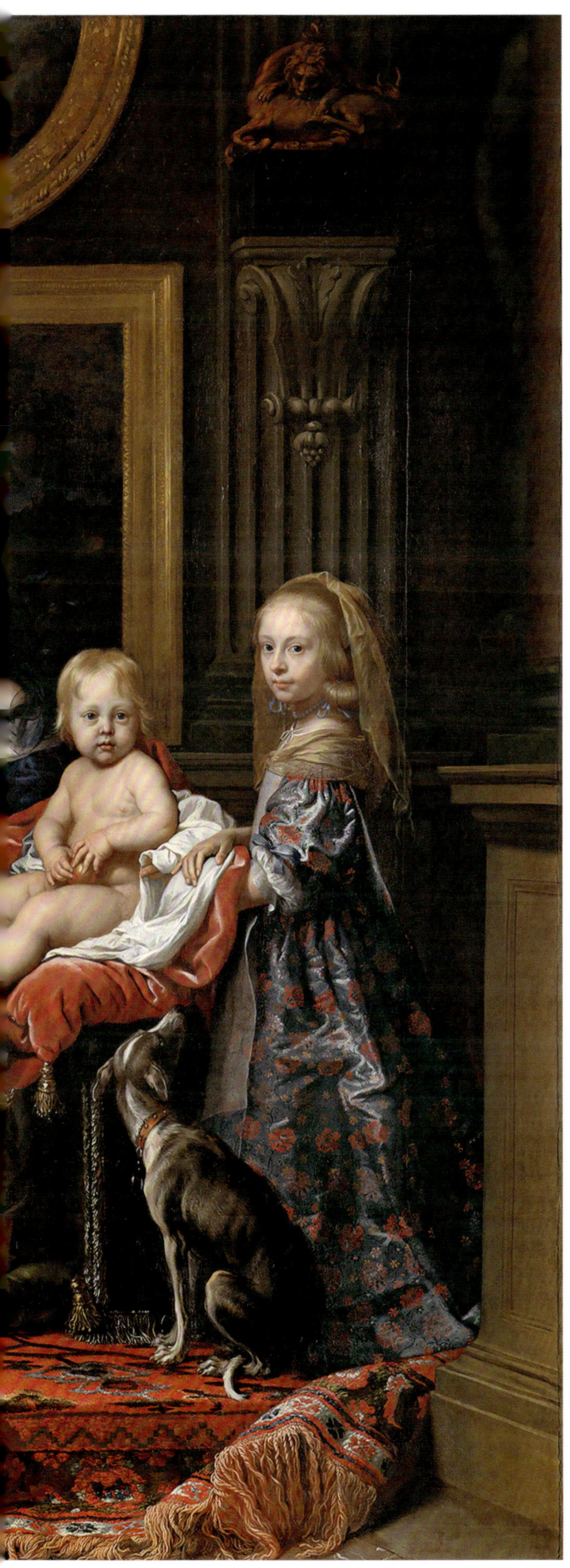

himself—the mirror next to Jabach reflects the artist at work, palette and brush in hand—also represents an intrusion of the public sphere upon this familial realm.

The composition clearly distinguishes these two worlds. As the patriarch, Jabach presides over the public, masculine domain of art and learning. He looks toward his growing family while gesturing at the objects around him, including a large celestial globe and a bust of Minerva, goddess of wisdom and the arts, which symbolize his erudition and his interests as a collector. His wife, Anna Maria, surrounded by the couple's children and pets, reigns over the family's private realm. It is the elder son and heir, Everhard V, inquisitively peering over his father's shoulder, who connects Jabach with his family. Other gestures and gazes link the figures and express their affective bonds. The portrait was probably occasioned by the baptism of the youngest child, Heinrich, portrayed nude and seated on a velvet cushion on his mother's lap—perhaps Le Brun's deliberate evocation of Renaissance images of the Madonna enthroned with the infant Christ. The portrait is at once a celebration of domestic harmony and a declaration of the continuity of the family line, ensured by the recent birth of Heinrich, the "spare" to his elder brother's "heir."

The emphasis on male lineage in the Jabach portrait recalls royal family portraits made in Europe during the sixteenth and seventeenth centuries, which served a dynastic purpose in representing the line of succession of the monarchy, be it Tudor, Bourbon, or Hapsburg. In Mughal India, by contrast, portraiture was largely a private pleasure for its emperors; albums of miniatures were shared only with family and close friends. Portraiture had emerged there in the sixteenth century, reflecting both the influence of European art and the taste of Emperor Akbar (ruled 1556–1605), who started the practice of commissioning portraits of himself and his entourage. The Shah Jahan Album, begun about 1620 by Emperor Jahangir (ruled 1605–27) and continued by his

29. Charles Le Brun (French, 1619–1690). *The Jabach Family*, ca. 1660. Oil on canvas, 9 ft. 2¼ in. × 10 ft. 9⅛ in. (280 × 328 cm). Purchase, Mrs. Charles Wrightsman Gift, in honor of Keith Christiansen, 2014 (2014.250)

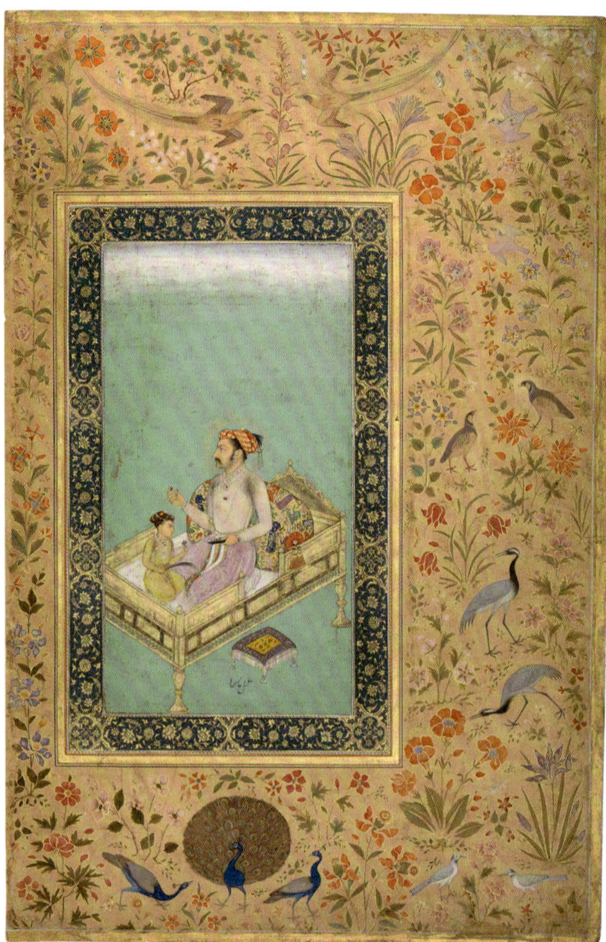

30. Nanha (Indian, act. ca. 1582–1635). *The Emperor Shah Jahan with his Son Dara Shikoh*, folio from the Shah Jahan Album, ca. 1620. Ink, opaque watercolor, and gold on paper; margins: gold and opaque watercolor on dyed paper, 15⅜ × 10⅜ in. (38.9 × 26.2 cm). Purchase, Rogers Fund and The Kevorkian Foundation Gift, 1955 (55.121.10.36)

descendants, includes portraits of the emperors, their courtiers, and others in the imperial orbit. One of its folios depicts Jahangir's son, the future emperor Shah Jahan, in the company of his favorite son, five-year-old Dara Shikoh (fig. 30). In this intimate scene, the two are absorbed in quiet contemplation of emeralds and rubies, reflecting Shah Jahan's passion for collecting gemstones and jewelry. Seated together on a golden throne, the bejeweled figures are portrayed with their heads in strict profile, a portrait format Shah Jahan favored. His images are characterized by their idealized, even iconic, aspect, a marked departure from Akbar's preference for expressive, naturalistic likenesses. The golden nimbus encircling Shah Jahan's head here and in other portraits in the album signals his status as heir to the imperial throne and evokes religious imagery from Christian, Hindu, and Buddhist traditions, all of which were then circulating in the Mughal court. The image's formality reflects Shah Jahan's taste in portraiture, but the father and son's shared activity imbues it with an intimacy that accords with its function in a private family album.

Like the Mughal emperors some three centuries before them, Britain's Queen Victoria and her consort, Prince Albert, amassed portraits as records of their family life. Unlike the Mughal rulers, however, Victoria capitalized on portraiture to shape her public persona. As early as the 1840s the royal couple, avid consumers of the new medium of photography, commissioned photographs of themselves and their growing family (the queen would bear nine children between 1840 and 1857) for their private enjoyment; like the Mughal miniatures, the photos were assembled in albums. In 1860 they invited the British photographer J. J. E. Mayall to photograph them and several of their children at Buckingham Palace and granted permission to release from this session a series of fourteen *cartes de visite*, or calling cards, inexpensive and small-scale portraits mounted on card stock. (The French photographer A. A. E. Disdéri had patented a system for the mass production of *carte de visite* portraits in 1854.) Marketed to the public as the Royal Album, hundreds of thousands of these sets were reportedly sold across Britain and abroad, fueling "cartomania," an international frenzy for such portraits of friends, family, and celebrities. For the first time the public had access to photographs of the British monarch and her family; the queen became a celebrity in large part thanks to the widespread circulation of her image.

The photographs in the Royal Album reveal a private side of the queen, showing her as a doting wife and mother in tableaux evocative of the era's middle-class

Opposite: Detail of figure 30

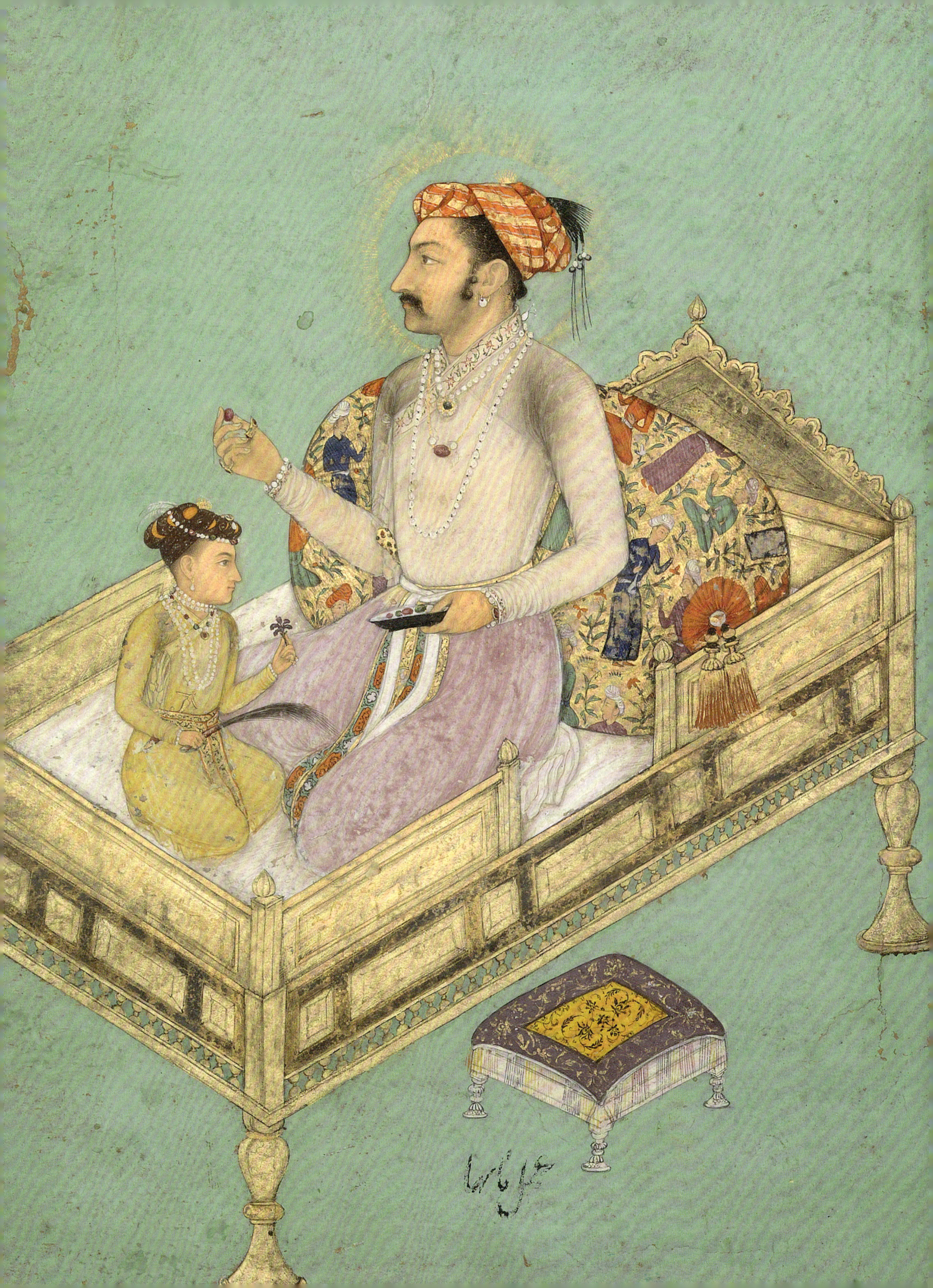

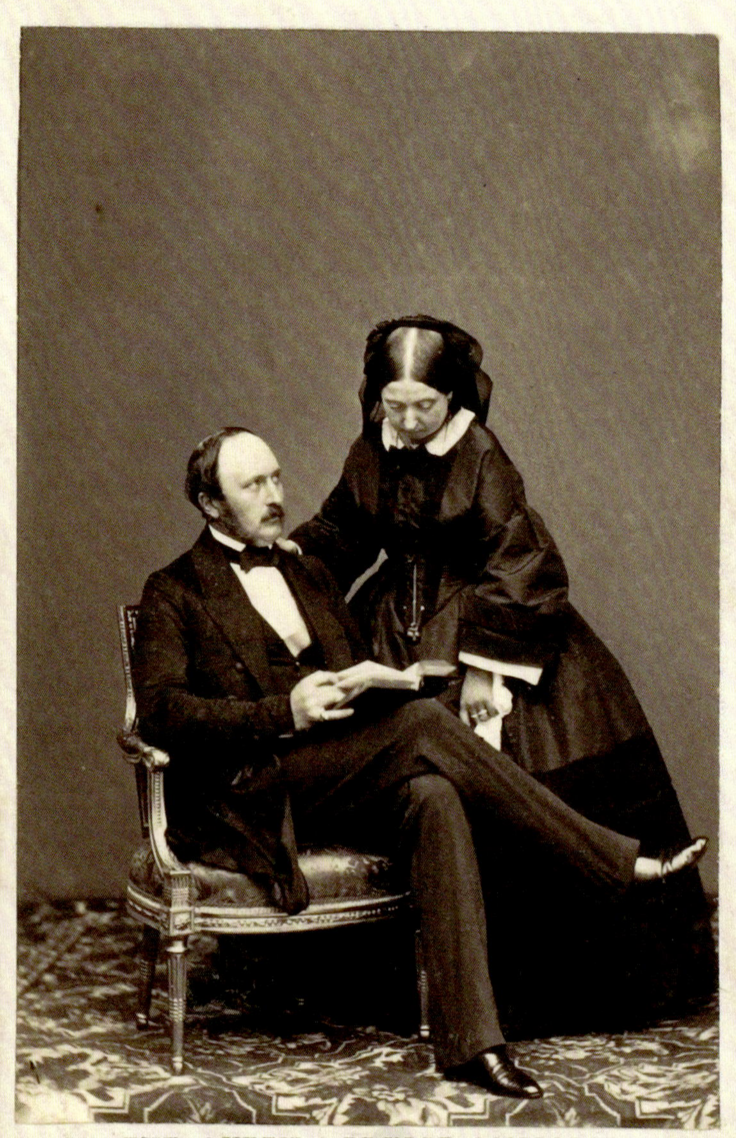

THE QUEEN & PRINCE CONSORT.

domestic ideal, conspicuously free of any sign of her royal status. In one, she appears to have interrupted her husband's reading in a staged scene that blurs the sitters' dual roles, wife/sovereign and husband/subject (fig. 31). Mayall, whom Victoria would name court photographer, issued a second set of royal portraits in 1861 in response to public demand for affordable images of the queen and her family, whom he photographed throughout the decade. "Queen Victoria never fully reconciled her private role as wife and mother with her public persona as queen and empress," the historian David Cannadine observed, and photographs from later in her reign emphasized her sovereignty. Nevertheless, Victoria's innovative bid to humanize the monarchy for her subjects through relatable photographs of the royal family proved prescient: today's royals similarly deploy social media, shaping their public images by selectively offering the world a glimpse into their private lives.

Photographs like Mayall's embody an evolution in European royal family portraiture aptly termed "the domestication of majesty" by the historian Simon Schama, as formal dynastic messaging gave way to more intimate imagery. This iconographic shift was informed by the emergence, in England in the 1720s and 1730s, of a new type of group portrait known as the conversation piece. These small-scale, informal works depict family members or friends interacting in domestic interiors, often engaged in such ordinary pursuits as drinking tea, playing cards, or making music, which provide a narrative underpinning to the scene. Other conversation pieces are set outdoors, presenting their sitters as members of the landed gentry. These portraits, whose subjects were not public figures, were considered private in nature, meant to be seen by friends and family in the sitters' homes rather than in public exhibitions. By midcentury the rising cultural current of sensibility, which extolled the virtues of loving mothers and devoted fathers, found visual expression in this mode of portraiture. A conversation piece by Francis Wheatley, traditionally identified as a portrait of the Saithwaite family, paints a picture of eighteenth-century domestic bliss (fig. 32). Mother and child appear to have just returned from a walk outdoors, a narrative that reflects the promotion of the natural world and its affective power in the period's sentimental literature. In response to this welcome interruption, the father abandons his reading to look upon his family with satisfaction. Beyond its function as an image of familial harmony, the conversation piece showcases its sitters' social status and fashionable taste. Thus, Wheatley paid equal attention to rendering the room's modish decor: the medallion-patterned Turkish carpet, the damask-upholstered sofa, and the Neoclassical vase atop the carved mantelpiece all signal the family's affluence.

The conversation piece as a subset of portraiture was largely a phenomenon in eighteenth-century British art. More generally, in Britain and elsewhere, after about 1770 the family portrait was marked by an increasing informality and the depiction of emotional bonds. With the invention of photography in 1839 and changing tastes, however, the currency of the commissioned painted family portrait diminished. Contemporary artists reengaging with family portraiture often choose their own subjects, in a reversal of the traditional process, as seen in the work of photographers Tina Barney, Deana Lawson, and Thomas Struth.

Struth, who has been photographing families since 1985, investigates the differences within and across families that make each unique (fig. 33). His sitters, who include but are not limited to his relatives and friends, range from his native Germany to Scotland, Brazil, the United States, and Japan, allowing for a cross-cultural exploration of the family as the basic unit of society. In that sense, public and private merge in Struth's body of work: "With every photo of a family, the relationships interest me in two respects," he explained. "First the relationships of people, who at that moment live in these places, with their own history. And also in the way that the pictures can go beyond that and give examples of particular ways of life." In most of these works, Struth and the family choose the setting together; individual members then "find their own place" during the sittings,

31. John Jabez Edwin Mayall (British, 1813–1901). *The Queen and Prince Consort*, 1860. Albumen silver print, image 3½ × 2¼ in. (8.7 × 5.7 cm). Gilman Collection, Gift of The Howard Gilman Foundation, 2005 (2005.100.382 [76])

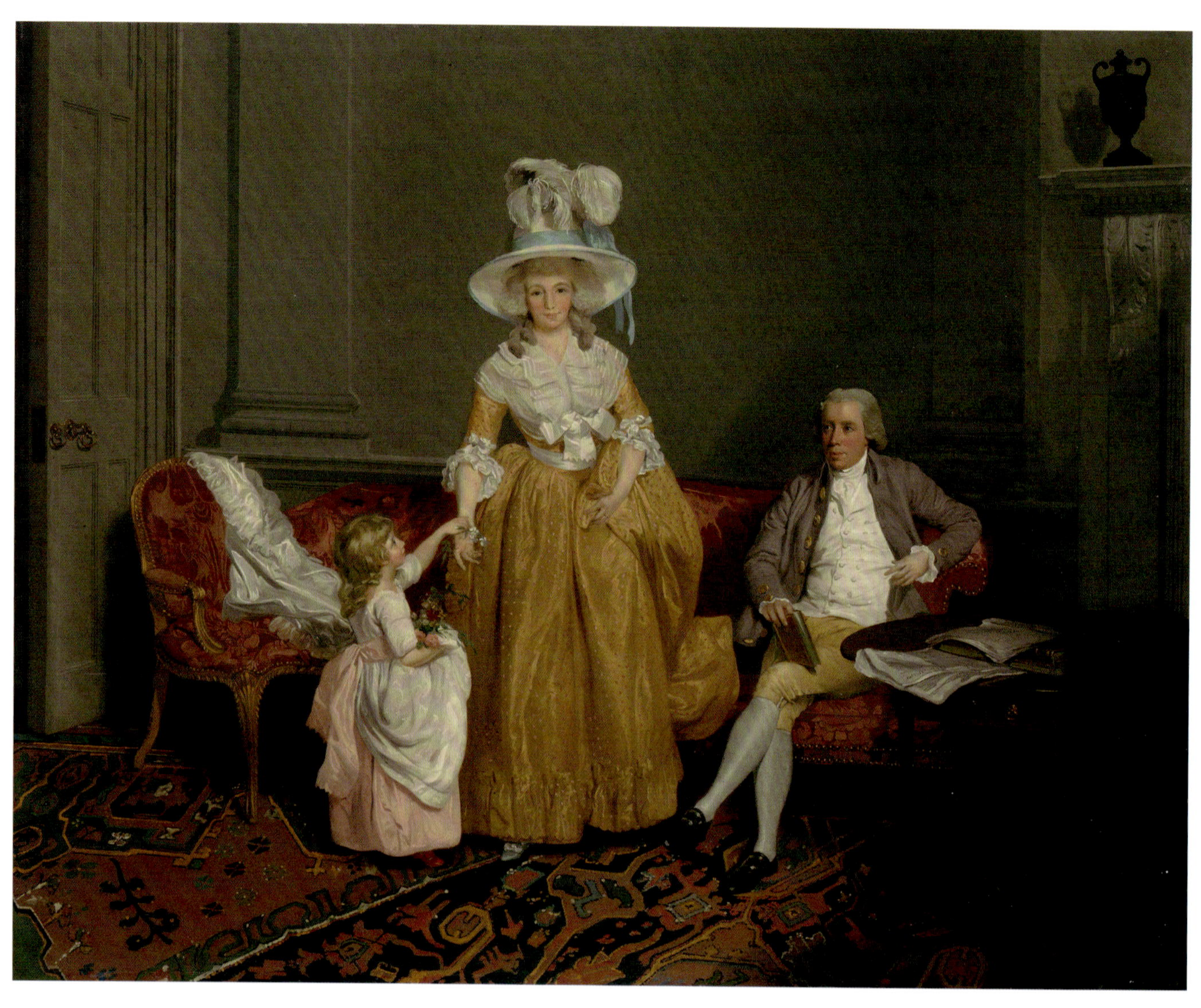

32. Francis Wheatley (British, 1747–1801). *The Saithwaite Family*, ca. 1785. Oil on canvas, 38¾ × 50 in. (98.4 × 127 cm). Gift of Mrs. Charles Wrightsman, 2009 (2009.357)

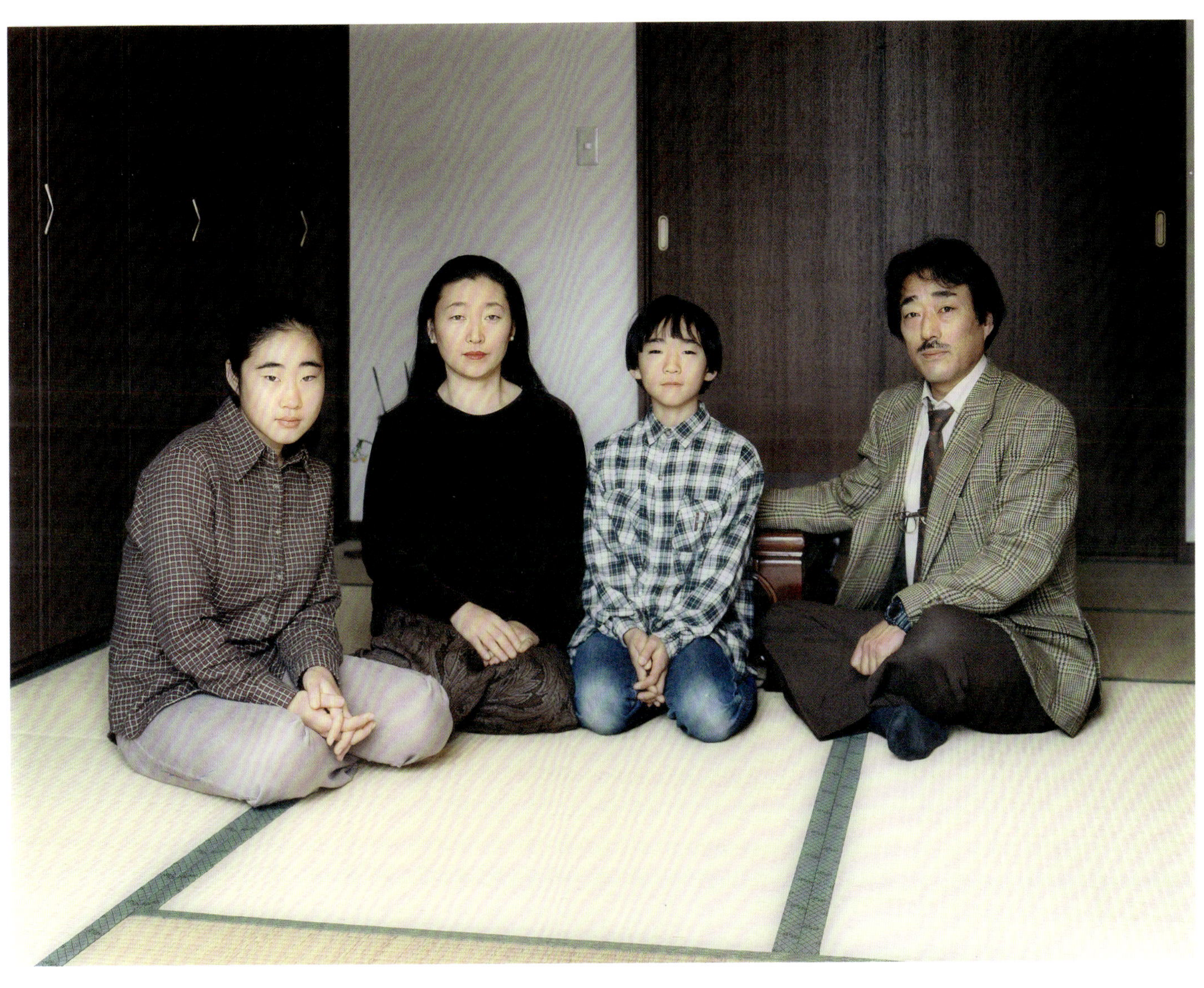

33. Thomas Struth (German, b. 1954). *The Okutsu Family in Tatami Room, Yamaguchi*, 1996. Chromogenic print, 58¼ × 69¼ in. (148 × 175.9 cm). Purchase, Harriett Ames Charitable Trust Gift, 2000 (2000.104)

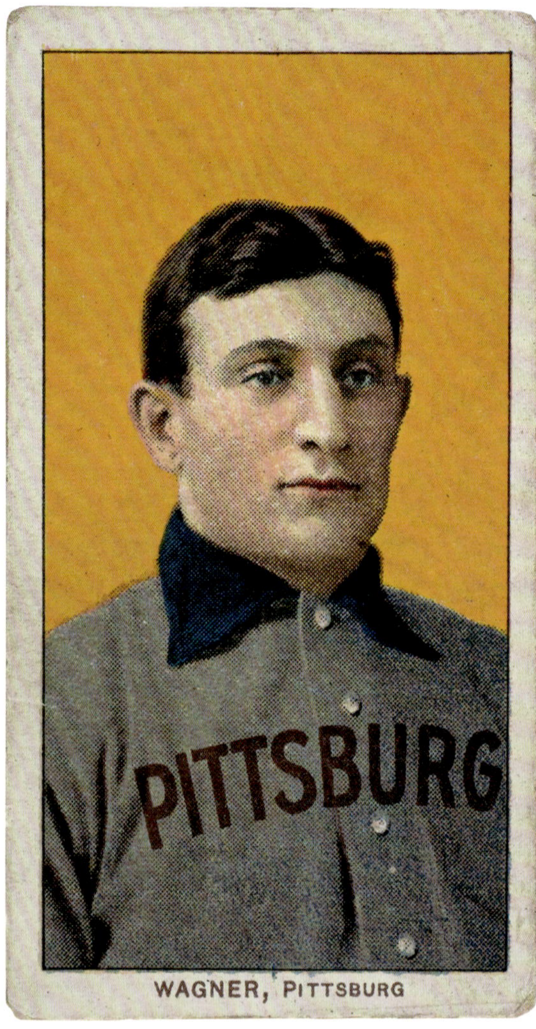

34. *Honus Wagner, Pittsburgh, National League, from the White Border series (T206)*. American, 1909–11. Commercial lithograph, sheet 2⅝ × 1½ in. (6.7 × 3.7 cm). The Jefferson R. Burdick Collection, Gift of Jefferson R. Burdick (63.350.246.206.378)

according to the photographer, who requires his subjects to look directly into the camera, not at him. The relatively long exposure time, ranging from a half second to eight seconds, contributes to the stillness that permeates Struth's portraits. Interaction among the sitters is minimal if not entirely absent; their deliberately neutral affect, characteristic of Struth's aesthetic, compels us to scrutinize the portrait for the slightest nuances of body language and expression as clues to the family dynamic.

In a 1996 photograph of the Okutsus sitting on mats in the tatami room at their home in Japan, meaning is conveyed through subtle gesture and pose. The mother and her two children form an intimate trio, their legs folded beneath them and their bodies almost imperceptibly touching; the father, wearing a jacket and tie, sits at slight remove from this group, the only one with his legs crossed. However, he extends his arm to place his hand on his son's back, connecting the family both physically and psychologically. Still, the Okutsus' overall self-presentation is formal, which accords with the setting in their tatami room, traditionally used as a reception space, a site where the family's public and private lives converge. In another photograph of the family, the father has exchanged his jacket and tie for a sweater, and the mood is more intimate and relaxed, in keeping with the private nature of the different room in which it is set (*The Okutsu Family in Western Room, Yamaguchi*, 1996).

Struth's ongoing series of family portraits—large-scale works intended for exhibition—makes public the private lives of ordinary people. Struth's inclusive practice recalls that of Alice Neel, who painted subjects she encountered in everyday life (see fig. 24). Their approach runs counter to a focus on the likenesses of public figures that dates to antiquity, demonstrated by the busts of eminent poets and philosophers that figured in portrait collections in the ancient world; collectors during the Renaissance emulated this antique model. In early modern Europe, the concept of celebrity expanded to encompass a wider range of social types, from artists, writers, and political figures to performers and courtesans. The craze in the 1850s for *carte de visite* portraits of prominent individuals was soon followed by the revival of the trade card, or business card, which had originated in seventeenth-century Europe. In the 1880s lithographic portraits of athletes, inventors, military leaders, and other distinguished figures began to appear on small cardboard trade cards issued by American tobacco companies. A rising interest in baseball, coupled with the growing market for cigarettes, contributed to the popularity of trade-card portraits of ballplayers; they quickly became collectibles. The rarest and most sought-after baseball card is of Hall of Famer Honus Wagner, who was a shortstop for the

Pittsburgh Pirates from 1900 to 1917 (fig. 34). Just over two hundred such cards were issued before production ceased at Wagner's request; it has been suggested either that he objected to his image being used to sell tobacco to children or that he wanted a share of the profits. Framed by a white border, Wagner is portrayed in uniform and set against a solid-colored ground, with his last name and team printed along the bottom of the card, recalling the format and function of Hans Holbein's professional portraits of Hanseatic League merchants, some of which also include inscriptions (see fig. 10). The lithographic baseball card gave way in 1952 to a photographic likeness accompanied by the player's autograph; his statistics replaced the tobacco ads once found on the reverse. In the 1930s chewing-gum companies supplanted tobacco manufacturers as the leading producers of baseball cards, which were included in bubble-gum packaging, creating a new market among young people for these collectible portraits.

The avidity with which baseball and other cards were traded and collected speaks to the twentieth-century cult of celebrity—a subject that fascinated Andy Warhol, who is memorably said to have opined, "In the future, everyone will be world-famous for fifteen minutes." In 1962 the Pop artist began making photo-silkscreened portraits of famous people: athletes like Roger Maris and Muhammad Ali, movie stars like Marilyn Monroe and Elizabeth Taylor, and American icons like First Lady Jacqueline Kennedy. Warhol's ongoing engagement with celebrity led the art historian Robert Rosenblum to dub him "the court painter to the [19]70s." Warhol, who astutely cultivated his own celebrity persona, had become famous himself by the end of the 1960s, the subject of his own art and that of others. As the art historian Sam Hunter commented in 1969, "He is a celebrity created by and for the mass media, and an accomplice in the process." His New York studio, the Factory, was populated by an unconventional mix of socialites, underground-film performers, and musicians; it too became famous, as a symbol of 1960s counterculture.

In 1969 the photographer Richard Avedon captured Warhol and members of the Factory in a work that was groundbreaking in both subject and format, the first in a series of group portraits that redefined celebrity and its portrayal (fig. 35); he later described the people in these photomurals as embodying the "great movements that were breaking up and unifying the country." Avedon dispersed the larger-than-life figures over three separate frames, each delineated by the printed black borders of the negatives; together, the panels span more than thirty feet, a scale that was without precedent in his work. This friezelike arrangement reads as Avedon's riff on the line-ups of members of civic associations in sixteenth- and seventeenth-century Dutch group portraiture, which the photographer set out to "reinvent," as he recalled. A 1588 portrait of officers in Amsterdam's civic guard by Cornelis Ketel exemplifies this type, with male figures arrayed across the canvas according to rank, the highest-ranking officers at center (fig. 36). Avedon, however, rejected the traditional hierarchical arrangement of figures, placing the panel with Warhol on the right rather than at center, as he had planned. As a result, the portrait's most recognizable figure is marginalized at one end, his gaze directed outside of the frame. Avedon instead centered the portrait on a trio of male nudes, whose beauty and sexual openness he saw as emblematic of the convention-flouting Factory. This grouping simultaneously nods to representations of the mythological Three Graces in classical art and subverts their gendered norms. In the left panel, Candy Darling, the transgender actress and a favorite of Warhol at the time, appears opposite the actor Joe Dallesandro, their naked bodies flaunting the gender fluidity that the Factory embraced at the height of the sexual revolution.

The artifice of Avedon's photograph is undisguised. The figures are portrayed against an empty white studio backdrop with no attempt to hide the portrait's staged nature, down to the play of hand gestures Avedon choreographed. Several of the subjects appear twice, including the poet Gerard Malanga, whose figure bleeds from the second to the third frame. This imperfectly conjoined pair was a deliberate artistic choice that revealed the photomural to be a composite image based on multiple sessions, not a record of a single moment in time. The implied movement of several of the figures from one frame to another reflects what Avedon called "the passage of social time": the film director Paul Morrissey first appears at far

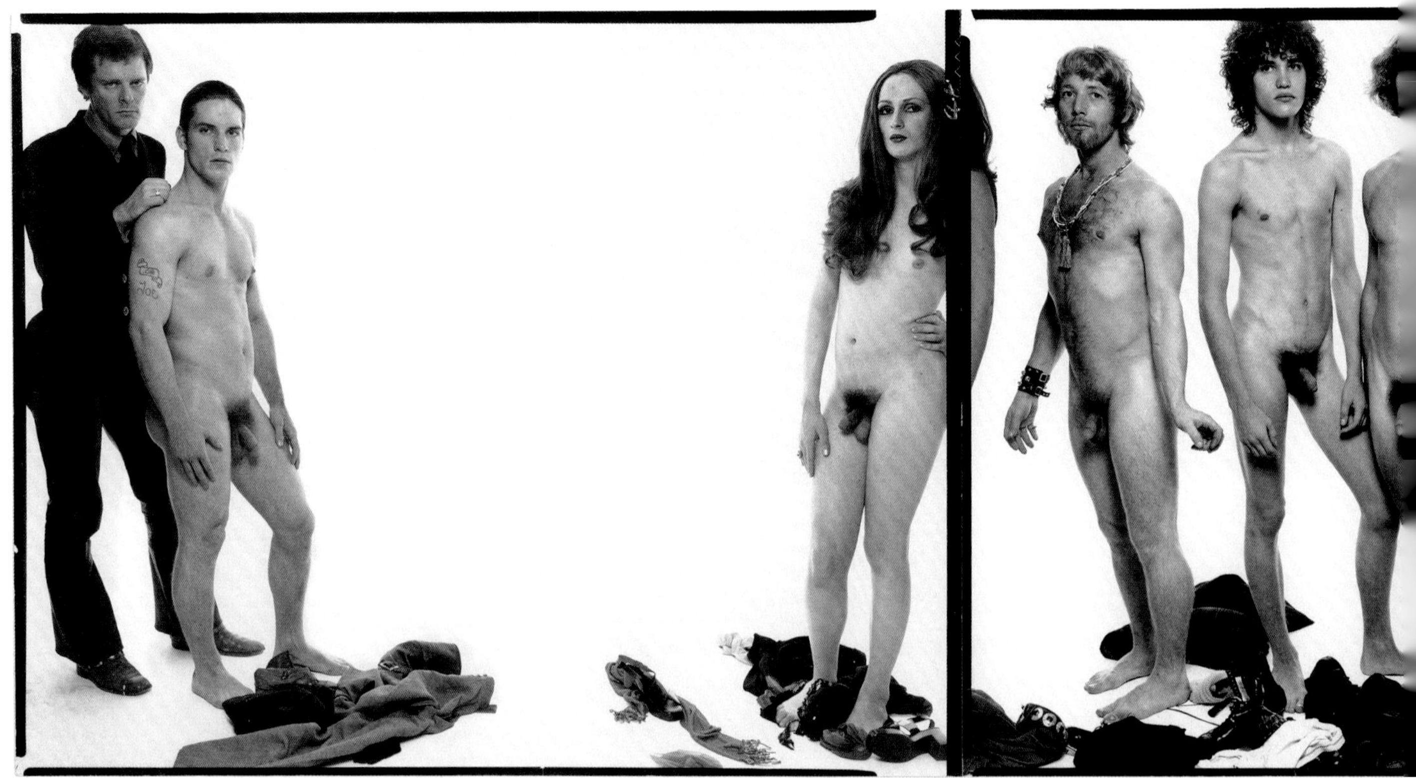

35. Richard Avedon (American, 1923–2004). *Andy Warhol and members of The Factory, New York City*, October 30, 1969. Gelatin silver prints, overall approx. 10 ft. 2 in. × 31 ft. 2½ in. (309.9 × 951 cm). Gift of the artist, 2002 (2002.379.3a–c)

left next to the nude Joe Dallesandro, then both reappear in the right panel, Morrissey lurking in the background and Dallesandro, fully dressed, standing next to Warhol.

When Avedon first exhibited this portrait, in his 1975 retrospective at Marlborough Gallery in New York, its frank presentation of male nudity and its overt sexuality were decried as shocking and sensationalistic, effects heightened by the photograph's monumental scale. Avedon deployed the same format across a range of subjects, from the antiwar activists known as the Chicago Seven to the members of the Mission Council, the chief strategists of the American war in Vietnam, his lens capturing the gravitas of contemporary history as incarnated by these larger-than-life figures. The critic for *Art in America* recognized the radicalism of Avedon's vision, declaring that the Mission Council portrait represented "a new kind of format for social imagery, one capable of containing complex feelings towards a critical historical issue." Avedon also prompted something of a renaissance in photographic group portraiture, as seen in Tina Barney's staged portraits of family and friends and Thomas Struth's large-format family portraits. In popular culture, Annie Leibovitz's celebrity-filled group portraits for the cover of *Vanity Fair* magazine's annual Hollywood issue draw upon Avedon's aesthetic.

Avedon's photograph of Warhol and his Factory "superstars," as they were known, also attests to the long-standing public fascination with the persona of the artist, which emerged soon after the development of self-portraiture in late fifteenth-century Europe. Once good-quality crystal mirrors became available, artists could use themselves as models. Charles Le Brun represents this innovation in his portrait of the Jabach family from about 1660, where his own likeness appears in a mirror; his reflected image reads as a signature of sorts and asserts his status as on par with that of his patron.

Similarly, Adélaïde Labille-Guiard's unambiguously feminine self-portrait of 1785, on the cusp of the French

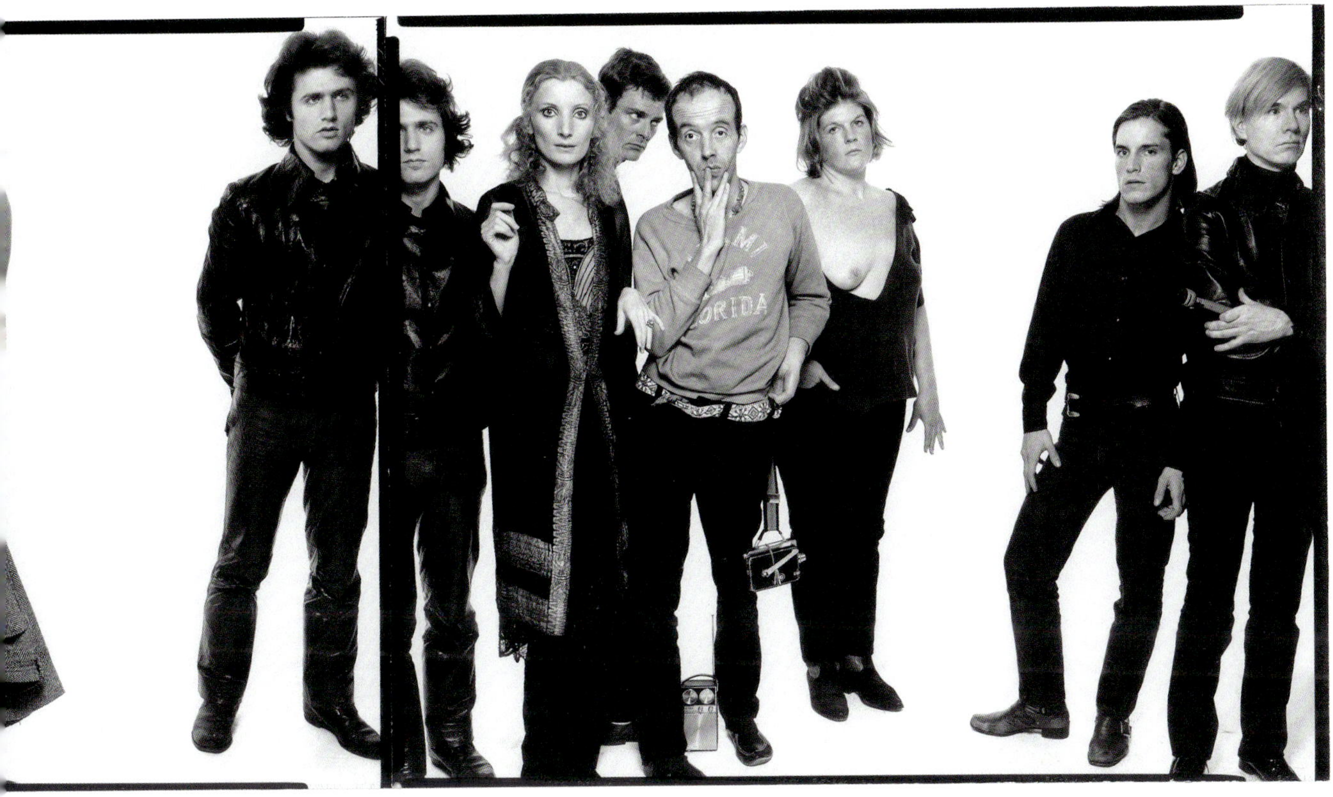

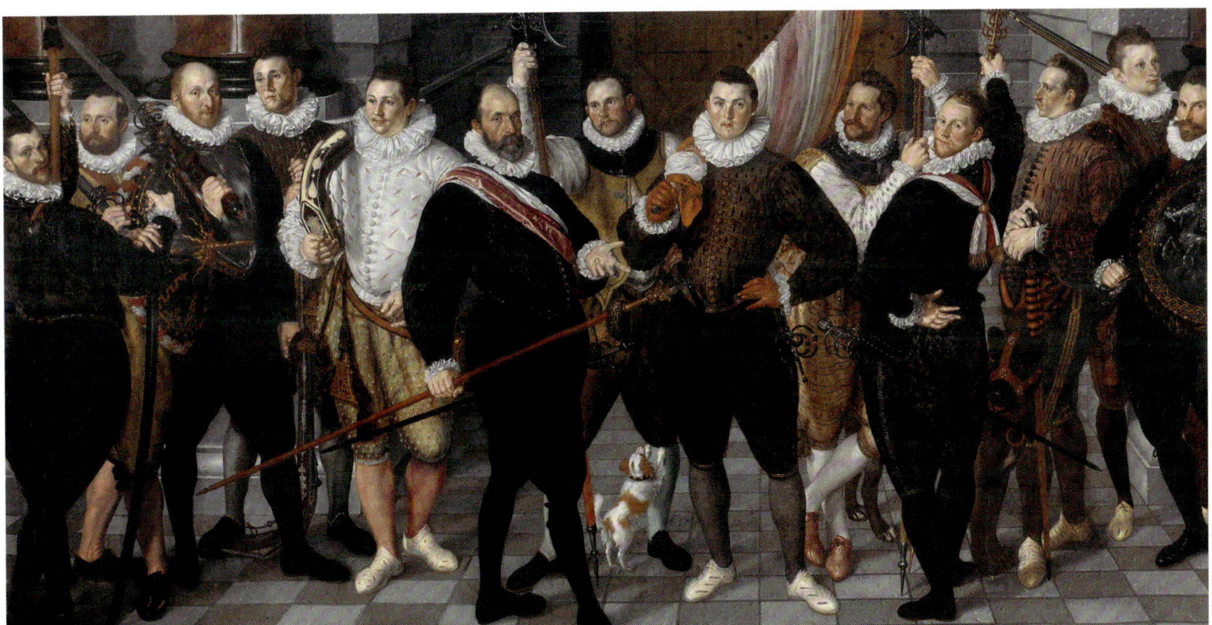

36. Cornelis Ketel (Dutch, 1548–1616). *The Company of Captain Dirck Jacobsz Rosecrans and Lieutenant Pauw*, 1588. Oil on canvas, 81⅞ in. × 13 ft. 5½ in. (208 × 410 cm). Rijksmuseum, on loan from the City of Amsterdam

Revolution, proclaimed her identity as a successful artist and, more broadly, asserted the ascendancy of professional women artists in France (fig. 37). Like Avedon's Factory portrait, the work was itself revolutionary in its subversion of gendered norms. Late eighteenth-century France generally disapproved of women pursuing careers as artists and publicly exhibiting their work. Social convention dictated that women's artistic pursuits be limited to drawing as a private pastime, and figure painting was deemed the exclusive purview of men. Labille-Guiard not only defied such dictums but signaled her ambitions through her painting's scale, as Avedon's photographic mural format would do some two centuries later. Her figures are lifesize—unprecedented in her oeuvre as a portraitist. Labille-Guiard depicted herself as an artist at work on an unseen canvas in her studio, paintbrush paused over palette, gazing outward in implicit acknowledgment of an audience beyond that of two of her students, with whom she shares the scene. Her signature, prominently inscribed on the easel's shelf, announces her authorship. The presence of her students asserts her other role as a teacher of women aspiring to be artists, then a rarity; in 1785, when this work was publicly exhibited at the state-sponsored Paris Salon, Labille-Guiard was one of only four women in the prestigious Royal Academy of Painting and Sculpture—the maximum number King Louis XVI would permit. He had imposed that quota in 1783 as a direct response to the exceptional admission of two women that year: Labille-Guiard and Élisabeth Vigée Le Brun. In this context, Labille-Guiard's portrayal of her students boldly challenges efforts to exclude women from the Academy. (From its founding in 1648 until its abolition in 1793, the Academy admitted some 550 artists, of whom 15 were women.) In the background, a bust of the artist's father and a statue of a vestal virgin, an ancient Roman maiden who vowed to remain chaste, seemingly observe the artist at work; these symbols of filial devotion and feminine modesty have been read as the artist's preemptive silencing of those who questioned the propriety of her professional choice. Eschewing artist's work clothes, Labille-Guiard improbably wears a fashionable silk *robe à l'anglaise* and a straw hat trimmed in ostrich feathers. Her sartorial selection might reflect a desire either to advertise her skill at rendering these varied materials to potential clients or to assert her femininity in defiance of her detractors, as the art historian Laura Auricchio has suggested. Although at least one reviewer in 1785 assumed that the work had been painted by a man because of the "vigor" and "force" of its handling, Labille-Guiard's mastery of the "masculine" Neoclassical style attested to artistic equality in the public forum of the Salon.

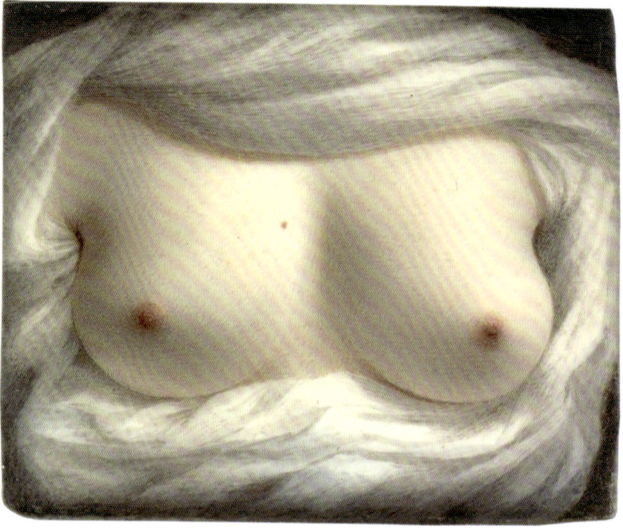

38. Sarah Goodridge (American, 1788–1853). *Beauty Revealed*, 1828. Watercolor on ivory, 2⅝ × 3⅛ in. (6.7 × 8 cm). Gift of Gloria Manney, 2006 (2006.235.74)

As a vehicle for self-promotion, Labille-Guiard's self-portrait had an inherently public function. Other self-portraits were private enterprises, such as the intimate work from 1828 by the Boston-based miniature painter Sarah Goodridge (fig. 38). On a thin sliver of ivory that fits in the palm of a hand, Goodridge painted her breasts—and only her breasts—with portraitlike specificity, down to the lone mole or freckle on the upper quadrant of her right breast. Her subject suggests an explicitly erotic variant of "lover's eyes," miniature eye

37. Adélaïde Labille-Guiard (French, 1749–1803). *Self-Portrait with Two Pupils, Marie Gabrielle Capet (1761–1818) and Marie Marguerite Carreaux de Rosemond (d. 1788)*, 1785. Oil on canvas, 83 × 59½ in. (210.8 × 151.1 cm). Gift of Julia A. Berwind, 1953 (53.225.5)

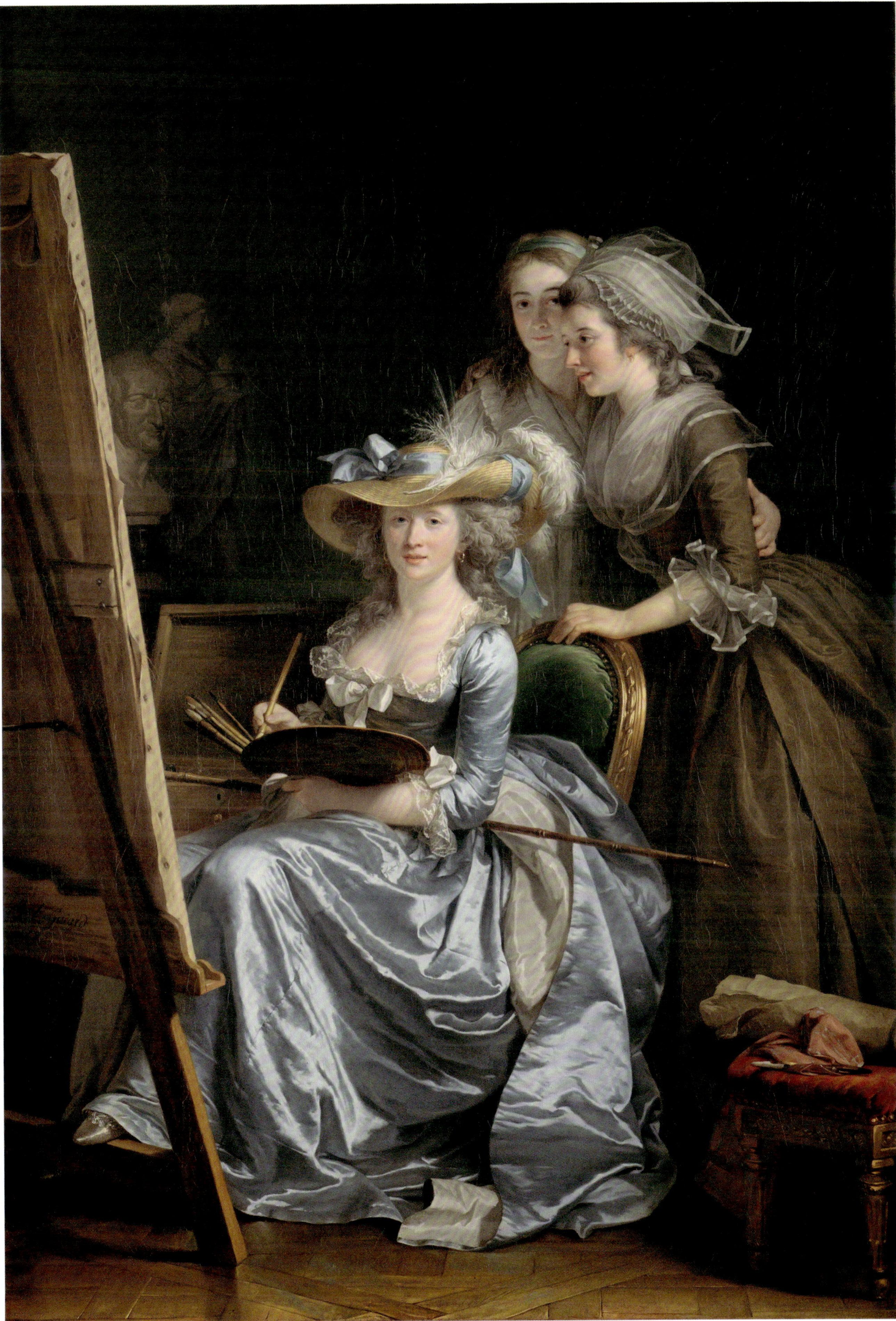

portraits first popularized in France and in vogue from 1790 to 1820 throughout Europe. Such portrait miniatures were exchanged as tokens of love or remembrance and carried close to the body or worn as jewelry. The subjects of these synecdochal portraits, typically painted from life, were known only to their recipients. Miniature mouths and, occasionally, a hand figure as variants of the "lover's eye" theme; Goodridge's miniature, though, is unique in its subject. She depicted her breasts swathed in white fabric, as if presented on a cushion, evoking the painted clouds often used to frame eye portraits. Goodridge gave this miniature, housed in a small box, to the American statesman and orator Daniel Webster in 1828, the year his first wife died. Although the nature of their relationship remains unknown, Webster never parted with Goodridge's gift.

Self-portraits served a different but also essentially private purpose for Vincent van Gogh, who painted thirty-five of them in just three and a half years. Like Rembrandt, whom he rivaled in both the sheer quantity and the expressive and stylistic range of his self-portraiture, Van Gogh assumed different personae in his work, from a Buddhist monk to a Dutch peasant. Unlike Rembrandt, Van Gogh was not famous in his lifetime, and there was no demand for his likeness. He offered some of his self-portraits in exchange for those of his fellow artists or, like Goodridge's miniature, as gifts to family and friends; others served as vehicles for artistic experimentation.

During his two-year sojourn in Paris, from February 1886 to February 1888, Van Gogh painted more self-portraits than at any other time in his brief, ten-year career, determined to succeed at portraiture. "What I'm most passionate about, much more than all the rest in my profession—is the portrait, the modern portrait," he wrote in an 1888 letter. The artist also reported to his brother Theo that he had bought a mirror, "so if I lacked a model I could work from my own likeness." For Van Gogh, the goal of the "modern portrait" was not to achieve a photographic likeness but rather to capture character through the expressive use of color. Indeed, those who knew Van Gogh noted how unlike his self-portraits he appeared; the artist himself addressed this disjuncture between image and subject, saying, "to my mind the same person supplies material for very diverse portraits." In this, the artist prefigures the self-transformations of Cindy Sherman (see fig. 48) and other shape-shifting contemporary artists.

A self-portrait as a working painter, wearing a blue smock and the straw hat he donned when painting outdoors, belongs to a group of seven head studies Van Gogh painted from mid-July to August 1887 (fig. 39). Attesting to the works' personal, experimental nature, all were painted quickly (likely in a single session) on the reverse of used canvases. Van Gogh used his likeness in this body of work to experiment with both his handling of paint and the angled placement of the head. *Self-Portrait with a Straw Hat* reveals his assimilation of contemporary French avant-garde painting in its high-keyed palette and application of paint in varied, discrete touches, recalling both the Impressionist broken brushstroke and the pointillist technique of the Neo-Impressionist painters, whose art Van Gogh would have seen in Paris. Following the stylistic experimentation of this work and others painted that summer, Van Gogh adopted a larger format for his self-portraits in the fall of 1887, signaling a new, more ambitious vision for his work in this genre.

While the self-portraits by Van Gogh and Goodridge are private works, and Labille-Guiard's statement-making canvas of 1785 was an unambiguously public one, the private and the public intersect in the paintings of Njideka Akunyili Crosby: in mining her personal experience, the artist reflects that of other members of the African diaspora. Akunyili Crosby, who was born in Nigeria and now lives and works in Los Angeles, has described herself as "someone from multiple worlds." Her work evokes those varied identities, with references to her childhood in Nigeria in the 1980s and 1990s, her familial relationships and life in America, and the Western art-historical tradition in which she was trained. The quiet domestic interior depicted in *Mother and Child*, painted in 2016, exemplifies the autobiographical aspect of her imagery (fig. 40). The painting reads simultaneously as a self-portrait, a family portrait, and a study in twenty-first-century cross-cultural identity. The seated figure is that of the artist, who frequently appears in her

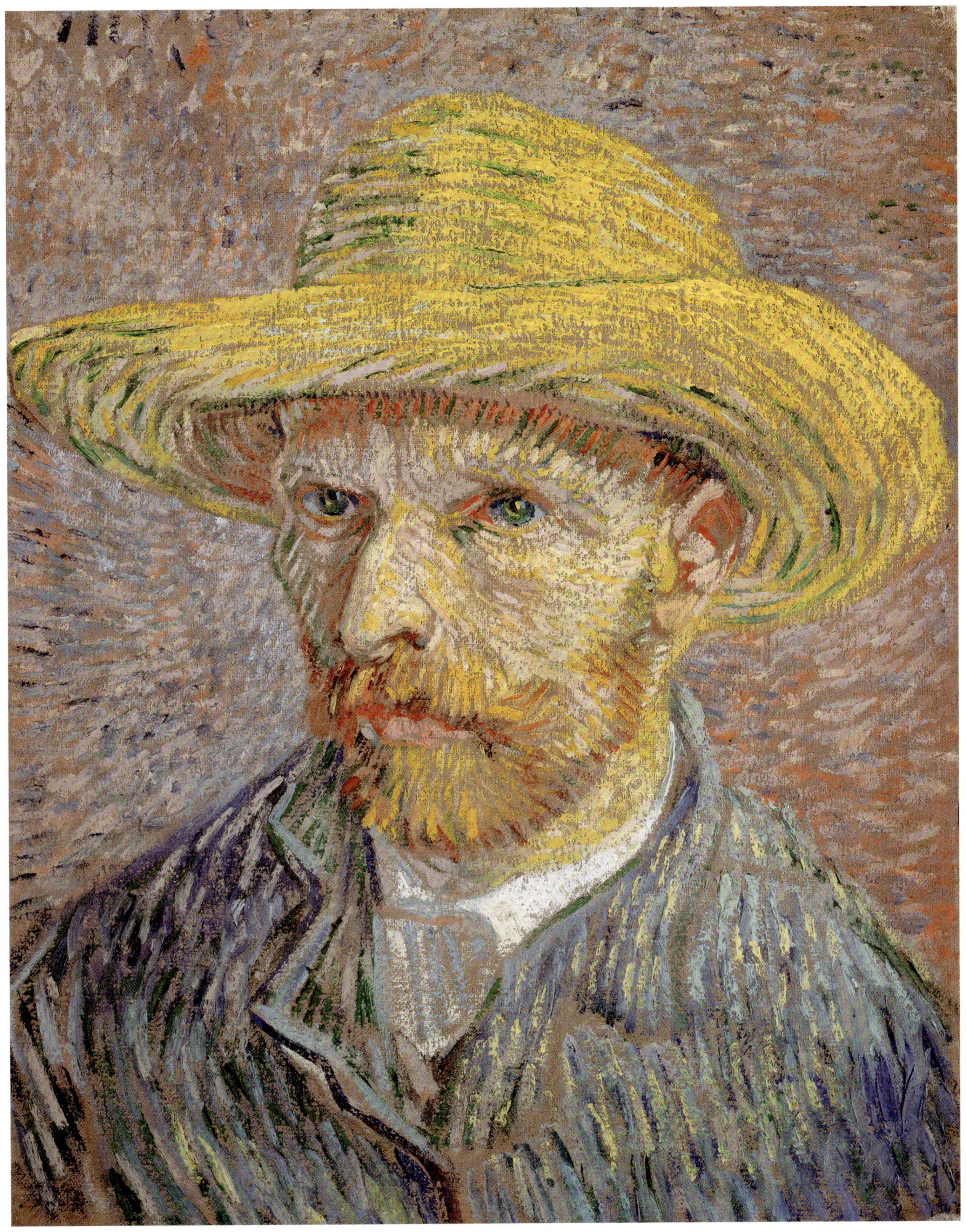

39. Vincent van Gogh (Dutch, 1853–1890). *Self-Portrait with a Straw Hat*, 1887. Oil on canvas, 16 × 12½ in. (40.6 × 31.8 cm). Bequest of Miss Adelaide Milton de Groot (1876–1967), 1967 (67.187.70a)

work; she shares the scene with the likeness of her recently deceased mother, Dora Akunyili, which repeats on the wallpaper (the portrait fabric made for her 2011 senatorial campaign), and a framed portrait of her maternal grandmother holding her youngest daughter (the artist's aunt). When this work was made, Akunyili Crosby herself was pregnant with her first child, adding another, unseen dimension to this commemoration of her matrilineage.

Mother and Child also alludes to the artist's multiple cultural identities: the traditional African portrait fabric and the terrazzo floor, which was popular in Nigerian homes in the 1990s, acknowledge her heritage; another autobiographical reference is the terrazzo pattern, which Akunyili Crosby created from transfer images of photographs she made of the floor in her family's village house. The composition also nods to the canon of Western art, which she studied in the United States: the small black-and-white painting of an empty interior with doors opening into other rooms is a copy of a painting by the Danish artist Vilhelm Hammershøi, which Akunyili Crosby juxtaposed with the open door in her own imaginary interior.

Akunyili Crosby's genre-defying, self-referential imagery manifests the artist's ongoing exploration of the "multiple worlds" intrinsic to her identity. Whether the subject is the artist herself, another individual, a family, or a celebrity, identity lies at the heart of portraiture. Identity can be fluid, however, as we will see next in portraits whose subjects assume a role, as well as in works that deliberately conjoin reality with fantasy, challenging the foundations of portraiture itself.

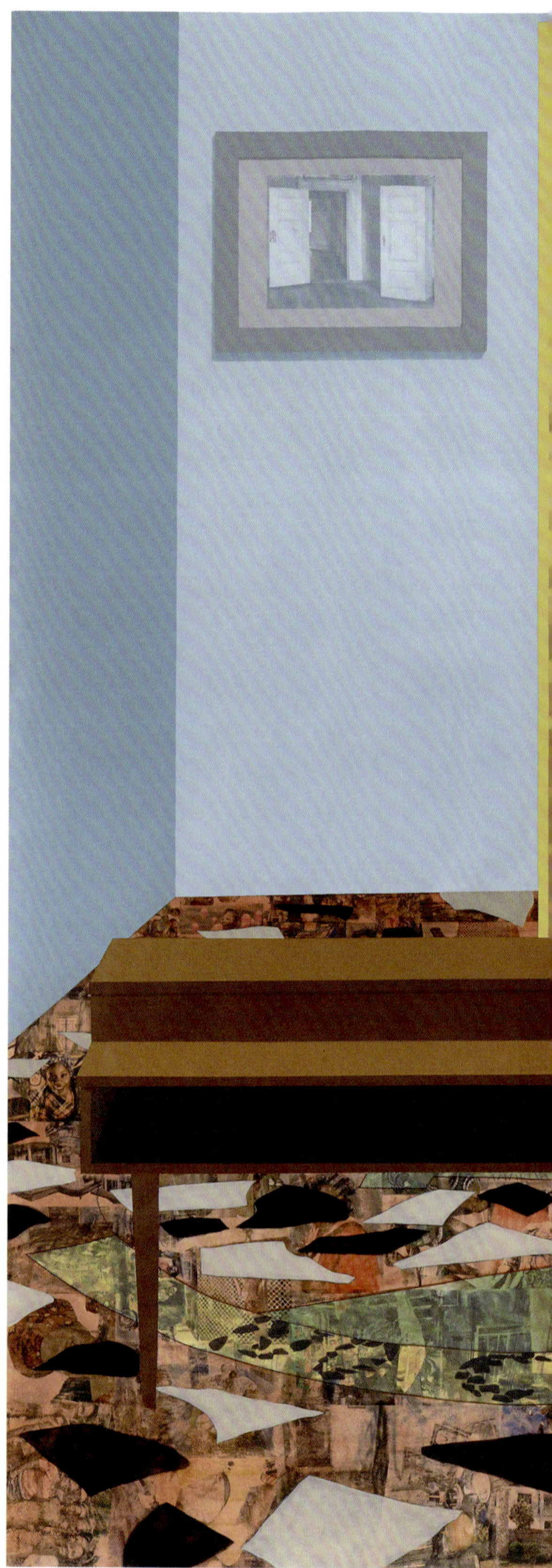

40. Njideka Akunyili Crosby (Nigerian, b. 1983). *Mother and Child*, 2016. Acrylic, transfer printing, colored pencil, cut and pasted paper, and printed fabric on paper, 95¾ in. × 10 ft. 4¼ in. (243.2 × 315.6 cm). Purchase, The Jacques and Natasha Gelman Foundation Gift, 2017 (2017.106)

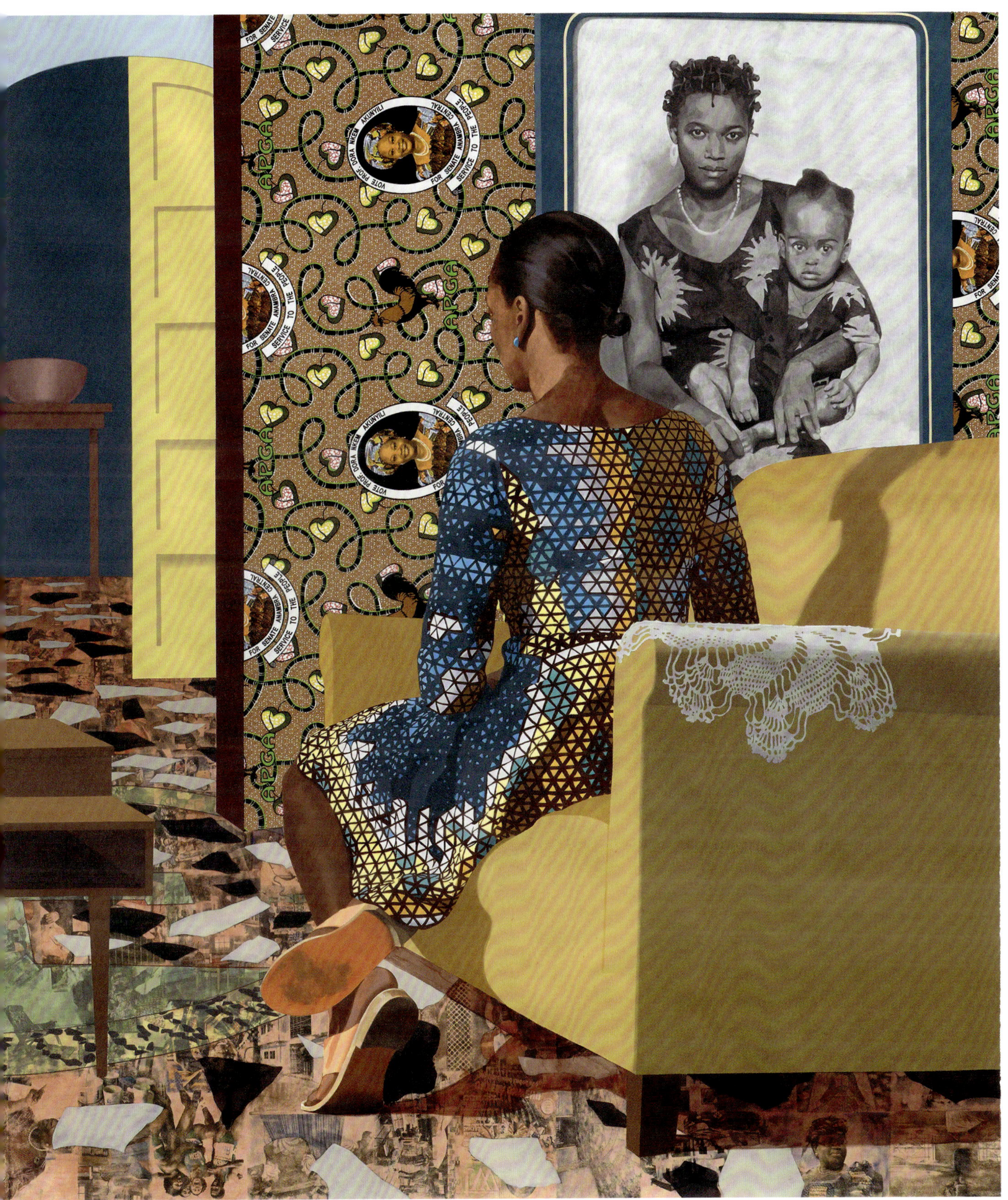
APGA
VOTE PROF DORA NKEM AKUNYILI
FOR SENATE ANAMBRA CENTRAL
SERVICE TO THE PEOPLE

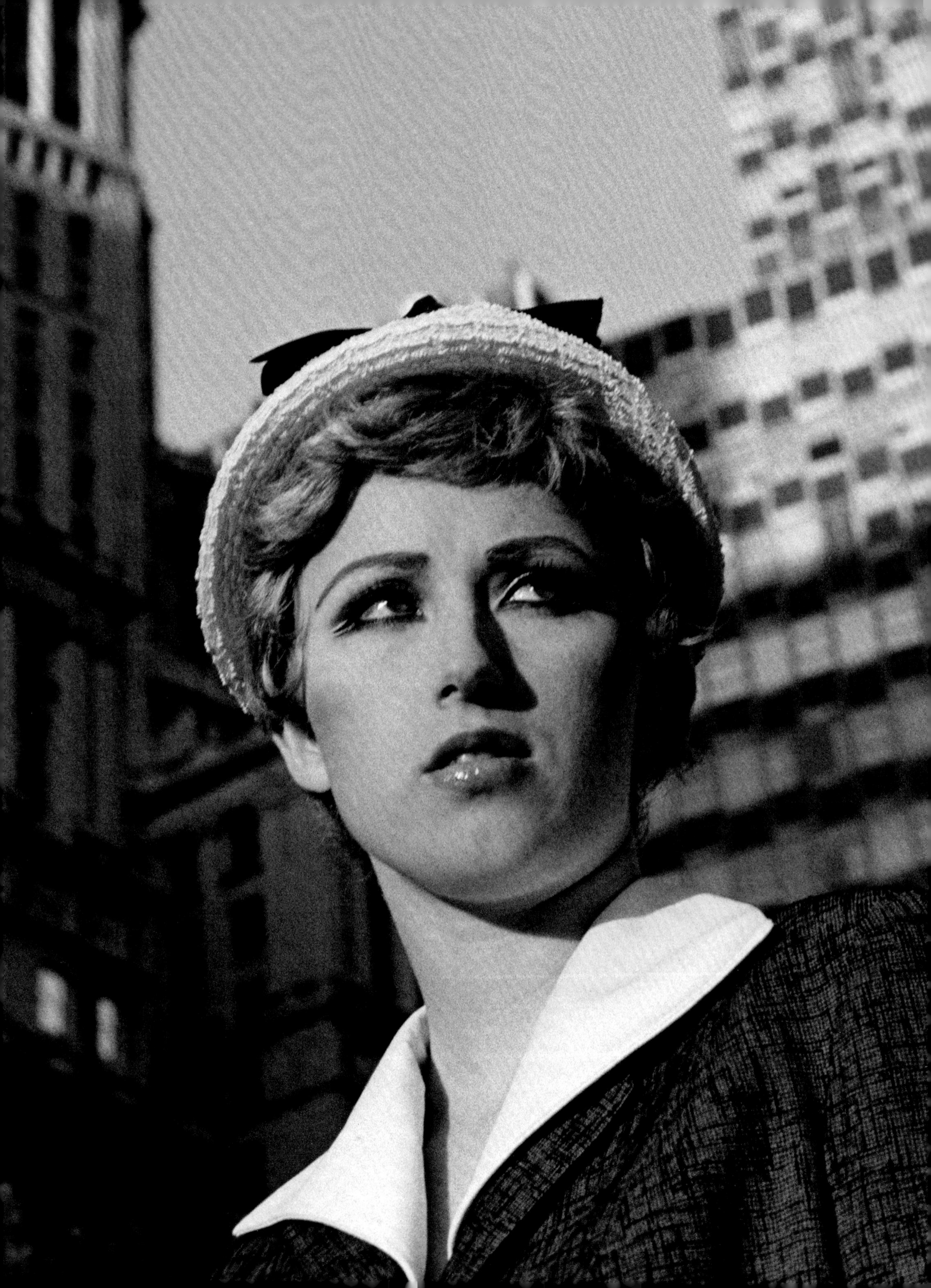

ROLE-PLAYING

As the representation of a specific individual, the portrait by definition conveys identity—even if the subject's name has been lost in the passage of time. That said, long before the advent of Photoshop and other means of altering appearances, the genre flirted with transforming, disguising, and even effacing likeness to craft identities that blur reality with fiction. We have already seen signs of artifice in the prevalence of idealization in portraiture, such as the perpetually youthful images of Emperor Augustus and Anthony van Dyck's flattering portrayals of seventeenth-century aristocrats, an approach emulated by successive generations of portraitists. Beyond such superficial dissimulation, portraiture has engaged throughout its history with identity's mutable and performative nature, from the social roles sitters adopt for a public audience to contemporary artists' shape-shifting personae.

The latter, more overt fictions can be traced to the costumed portraits that originated in early modern Europe. The *portrait historié*, or historicized portrait, which dates to the late fifteenth century, introduced role-playing to portraiture, with the sitter appearing as a figure from the Bible, classical mythology, or history. It thus aligned portraiture with history painting, the genre that, well into the nineteenth century, the European art establishment considered the highest form of art because it relied on the artist's imaginative power. Portraiture was deemed a lesser art that simply recorded what could be seen. A painting of the celebrated male soprano and musician Marcantonio Pasqualini, made in Rome by Andrea Sacchi in 1641, exemplifies the more elevated mode of historicized portraiture (fig. 42). Although his likeness was "most beautifully painted from life," according to a seventeenth-century commentator, the work was "not a simple portrait but a most beautiful conceit." Indeed, the composition is operatic in its staging, with Pasqualini dressed as a shepherd, posing as if playing a vertical harpsichord, or clavicytherium, and turning to acknowledge the audience. His performance transpires in a mythological realm: he shares the stage with Apollo, the god of music, identified by the lyre that he holds, and the satyr Marsyas, shown bound to a tree as punishment for failing in his musical challenge to Apollo. This narrative transforms the portrait into an allegory of music and enhances Pasqualini's status as a musician (as well as Sacchi's status as an artist). His talent is celebrated by no less than Apollo, who crowns him with a laurel wreath in recognition of his accomplishment. In

41. Cindy Sherman. *Untitled Film Still #21*, 1978 (detail of figure 48)

the earthly realm, the portrait serves as a thinly veiled form of self-promotion on the part of Pasqualini, who likely commissioned his portrait from Sacchi. The work's flattering classical allusions would have been understood among Pasqualini's friends and influential patrons in Rome, notably Cardinal Antonio Barberini, whose collection of musical instruments included an example of the rare vertical harpsichord Pasqualini plays here.

The performative aspect of this mode of portraiture mirrored contemporary elite forms of entertainment, such as the masques presented by costumed players at the court of Charles I in seventeenth-century England, the lavish entertainments staged by the French kings at the château of Versailles in the seventeenth and eighteenth centuries, and the masked balls that were popular on both sides of the Channel. Late in the eighteenth century, guests at the residence of Sir William Hamilton, the British ambassador to Naples, witnessed the spectacle of Emma Hart, the future Lady Hamilton, executing her celebrated "Attitudes," choreographed poses inspired by figures on the classical Greek vases in Hamilton's collection; her performances were such a sensation that they were memorialized in engravings published in 1794. In France, Queen Marie Antoinette enacted her pastoral fantasies costumed as a shepherdess at her private retreat at Versailles, which featured a working dairy—a precursor to contemporary cosplay. Eighteenth-century European portraiture is replete with depictions of aristocratic and royal sitters as shepherds and shepherdesses, vestal virgins from ancient Rome, goddesses and, occasionally, gods. Such disguises conveyed social standing, particularly for women, who did not have recourse to the military, political, and professional markers of status and rank deployed in portraits of elite men, as the art historian Gill Perry has noted. From the 1760s, the British artist Sir Joshua Reynolds championed this mode of "Grand Style" portraiture, ennobling his female sitters through classicizing costumes and allusions.

Jean Marc Nattier dominated the market for historicized portraits in France during the reign of Louis XV (1715–74). In 1756 he painted one Madame Bergeret de Frouville as Diana, virgin goddess of the hunt (fig. 43). Armed with Diana's trademark bow and quiver of arrows, Nattier's aristocratic sitter is portrayed in a landscape evocative of the goddess's sylvan haunts. The leopard skin knotted at her breasts is worn by other "Dianas" Nattier painted, which suggests that it was a studio prop. Cheeks rouged (like most of Nattier's fashionable female sitters), she appears in a state of dishabille, shimmering satin billowing beneath her. Her revealing white chemise is typical of the attire worn by female subjects in the artist's *portraits historiés*, no matter what role they were playing. By appearing "as Diana" rather than simply herself, the sitter was not bound by the strict rules of decorum that governed conventional portrait likenesses—hence, her provocative décolletage. The artist, too, was free to unleash his imagination, much as a history painter would in recreating scenes from mythology. This type of ostentatious artifice generated backlash from critics as tastes—and the political climate—changed in late eighteenth-century France, but artists would exploit the freedom such fictions accorded in portraiture and other genres well into the nineteenth century.

The elision of portraiture with history painting in the *portrait historié* recalls another hybrid type of figure painting, the *tronie* (a now obsolete Dutch word for "head" or "face"), popularized by Rembrandt and his students in the seventeenth-century Dutch Republic. These paintings of a cropped single figure, usually painted from life in the studio, are marked by their verisimilitude but were not intended as portraits of specific individuals. Rather, their subjects, often costumed, served as a vehicle for exploring different character types, facial expressions, and light effects. Unlike portraits, tronies were generally not commissioned, and contemporary collectors prized them as displays of bravura technique and artistic imagination. Portraitlike but not a portrait, the tronie is a figure of fantasy.

A close-up, bust-length study of a young woman, painted by Johannes Vermeer about 1665–67, is one such work (fig. 44); tellingly, until 2001, it was identified as a portrait, with scholars citing the clearly individualized

42. Andrea Sacchi (Italian, ca. 1599–1661). *Marcantonio Pasqualini (1614–1691) Crowned by Apollo*, 1641. Oil on canvas, 96 × 76½ in. (243.8 × 194.3 cm). Purchase, Enid A. Haupt Gift and Gwynne Andrews Fund, 1981 (1981.317)

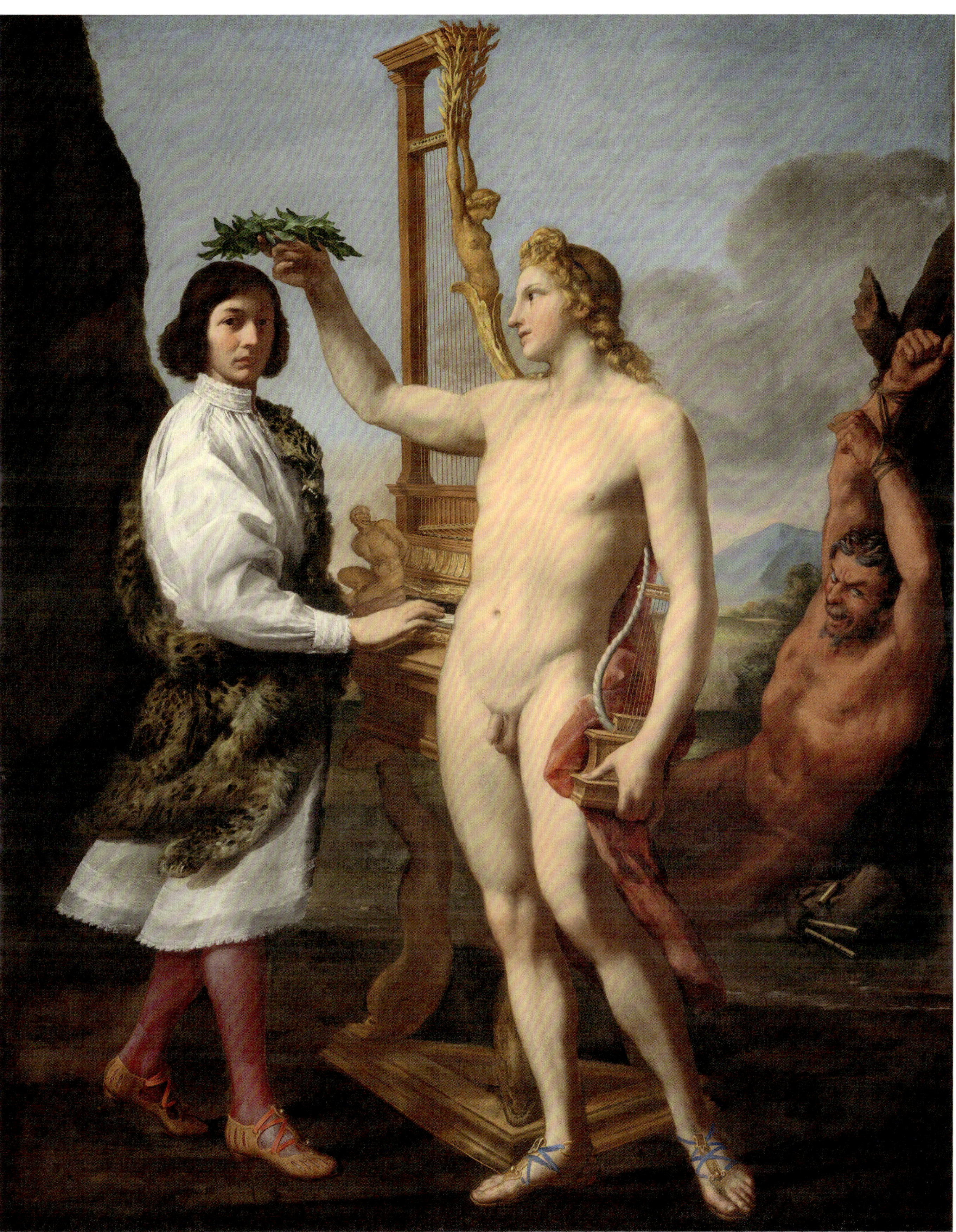

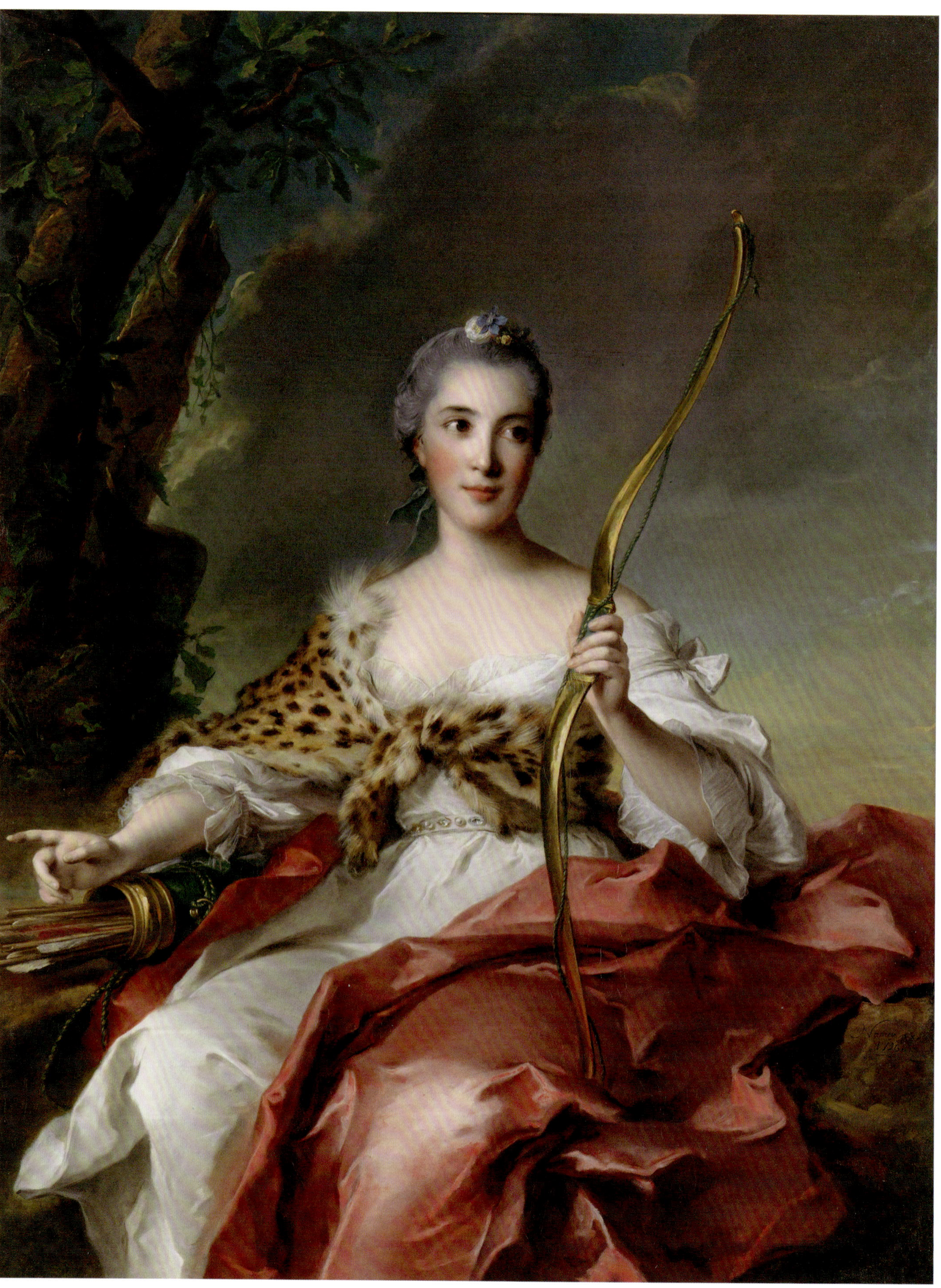

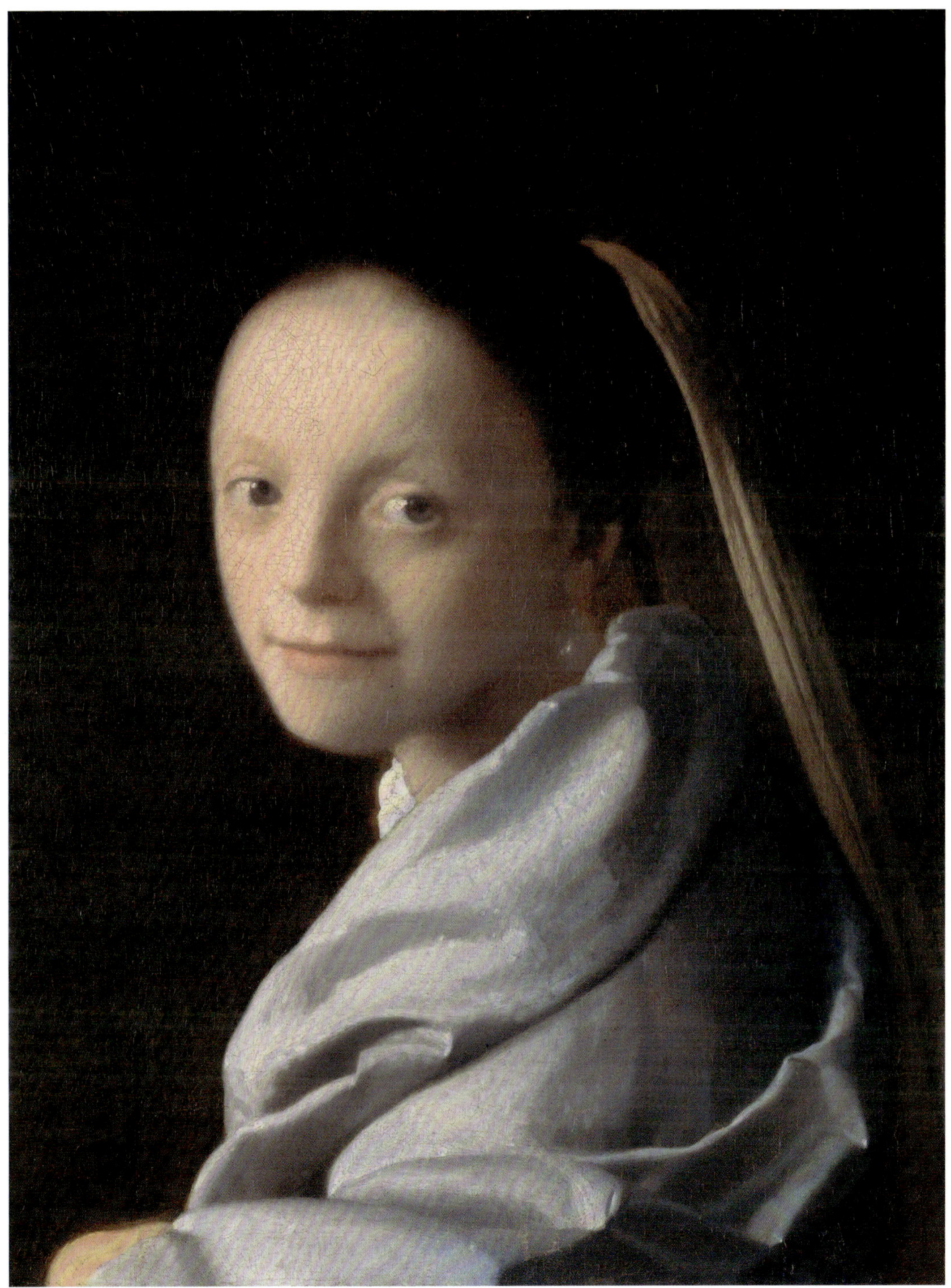

Opposite: 43. Jean Marc Nattier (French, 1685–1766). *Madame Bergeret de Frouville as Diana*, 1756. Oil on canvas, 53¾ × 41⅜ in. (136.5 × 105.1 cm). Rogers Fund, 1903 (03.37.3)

Above: 44. Johannes Vermeer (Dutch, 1632–1675). *Study of a Young Woman*, ca. 1665–67. Oil on canvas, 17½ × 15¾ in. (44.5 × 40 cm). Gift of Mr. and Mrs. Charles Wrightsman, in memory of Theodore Rousseau Jr., 1979 (1979.396.1)

treatment of the sitter's features, made more prominent by the fashionably shaved eyebrows and hairline. This work is now recognized as one of Vermeer's four known tronies, all of young women gazing outward, from the mid-1660s, which were probably painted from life. Among them, *Girl with a Pearl Earring* (Mauritshuis, The Hague) is nearly identical in scale and composition to the present work and has been seen as its pair. The artist's signature, with the initials in monogram, appears in the upper left corner of both canvases, indicating that they were painted with an eye to the art market rather than as studies for other works, as some tronies were. In both, the varied light effects were intended to showcase Vermeer's mastery to connoisseurs of painting; here they are expressed in the evocative play of light and shadow across the features, the glint of light on the pearl earring, and the tonal range of the deep folds of the wrap. A late seventeenth-century auction catalogue refers to one of Vermeer's tronies as clad in "antique garments." "Antique" then referred to any type of historicizing dress, such as the folds of silk draped over the figure's shoulders in the present work, which loosely suggest the drapery of classical statuary. The model's attire would have been understood by a seventeenth-century audience as a costume and not contemporary dress. As a virtuoso display of technical skill, Vermeer's young woman anticipates the so-called fantasy figures that Jean Honoré Fragonard would paint in Paris a century later, for example, *Woman with a Dog* (identified as Marie Émilie Coignet de Courson), from about 1769 (37.118). Portraitlike, Fragonard's paintings represent a range of social types, all clad in historicizing dress. These imaginative and expressively rendered figures are eighteenth-century variants of the tronie.

Both the tronie's fusion of the real with the imaginary and its evasion of strictly defined categories would echo more than two centuries later in a group of figure paintings Édouard Manet made in his Paris studio between 1862 and 1866 (fig. 45). By conflating portraiture with the lowly mode of genre painting, or scenes from everyday life, Manet's images of Victorine Louise Meurent confound the hierarchical categories of painting that had dominated European art for centuries. In a further subversion of pictorial convention, his paintings of Victorine were realized on the large scale usually reserved for history painting. In them, the model enacts scenarios, either costumed or, scandalously, in the nude. Although she remains recognizable by her auburn hair and pale complexion, her facial features read differently among the works, challenging the fundamental notion of the portrait as a record of an individual's likeness. The art historian Carol Armstrong characterized Manet's unconventional approach in his paintings of Victorine as "making the portrait strange." In an 1862 canvas Manet's model assumes the guise of a Spanish *espada*, or matador, the bullfighter tasked with killing the bull—itself a fiction as there were no female bullfighters in nineteenth-century Spain, which Manet's contemporaries would have known. She is outfitted from Manet's trove of studio props, including a sombrero and bolero jacket that appear in the artist's other Spanish-themed subjects from the early 1860s, and flourishes a bullfighter's cape. Adding to this multilayered fabrication, her pose conflates high and low source material: two sixteenth-century allegorical figures engraved by Marcantonio Raimondi after a history painting by Raphael and, as Armstrong posited, a contemporary *carte de visite* photographic portrait of the dancer Eugénie Fiocre as a matador. The bullfight is lifted directly from Francisco de Goya's *The Art of Bullfighting*, a set of prints published in 1815–16.

Notwithstanding its artifice, *Mademoiselle V . . . in the Costume of an Espada* reads as the most portraitlike of Manet's staged paintings of Victorine, as biographical information on the artist's model, published in 2023 by the anthropologist James Fairhead, affirms. "Mlle Victorine" was the stage name of a popular cancan dancer who appeared in an 1861 production at the Hippodrome in Paris that included a parody of bullfighting, though it is not known if she or another member of the all-female troupe danced in that scene. Manet, a regular at the Hippodrome, might well have been alluding to that

45. Édouard Manet (French, 1832–1883). *Mademoiselle V . . . in the Costume of an Espada*, 1862. Oil on canvas, 65 × 50¼ in. (165.1 × 127.6 cm). H. O. Havemeyer Collection, Bequest of Mrs. H. O. Havemeyer, 1929 (29.100.53)

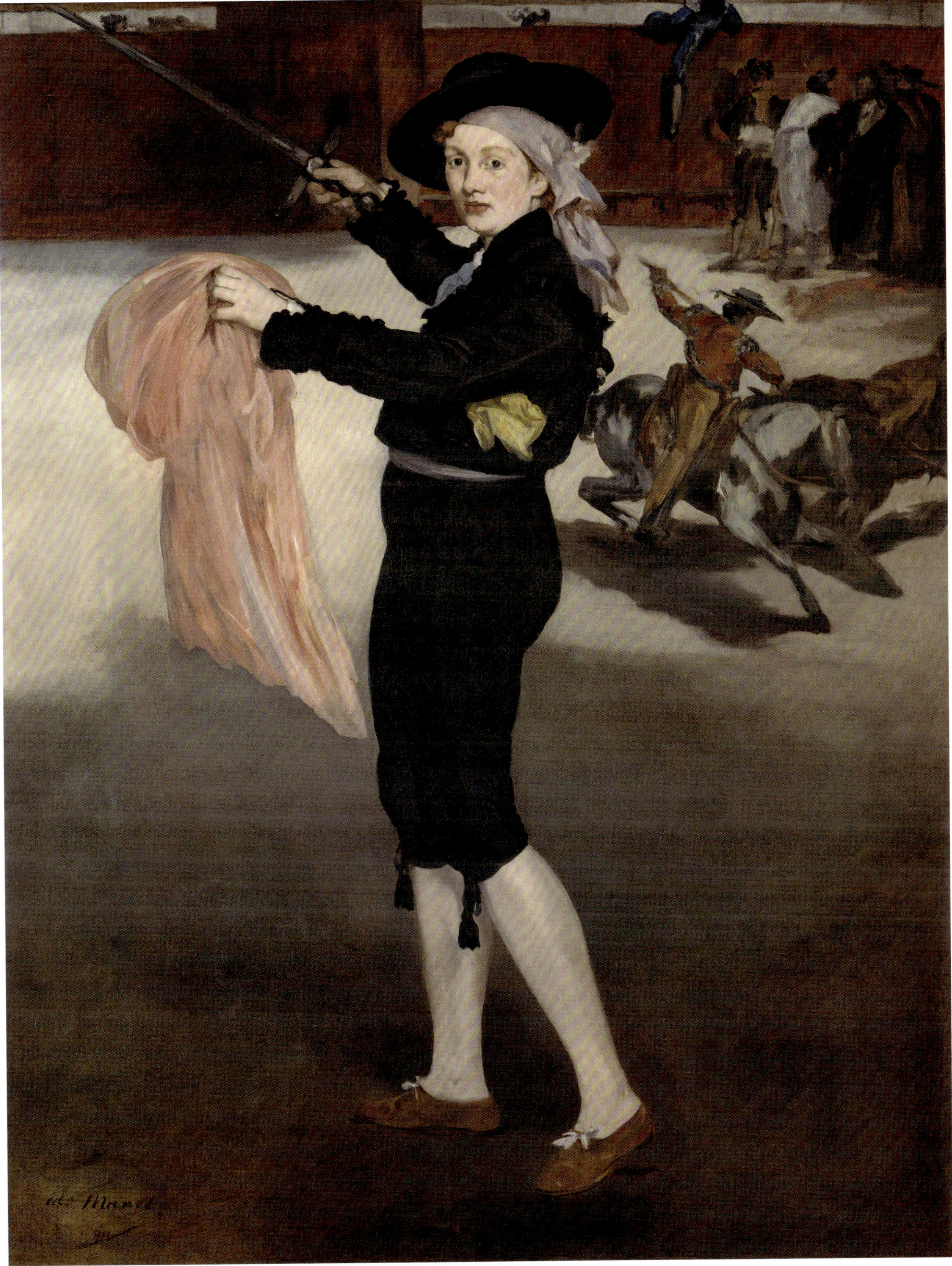

performance if not to a role played by his model when he painted Victorine cross-dressed as a matador in his studio the following year. The work's title can now be understood as Manet's nod to her stage name—that is, to her actual identity as a performer. Moreover, it is the only one of Manet's staged images of Victorine in which she is identified and in which it could be said that she plays herself, albeit in character. In his other paintings, her identity is subsumed in the service of the artist's modern narratives, subverting our expectations of portraiture.

Manet's radical approach to the portrait in his images of Victorine Meurent inspired his fellow avant-garde artists, including Claude Monet, whose model and future wife, Camille Doncieux, enacted various roles in his figure paintings of the 1860s and 1870s. In 1866 she assumed the identity of a fashionable Parisian in *The Woman in a Green Dress* (Kunsthalle Bremen). Its debt to Manet's precedent was recognized by contemporary commentators; like Manet's paintings of Victorine, Monet's image of Camille defies categorization, which the artist himself later acknowledged: "though I absolutely did not want to make a portrait but simply a Parisian figure of the era, the resemblance is total." All the figures in Monet's *Women in the Garden* of about 1866 (Musée d'Orsay, Paris), a composite painting inspired by contemporary fashion plates, are based on Camille. Similarly, a clearly identified and recognizable Camille plays a role in an 1873 work Monet staged in the garden of their rented house at Argenteuil (*Camille Monet on a Garden Bench*; 2002.62.1).

Role-playing is equally central to the contemporary practice of Kehinde Wiley, whose work engages in dialogue with Western art history. In Wiley's staged portraits, young Black and Brown men (and sometimes women) emulate the poses of canonical portrait subjects, who are inevitably White and in positions of power. By appropriating these painted and sculpted precedents—"hacking that language," to use Wiley's phrase—the artist claims their authority for subjects portraiture has historically marginalized. In his 2021 *Portrait of a Young Gentleman* (fig. 46), a Senegalese model borrows the hand-on-hip pose of Thomas Gainsborough's iconic 1770 portrait known today as *The Blue Boy* (Huntington Art Museum, Los Angeles). It is a work familiar to Wiley since childhood, lending personal resonance to his *Young Gentleman*. Wiley's subject projects the self-confident swagger of a young Black man in the twenty-first century. His "role," in Wiley's words, is "a little bit hippie, a little bit hobo, a little bit surfer bum," as reflected in his attire: tie-dyed T-shirt, Asics sport watch, and Vans Sidestripe, the quintessential California skateboard shoe. His outfit reads as a modern equivalent of the historicizing costume worn by Gainsborough's model or Victorine Meurent's matador garb.

Such explorations of artifice and role-playing in portraiture are not limited to the realm of painting. With the advent of photography, the photographic portrait was quickly harnessed to similar deceptions, challenging the new medium's apparent veracity. Only a year after Louis Daguerre invented the eponymous daguerreotype in 1839, a disgruntled competitor, Hippolyte Bayard, staged his own death, documented in the photograph *Self-Portrait as a Drowned Man*. That one-off event prefigured the long-running performance by Virginia Oldoini, Countess de Castiglione, in the studio of photographer Pierre-Louis Pierson. In Paris during the 1860s, when Manet was painting multiple Victorine Meurents, the countess was photographed in at least 188 different poses over the course of more than forty sittings. These works marked the creative climax of an artistic collaboration between the photographer and his subject that ultimately spanned almost four decades. Her yearslong exploration of her photographic image recalls Rembrandt's sustained engagement with his own likeness (see fig. 14). However, her portrait enterprise, unlike Rembrandt's, has been attributed to narcissism, which suggests a misogynistic dismissal of her creative agency. Like Rembrandt, the countess experimented with identity, trying on different personae and roles. Pierson's photographs show

46. Kehinde Wiley (American, b. 1977). *A Portrait of a Young Gentleman*, 2021. Oil on linen, image 70½ × 49⅛ in. (179.1 × 124.8 cm). Collection of the Huntington Library, Art Museum, and Botanical Gardens, Los Angeles; Commissioned through Roberts Projects, Los Angeles; Gift of Anne F. Rothenberg, Terry Perucca and Annette Serrurier, and the Philip and Muriel Berman Foundation. Additional support was provided by Laura and Carlton Seaver, Kent Belden and Dr. Louis Re, and Faye and Robert Davidson

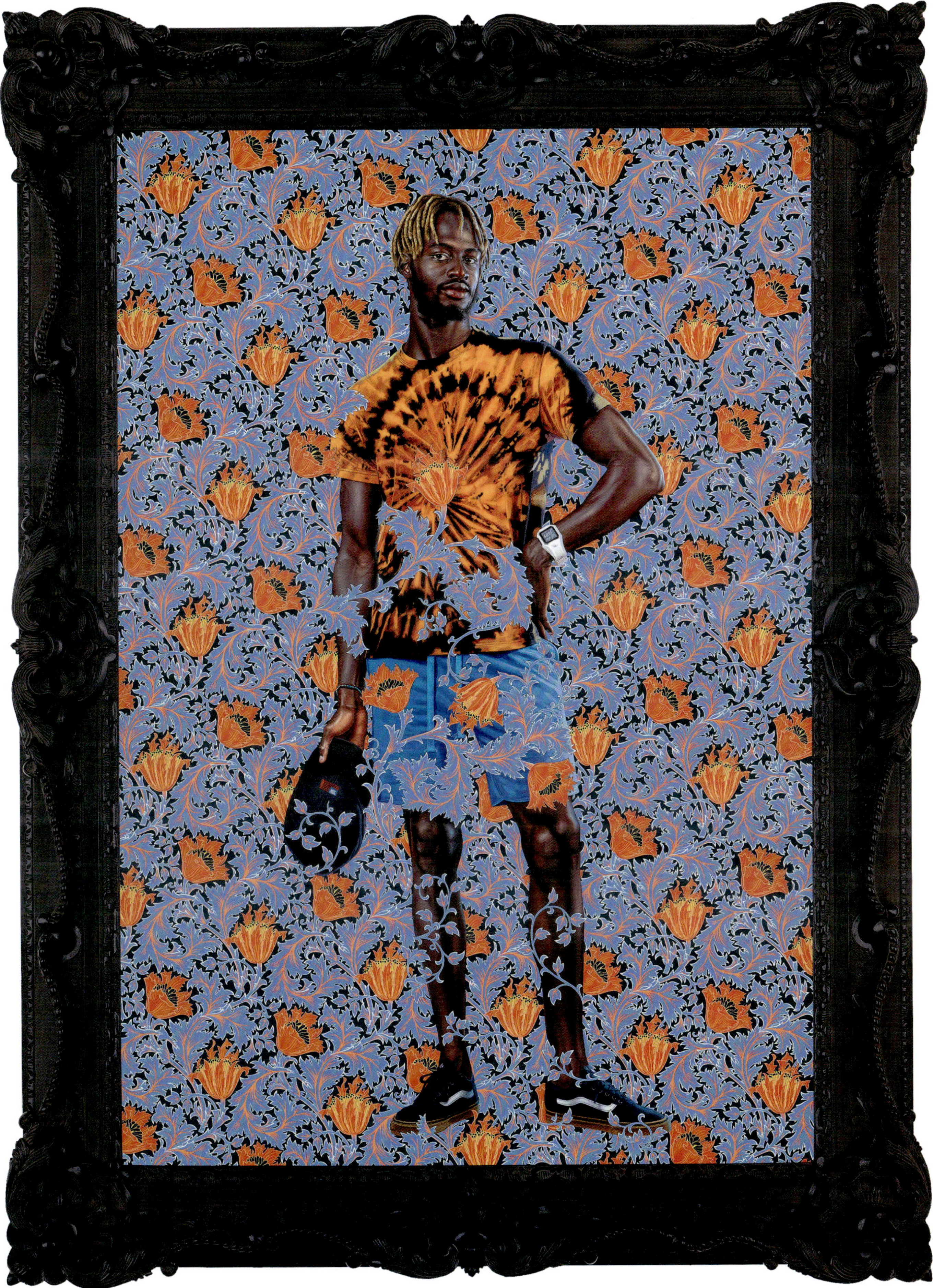

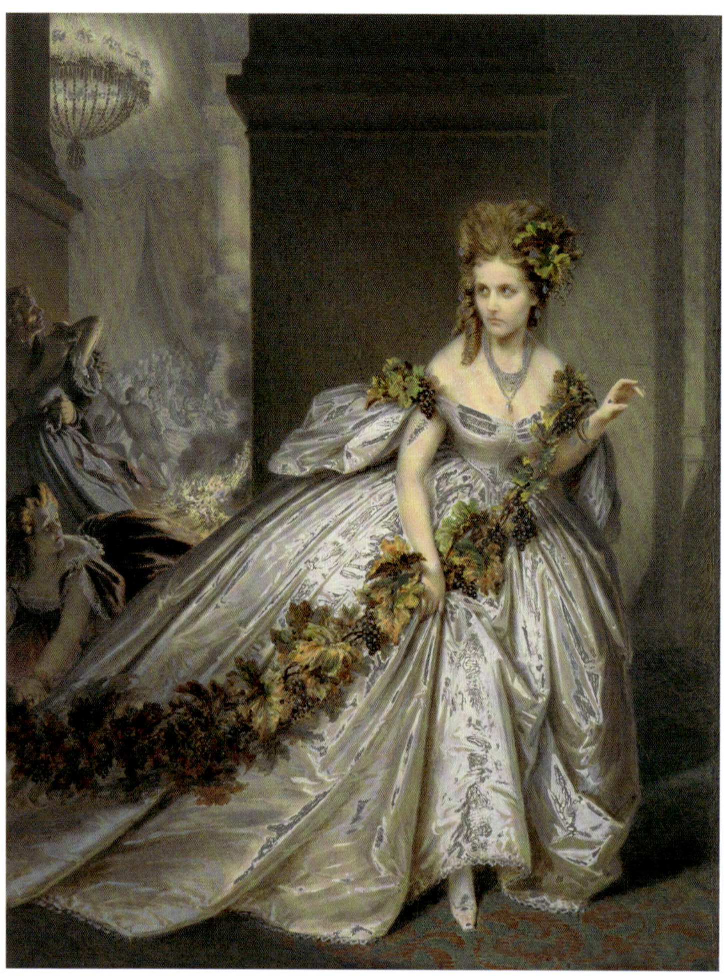

47. Pierre-Louis Pierson (French, 1822–1913), photographer; Aquilin Schad (Austrian, 1817–1866), painter. *La Frayeur*, 1861–64. Salted paper print from glass negative with applied color, 22½ × 17⅜ in. (57 × 44 cm). Purchase, The Camille M. Lownds Fund, Joyce F. Menschel Gift, Louis V. Bell and 2012 Benefit Funds, and C. Jay Moorhead Foundation Gift, 2015 (2015.395)

her assuming conventional portrait poses, playing a character—either in or out of costume—and performing a range of attitudes in mise-en-scènes that she staged for the photographer's lens.

Many of her images allude to actual events in her life, including *La Frayeur* (*Fright*), a painted photograph of 1861–64, which shows the countess in a satin ballgown that she reportedly also wore to a gala at the British Embassy in Paris in April 1866 (fig. 47). Renowned as a great beauty, she was frequently sighted at such entertainments. Pierson's studio specialized in painted photographs, then in vogue; in such hand-colored works, touches of gouache or watercolor were intended to enhance the original black-and-white photograph. However, the countess exploited these effects, transforming the reality of the photographic portrait into a painted fiction. Here, the painted ballroom scene entirely obscures the original studio background, and the dress has been extensively overpainted to create the effect of shimmering satin. The countess established the setting in notes to the painter on the back of a photographic print that served as a study for the final work: "The remains of a ball where a fire has started. A chandelier on the floor, the assembled company in flight. White satin dress, with high sheen, black and red grapes, dark green and red leaves." The result, as painted by Aquilin Schad, is a curiously hybrid work: both photograph and painting, at once real and imaginary. The altered photographic print is not unlike today's digitally manipulated imagery, a kind of nineteenth-century Photoshop.

In *Fright*, as in her other photographic portraits, the countess is the protagonist in a drama of her own creation; as Pierson later recalled, it was she who controlled her image. At the height of their collaboration in the

1860s, she was a public figure, notorious for her short-lived liaison with Emperor Napoleon III, yet the photographs were made for her private use; the countess selectively offered her likenesses to family members and others in her immediate circle, but most remained known only to her and Pierson until after her death in 1899.

The portraits the Countess de Castiglione staged for the camera are effectively a form of performance art. The photographs have also been likened to self-portraits, in recognition of the sitter's agency in the creation of her image. By the time of her death, she and Pierson had generated more than four hundred portraits, whose inherent artifice challenges the centrality of identity in portraiture. Nearly a century later Cindy Sherman began her own exploration of the ways identity is constructed, through staged photographs in which she serves as both photographer and model. Although her images are often referred to as self-portraits, Sherman rejects that label: "I feel anonymous in my work. When I look at the pictures, I never see myself; they aren't self-portraits. Sometimes I disappear." Rather, by embodying these imagined "characters," as Sherman refers to her subjects, the photographer engages with female stereotypes perpetuated by mass culture, ranging from starlets and centerfolds to socialites.

In 1977, when photography was increasingly transgressing the boundaries of verisimilitude, Sherman, then twenty-three, realized the first in a series of seventy black-and-white photographs that would span three years and launch her career. The series was inspired by film stills, inexpensive publicity photos taken on the set of a movie, which were widely used promotional tools during the middle of the last century; Andy Warhol's iconic 1962 silk-screened portrait of Marilyn Monroe was based on a publicity photo for the 1953 film *Niagara*. The series, Untitled Film Stills, culls from a range of midcentury cinematic genres, including Hollywood B movies, Italian neorealism, and film noir; it conjures the work of such directors as Alfred Hitchcock, Douglas Sirk, and Michelangelo Antonioni. In Sherman's 8-x-10-inch photographs, whose scale and glossy black-and-white format match that of the midcentury film still, the artist enacts such stock female roles as "the trashy has-been" (her words), the dissolute housewife, and the ingenue. In *Untitled Film Still #21*, from 1978, Sherman, wearing a blonde wig, calls to mind a young Grace Kelly in a Hitchcock thriller, playing an office worker seemingly trapped as the walls of the city close in around her (fig. 48). That undercurrent of anxiety is echoed in two related urban scenes (#22 and #23)—a group Sherman calls the "city girl" pictures, in which she casts herself in the same part.

Many of the photographs in the series are deliberately grainy, intended to evoke their pop-culture source material, as Sherman explained: "I wanted them to seem cheap and trashy . . . I didn't want them to look like art." The staged scenarios are evocations rather than re-creations of actual films, their narratives deliberately ambiguous. Sherman's overt use of makeup, wigs, and thrift-store clothes emphasizes the artificiality of her subjects and of the works themselves. Her convincing performances as an actor playing a range of roles prompted Andy Warhol to comment that Sherman was "good enough to be a real actress."

In subsequent series, her self-transformations became more radical with the use of prosthetics and, more recently, digital manipulation. These developments allow the artist to more fully inhabit her fictive identities by further effacing her own appearance, an emphatic rejection of the portrait as likeness. She has even portrayed male subjects, notably in her History Portraits (1989–90) and Men (2019–20), exploring gender fluidity and the artifice of masculine stereotypes through the latter's markedly androgynous characters.

Like Sherman, the contemporary artist Zhang Huan has served as his own model. But while Sherman adopts different personae to upend gender stereotypes, Zhang until 2005 used his body as a medium to explore his own identity in performances that were photographically documented by collaborators. As he explained, "The body is the proof of one's identity, so the corporeal self is the most essential component in my works." *Family Tree*, made less than three years after Zhang's 1998 move to the United States from his native China, focuses on the artist's visage, the locus of portraiture, to express the tension between individual and cultural identities (fig. 49). Nine closely cropped photographs of Zhang's face, identical in size and arranged in a grid, document the

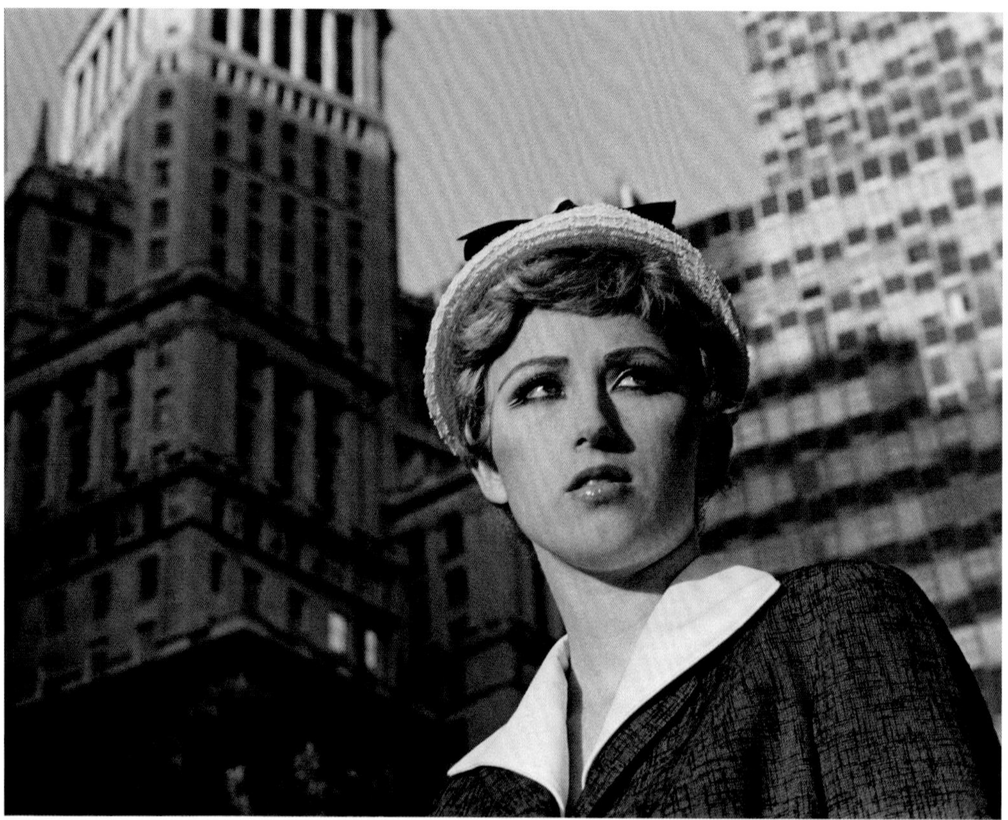

48. Cindy Sherman (American, b. 1954). *Untitled Film Still #21*, 1978. Gelatin silver print, 7⅜ × 9½ in. (18.7 × 23.9 cm). Purchase, The Horace W. Goldsmith Foundation Gift, through Joyce and Robert Menschel, 1992 (1992.5147)

progressive effacement of his features as three calligraphers covered his face with Chinese characters over the course of a single day. Both the medium and the text reflect the artist's cultural identity: ink has been the dominant medium in Chinese painting and calligraphy for more than two thousand years, and the words the artist selected reference a traditional Chinese fable, "Moving a Mountain." The text also alludes to the ancient Chinese practice of physiognomy, in which facial features are mapped as markers of both personality and destiny; physiognomy as an expression of character has long informed traditional Chinese portraiture (see fig. 12). In *Family Tree*, the Chinese characters, clearly legible on Zhang's face at the outset, ultimately dissolve into a wash of ink that obliterates his appearance, his cultural heritage subsuming his individual identity, a manifestation of Zhang's experience as a foreign-born resident of the United States. As the artist concluded, "I disappeared."

Family Tree and other conceptual works in which Zhang used his body to interrogate his identity align with the tradition of self-portraiture; their creation at seminal moments of Zhang's life particularly recalls how Vincent van Gogh turned to self-portraiture to assert his professional identity at a time of personal crisis (*Self-Portrait with Bandaged Ear*, 1889, The Courtauld, London). Zhang's work also foregrounds the portrait's performative aspect, which underlies all forms of role-playing explored in this chapter. Costumed subjects as varied as Nattier's eighteenth-century aristocrats and Sherman's "city girls" reveal the malleability of likeness and identity, highlighting the inherent tension in portraiture between truth and artifice.

49. Zhang Huan (Chinese, b. 1965). *Family Tree*, 2001. Nine chromogenic prints, each 21 × 16½ in. (53.3 × 41.9 cm). Yale University Art Gallery, New Haven, Leonard C. Hanna, Class of 1913, Fund

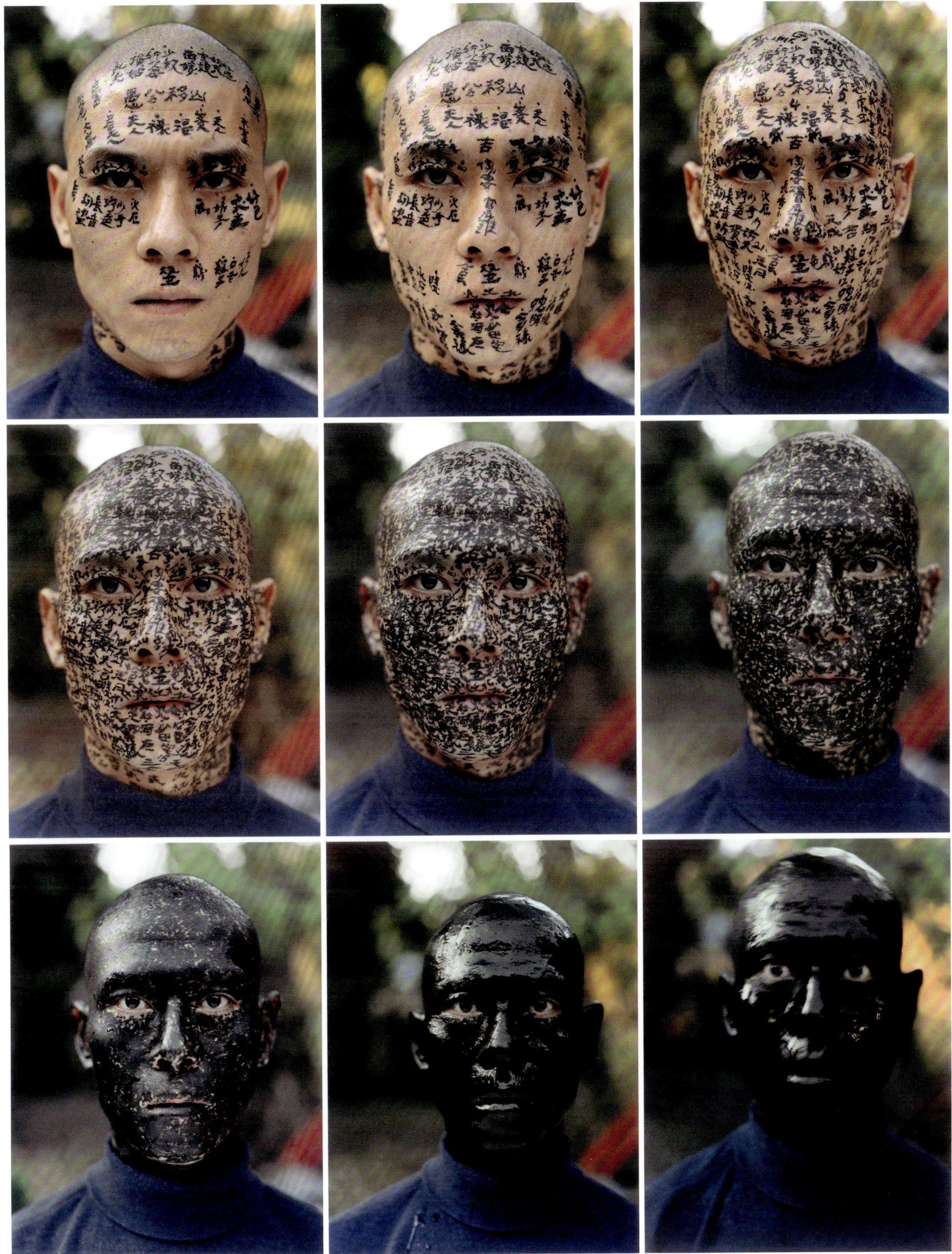

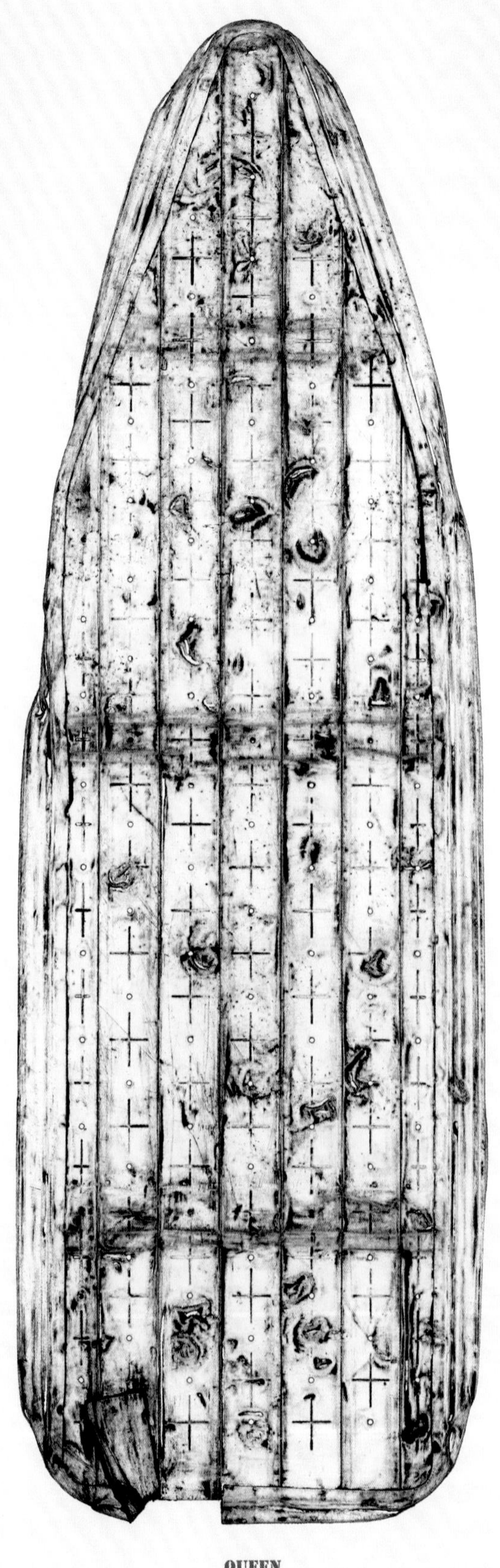

QUEEN

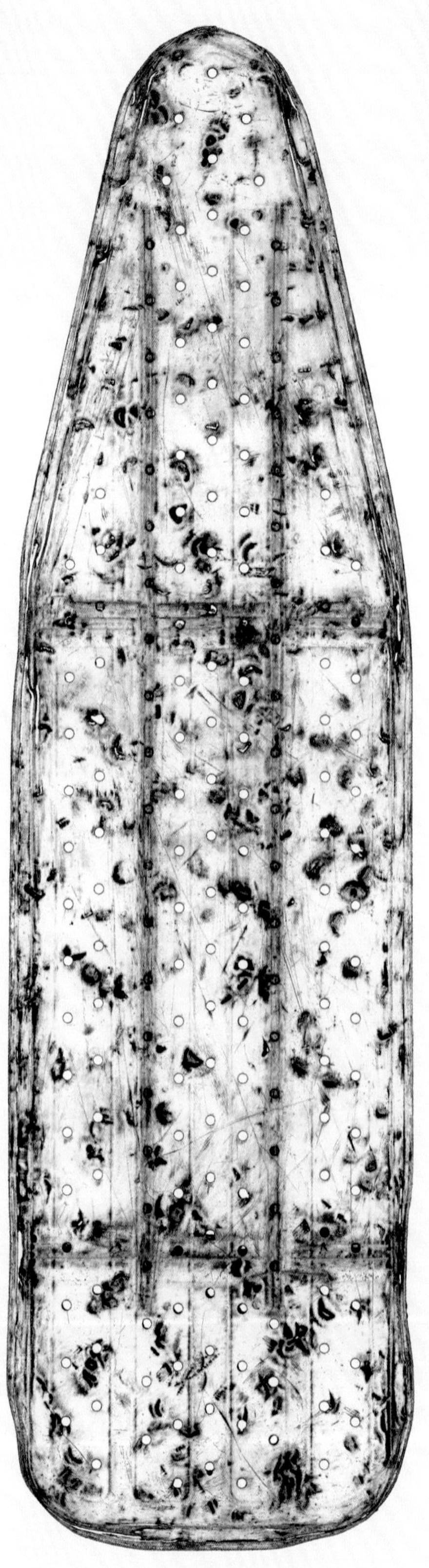

ANNA MAE

SUBVERSIONS

Across its long history, the portrait has subverted our expectations of how it should look, whom it should represent, and even what it depicts. Challenges to the status quo emerged in works that conflate portraiture with figure painting (see fig. 44), exaggerate the subject in caricature (see fig. 13), and depict previously marginalized subjects, as did Alice Neel's "pictures of people." The narrative of portraiture has continued to expand over the last century, and artists have increasingly rebelled against its canon, defying its privileging of likeness and Western standards of beauty while addressing its representational lacunae.

In the final decades of the nineteenth century, European artists adopted an increasingly subjective approach to the portrait, in keeping with a new emphasis on the expressive aspect of painting. Vincent van Gogh channeled the persona of a Buddhist monk in his austere *Self-Portrait Dedicated to Paul Gauguin* of 1888 (Harvard Art Museums, Cambridge, Mass.); later that year, Gauguin realized a portrait of Van Gogh painting sunflowers, a favorite motif, commenting that the work represented his attempt to "convey something of [the subject's] inner character" (Van Gogh Museum, Amsterdam). In 1905 Henri Matisse caused a sensation at the Salon d'Automne in Paris with his visible brushwork and palette of bold, nonnaturalistic colors in *Woman with a Hat*, a portrait of his wife, Amélie (San Francisco Museum of Modern Art). Such disruptors of the tradition of portraiture set the stage for the twentieth century and beyond.

Abstract tendencies in art that emerged about 1900 particularly challenged the primacy of likeness in portraiture. In this context, Pablo Picasso's portrait of the American writer Gertrude Stein, begun in the winter of 1905–6 and completed the following summer, has been called "transformative" by the Picasso scholar William Rubin (fig. 51). In her memoir Stein recounted the evolution of her portrait in near-mythical terms, grandiosely claiming to have sat for the artist more than ninety times. She recalled a sitting near the end of winter in which a frustrated Picasso "painted out the whole head" and abandoned the canvas, claiming that he could no longer "see" his subject. Technical analysis of the painting reveals that Picasso did in fact rework the head multiple times, while making only minor changes to the rest of the portrait; moreover, the head as it now appears was likely realized in a single session, lending credibility to Stein's

50. Willie Cole. *Five Beauties Rising*, 2012 (detail of figure 54)

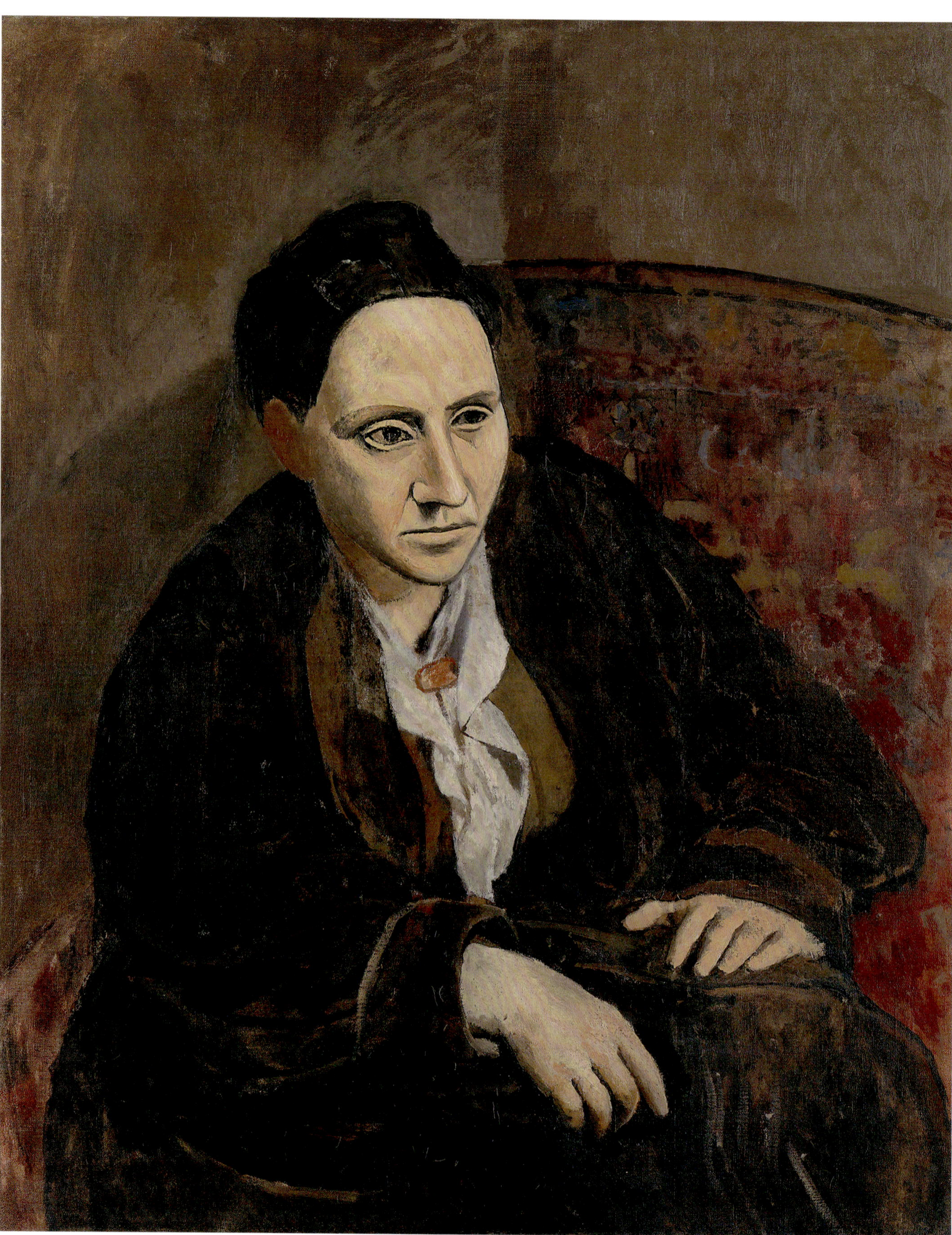

claim that the artist painted it quickly and without the presence of his model. The head's pronounced angularity and stylized features are noticeably at odds with the rounded forms of the figure. Stein's masklike face, with its almond-shaped eyes and the unbroken line from the brow to the tip of the nose, conjures sculptural prototypes from ancient Iberia and twelfth-century Spain that Picasso had recently discovered. Its faceted planes appear to have been modeled by chisel rather than by brush. That Picasso's portrait failed to satisfy contemporary expectations of likeness is borne out in the artist's response to its early reception, as Stein recalled: "Yes, he said, everybody says that she does not look like it but that does not make any difference, she will." In the aftermath of Picasso's portrait, Stein consciously styled herself after her painted likeness, which remains embedded in the public imagination as the defining image of "Gertrude Stein." In Stein's inimitable words, "For me, it is I, and it is the only reproduction of me which is always I, for me."

Picasso's iconic portrait of Gertrude Stein signaled a radical shift from a "perceptual" to a "conceptual" mode of portraiture, to borrow Rubin's characterization. Painting Stein's face in her absence, Picasso abandoned the fidelity to appearance implicit in the traditional practice of painting a portrait from life; resemblance gave way to the artist's subjective response to his sitter, fundamentally redefining portraiture. The critic Marius de Zayas recounted a 1910 conversation in which Picasso commented, "the picture should be the pictorial equivalent of the emotion produced by [the subject]." Seventy years later the painter Eric Fischl saw in the portrait of Gertrude Stein a projection of its artist, observing that in the sitter's face, "both she and Picasso reside." Indeed, a self-portrait Picasso painted in late 1906, after he had finished Stein's portrait, mirrors his masklike rendering of her visage (*Self-Portrait with Palette*, Philadelphia Museum of Art).

With the emergence of Cubism a few years later, Picasso continued to push portraiture toward the expressive possibilities of abstraction. In a group of portraits painted in 1910, he reduced the figures to a series of monochromatic, faceted planes, barely tethered to external appearance but each still individually recognizable. Between 1912 and 1914 Picasso realized a group of works intended, as he put it, to "sing" his love for Eva Gouel, which culminated with the magisterial *Woman in a Chemise in an Armchair* (fig. 52). Rendered in the collage-like idiom of Synthetic Cubism, the image of Picasso's lover verges on abstraction, yet it exudes an undeniable eroticism, from the provocative pose, emphasized by the placement of her scalloped chemise, to the depiction of such titillating details as nipples and underarm hair. In one of the studies for the painting, Eva's features and hair, falling in soft waves, are recognizable. In the final canvas, though, all that remains to individualize the figure is the stylized depiction of the sitter's long hair. Her facial features have been abstracted to a razor-thin cruciform. In transcending likeness to express Picasso's emotional response to his sitter, the work epitomizes the "conceptual" portrait.

For Picasso, painting a portrait was personal; disdainful of commissions, he said, "I cannot make a portrait of just any person." His contemporary the American artist Marsden Hartley expressed a similar view: "Everything I do is attached at once + directly to personal experiences." Hartley began painting his War Motifs series in Berlin, just months after the outbreak of World War I, in response to the battlefield death of his friend and probable lover Karl von Freyburg, a lieutenant in the German army. *Portrait of a German Officer* (fig. 53), the first work in this series, has the effect of a painted collage that suggests a figure standing against a black ground, the color of mourning in Western culture. The lower part of the head is evoked by a semicircle at the top and the torso by an array of flags and other military regalia, including the black-white-and-red imperial flag (its colors reversed); it is flanked by a plumed helmet and the silver tassels of a Prussian officer's sash. Hartley also individualized the work with objects, numbers, and letters that refer to Von Freyburg: the initials "Kv.F" in the lower left

51. Pablo Picasso (Spanish, 1881–1973). *Gertrude Stein*, 1905–6. Oil on canvas, 39⅜ × 32 in. (100 × 81.3 cm). Bequest of Gertrude Stein, 1946 (47.106)

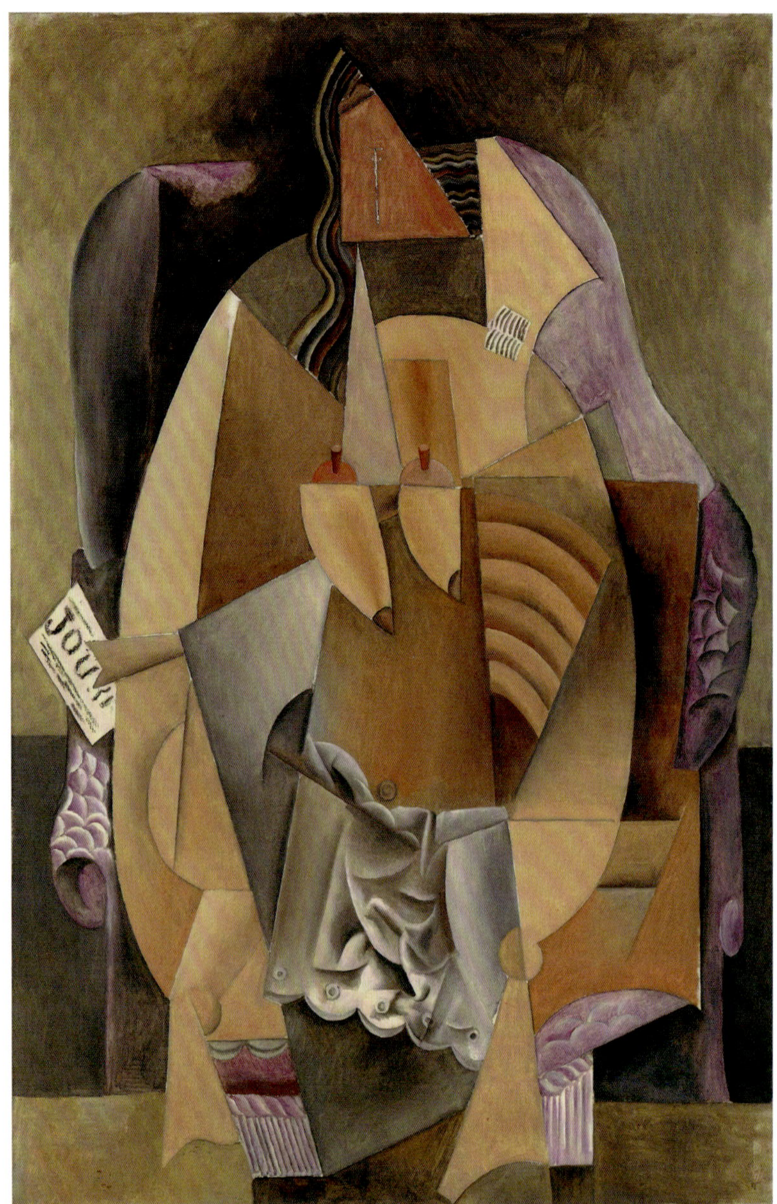

52. Pablo Picasso (Spanish, 1881–1973). *Woman in a Chemise in an Armchair*, late 1913–early 1914. Oil on canvas, 59 × 39⅛ in. (149.9 × 99.4 cm). Leonard A. Lauder Cubist Collection, Gift of Leonard A. Lauder, in celebration of the Museum's 150th Anniversary, 2019 (2019.593)

corner, depicted as if embroidered on the shoulder board of a military uniform; the "24," Von Freyburg's age at his death; and the larger-than-lifesize Iron Cross (which Von Freyburg was posthumously awarded for bravery) enclosed in a red circle within the triangle at the top of the canvas, as if pinned on the officer's chest. The Iron Cross appears in other canvases in the War Motifs series. Hartley attached personal significance to such objects; he would keep a pair of Von Freyburg's silver epaulets for the rest of his life, and he brought *Portrait of a German Officer* with him when he departed for New York in 1915.

Hartley realized two other abstract portraits of Von Freyburg among the twelve canvases that constitute his War Motifs series; in both, a centrally placed plumed helmet represents the subject's face. Rejecting likeness as a necessary component of portraiture, Hartley's use of symbolic objects to identify Von Freyburg recalls the traditional role of attributes to denote the sitter's power,

Opposite: 53. Marsden Hartley (American, 1877–1943). *Portrait of a German Officer*, 1914. Oil on canvas, 68¼ × 41⅜ in. (173.4 × 105.1 cm). Alfred Stieglitz Collection, 1949 (49.70.42)

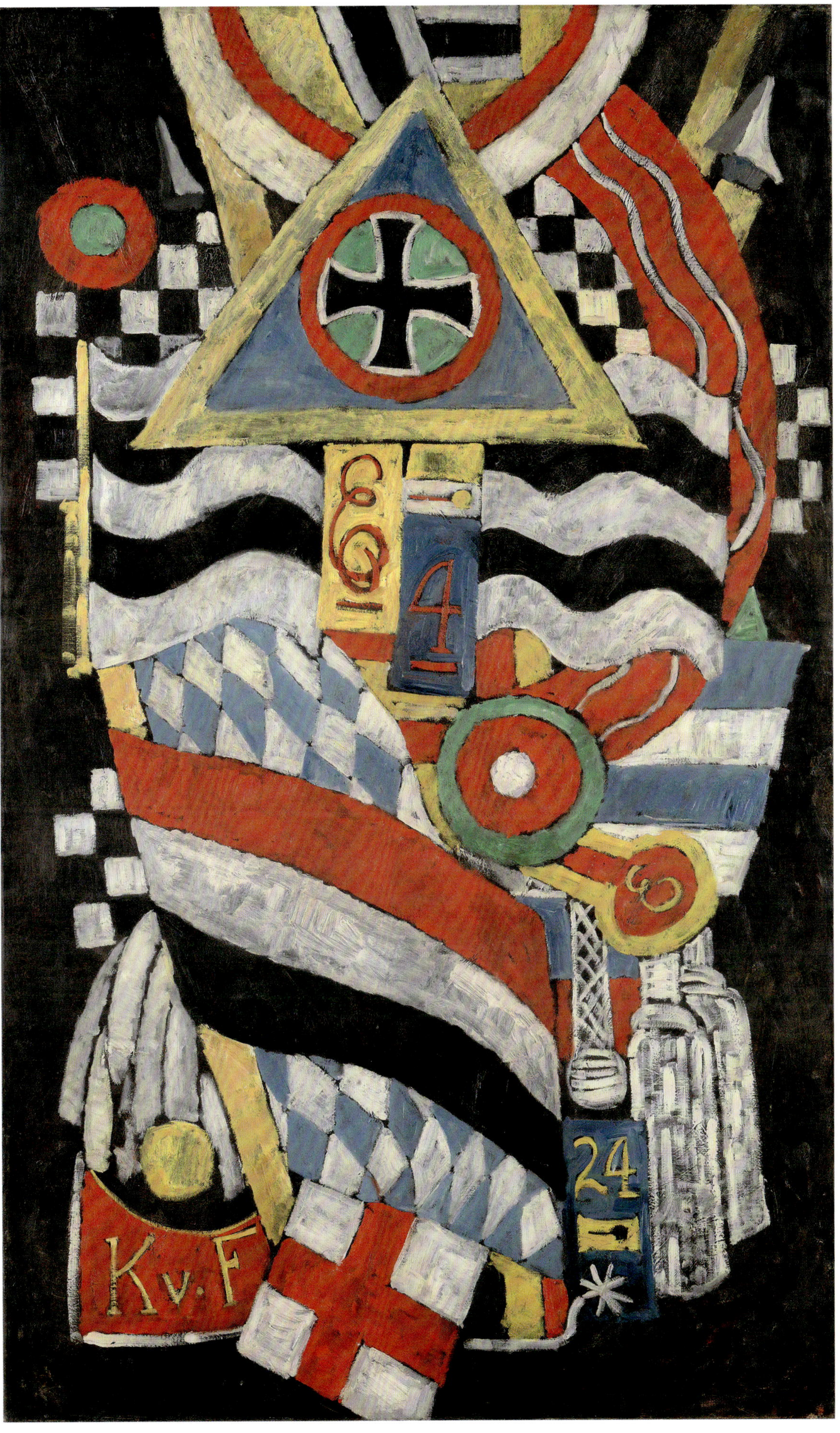
24
Kv. F

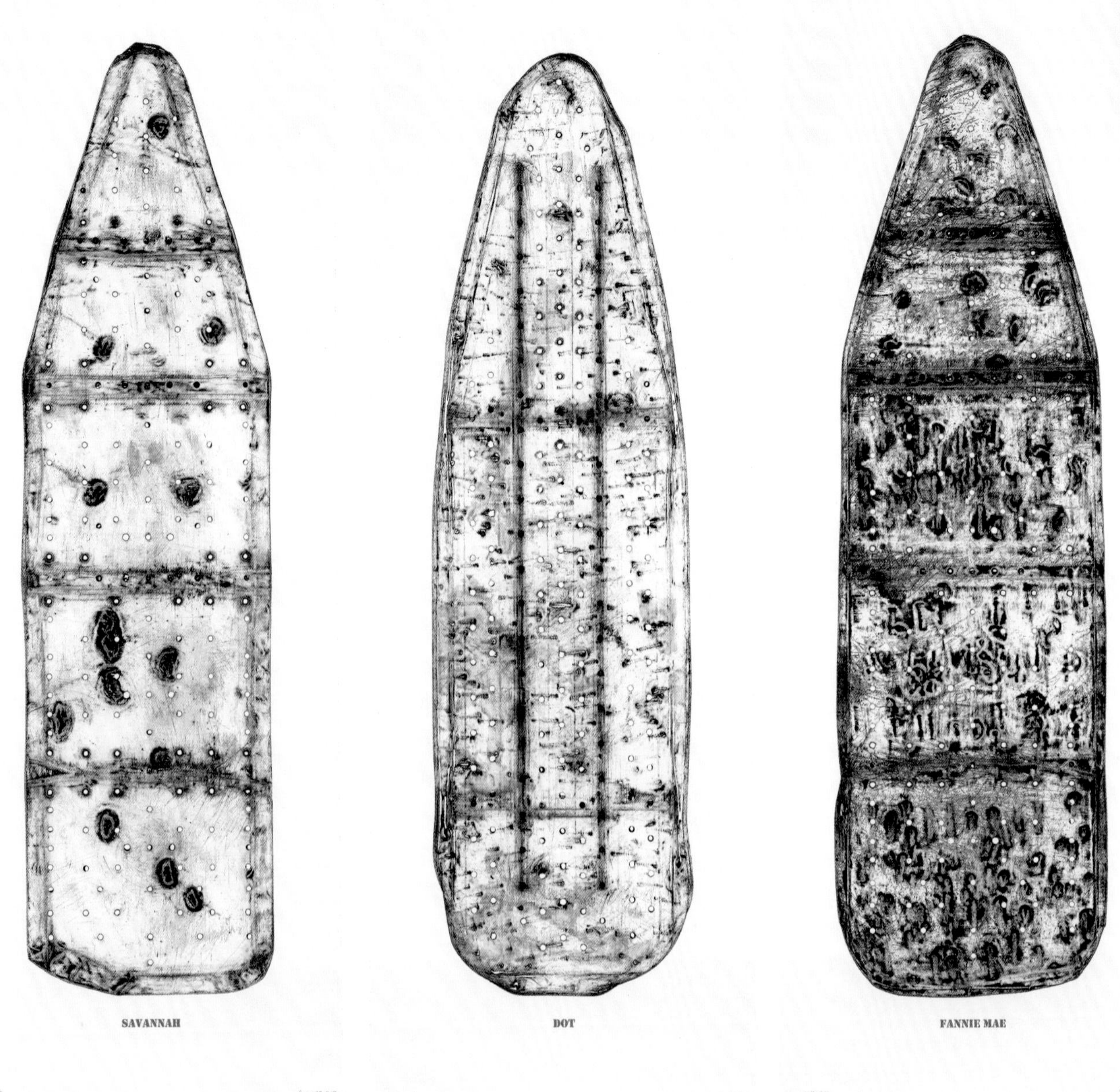

status, or profession, as in Hans Holbein's *Portrait of Georg Gisze* and François Gérard's Napoleon (see fig. 19). Similarly, Van Gogh produced symbolic portraits in two paintings he made in the Yellow House in Arles in 1888, which he was then sharing with Paul Gauguin. The paintings of the two artists, each represented by a chair, clearly reflect their distinct personalities: one is a simple pine chair, shown in daylight, with a pipe and a bag of tobacco atop its rush seat; the other is a carved walnut chair, shown at night in a gaslit interior, with a burning candle and two modern novels on its seat. Not long after Gauguin's abrupt departure, Van Gogh recalled the latter work as a reference to his absent friend: "I tried to paint 'his empty place.'"

A sense of portraiture in absentia likewise infuses the photographs Catherine Opie made in 2011 inside Elizabeth Taylor's Bel Air, California, mansion, whose address, 700 Nimes Road, gave the series its name. "I was making a portrait of Elizabeth Taylor through her home," Opie said. These still-life photographs, at once detached and intimate, create a symbolic portrait of the Hollywood star that seems to reveal more about her than would a traditional

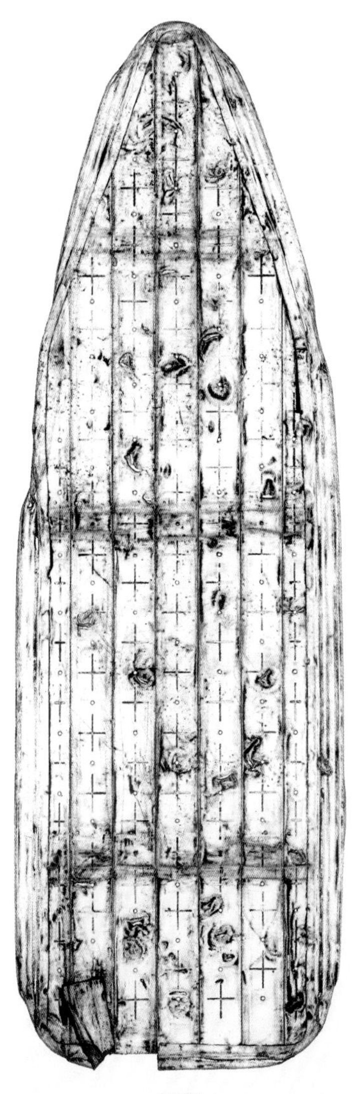

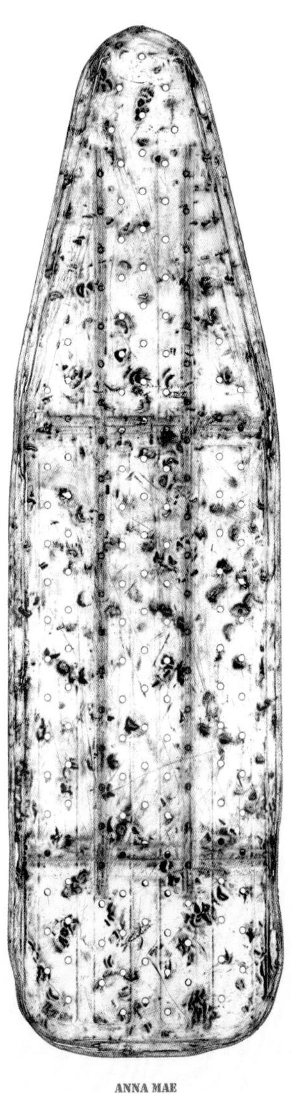

54. Willie Cole (American, b. 1955). *Five Beauties Rising*, 2012. Suite of five prints; intaglio and relief, each 63½ × 22½ in. (161.3 × 57.2 cm). John B. Turner Fund, 2021 (2021.258a–e)

celebrity portrait. The actress, whom Opie never met, died while the photographer was at work on the project, lending the objects in the photographs—including Taylor's jewels and Oscar statuettes, the contents of her closets, and ordinary bedside clutter—an unintended poignancy as mementos of a life recently ended.

Everyday household items like shoes and steam irons similarly acquire a charged meaning in the work of Willie Cole; he transforms such quotidian objects into sculptural and printed works that evoke both his childhood in Newark, New Jersey, and the broader African American experience. *Five Beauties Rising*, a set from a 2012 series of twenty-eight prints of vintage ironing boards, commemorates his grandmother, great-grandmother, and the countless other Black women of their time who were domestic workers (fig. 54). Each print bears the etched impression of a flattened steel ironing board that was hammered, scratched, dragged, and distressed. Floating vertically against a neutral background, the printed ironing board connotes a standing figure depicted in the full-length format popularized by Anthony van Dyck in the seventeenth century for his royal and aristocratic sitters

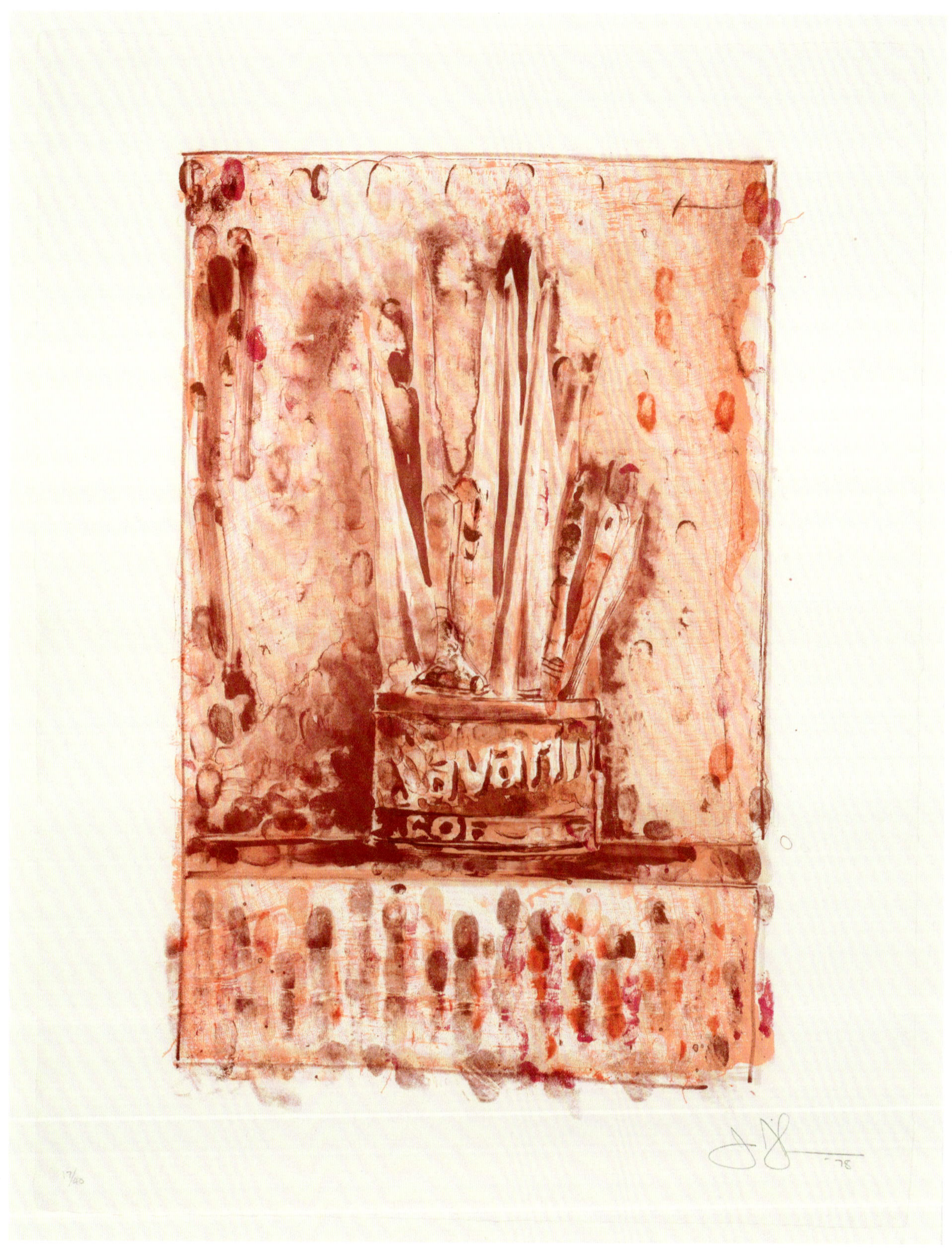

55. Jasper Johns (American, b. 1930). *Savarin 3 (Red)*, 1978. Lithograph, sheet 26 × 19⅞ in. (66 × 50.5 cm). John B. Turner Fund, 1978 (1978.581)

(see fig. 21). These upright, portraitlike forms project monumentality. Each of the prints bears a name, printed in relief at the base; some of the names are those of Cole's ancestors and others, like "Anna Mae" and "Dot," were common among Black women in the first half of the twentieth century. Cole's naming humanizes the inanimate objects, further aligning the Five Beauties with portraiture. Equivalent to the individual likenesses captured in portraits, the surface topography of each print is unique, from the densely inked surface of the ironing board in "Fannie Mae," with its pronounced skeleton of horizontal and vertical struts, to the more subtle striations of "Queen" and the delicate pattern in "Anna Mae," created by the board's perforations and surface markings.

An everyday object also recurs in the work of Jasper Johns as a stand-in for a likeness, this time that of the artist. A Savarin coffee can containing paintbrushes first appeared in Johns's work in 1960, in the form of a painted bronze sculpture that remains in the artist's possession. The coffee can as self-portrait reappeared in his printed and graphic works of the late 1970s and 1980s, including *Savarin 3 (Red)*, a 1978 lithograph (fig. 55). Here Johns paired it with another recurrent motif, his own hand, which appears in overlapping impressions across the lower register. Art historians have suggested that Hartley's symbolic visual language was a precedent for some of Johns's autobiographical imagery.

The self-referential aspect of *Savarin 3 (Red)* is underscored by both Johns's fingerprints, pressed or dragged across the background of the lithographic plate, and the multiple imprints of his hand along the lower register. These markings manifest the concept of "the artist's hand" in the creation of a work of art. The red-inked handprints also evoke the stenciled hands found on prehistoric cave walls, which similarly read as symbolic self-portraits of their unknown creators.

Johns's unconventional self-portraits coincided with other disruptive currents in portraiture in the middle decades of the twentieth century, notably a defiance of long-accepted standards of appearance. In the early 1960s Francis Bacon began making portraits of close friends that featured extreme anatomical and expressive distortions, as also seen in his self-portrait (see fig. 15). Bacon's friend Lucian Freud, who had been painting portraits for some twenty years, in 1966 issued his own challenge to portraiture's norms, painting the first of what he called "naked portraits" in his London studio. These portraits of family members, friends, and models reveal Freud's fascination with the body as a physical form. Their nudity was radical in portraiture, whether the subject was the mountainlike performance artist Leigh Bowery, seen from behind seated on a low ottoman (fig. 56), or Freud's long-limbed assistant, David Dawson, shown splayed on his back on the studio bed alongside the artist's whippet (*Sunny Morning—Eight Legs*, 1997, The Art Institute of Chicago). In Freud's handling of paint, the flesh, musculature, and pulsating veins of his nude sitters became palpable, as the artist jettisoned the centuries-long current of idealization in Western portraiture in favor of an unsparing and, at times, harsh, realism. "I'm not trying to make a copy of the person," the artist explained in 2009. "I'm trying to relay something of who they are as a physical and emotional presence. I want the paint to work as flesh does."

Freud's equation of paint and flesh acquires new meaning in the work of Jenny Saville, who likens paint to "liquid flesh." The artist, who cites Freud among her earliest artistic influences and shares his intense engagement with corporeality, primarily paints female nudes, often larger than life, that transgress conventional beauty: one group of portraits features bodies that bear the marks of reconstructive surgery. "Beauty is always associated with the male fantasy of what the female body is," she said in a 1994 interview. "It's just what women think is beautiful can be different." Saville based *Still* on a photograph from a forensic science book. The painting depicts a woman's head as seen under the icy glare of a morgue's examination lights (fig. 57). The unconventional subject recalls a portrait type known as the death mask, a wax or plaster cast of a mold made from a deceased person's face. The head, its swollen features and bruised flesh suggesting prior violence, fills a massive canvas, nine feet by twelve; the effect is simultaneously confrontational and intimate. Saville's sensual, painterly brushwork, at odds with the work's morbid subject, creates another dichotomy. The work's title and its horizontal orientation conjure still-life painting; the French term for that genre, *nature morte*

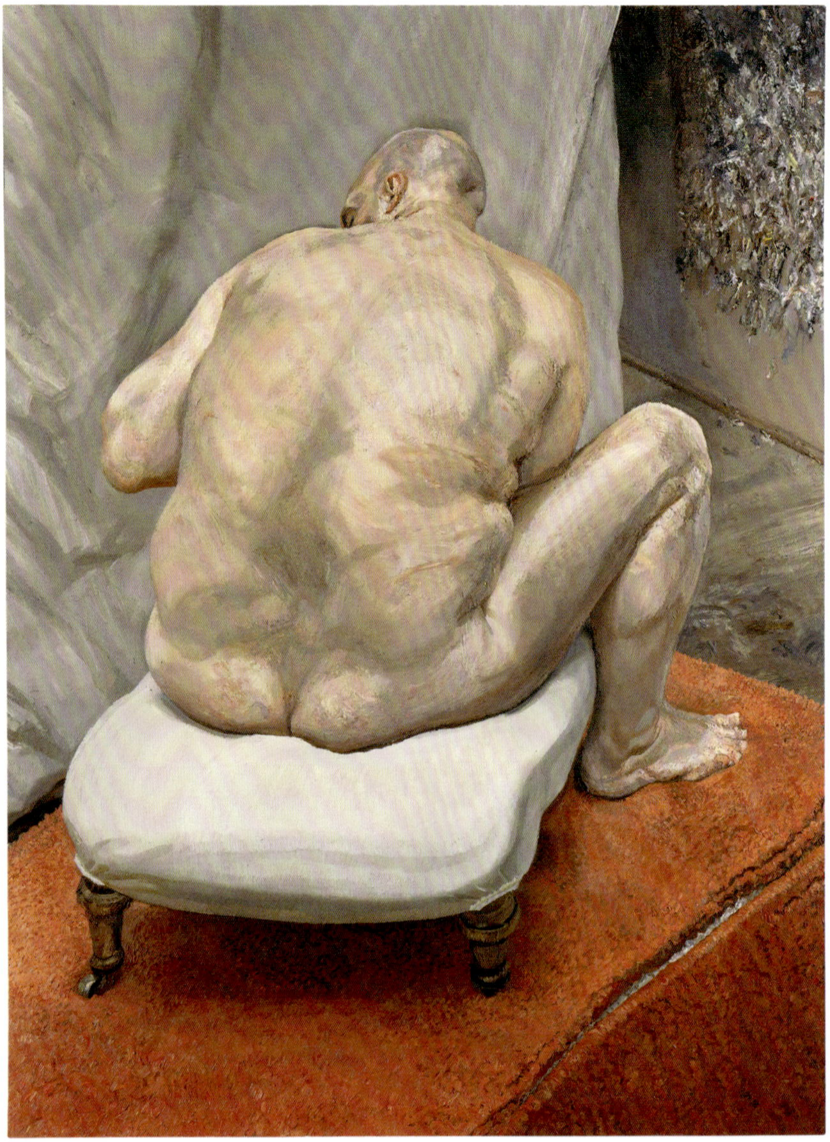

56. Lucian Freud (British, b. Germany, 1922–2011). *Naked Man, Back View*, 1991–92. Oil on canvas, 72 × 54 in. (182.9 × 137.2 cm). Purchase, Lila Acheson Wallace Gift, 1993 (1993.71)

(literally, "dead nature"), is here particularly apt. *Still* recalls some of the more macabre variants of still life, notably paintings of the severed head of Saint John the Baptist on a platter found in Renaissance and Baroque art, as well as Théodore Géricault's painted studies of body parts that he borrowed from a morgue in preparation for his 1818–19 *Raft of the Medusa* (Musée du Louvre, Paris).

Still suggestively pairs with Saville's *Reverse* (2002–3, collection of Larry Gagosian), another oversize close-up of a woman's head—this time, Saville's—turned outward on a reflective surface. Where *Still*'s palette is cool and bloodless, *Reverse*, all saturated reds, pulsates with life. While *Reverse* is a self-portrait, Saville considers her figurative paintings beyond such "traditional" (her word) categorizations: "If they are portraits, they are portraits of an idea or a sensation. . . . There's no personality as such." In this sense, *Still* and *Reverse* are descendants of Picasso's "conceptual" portraits.

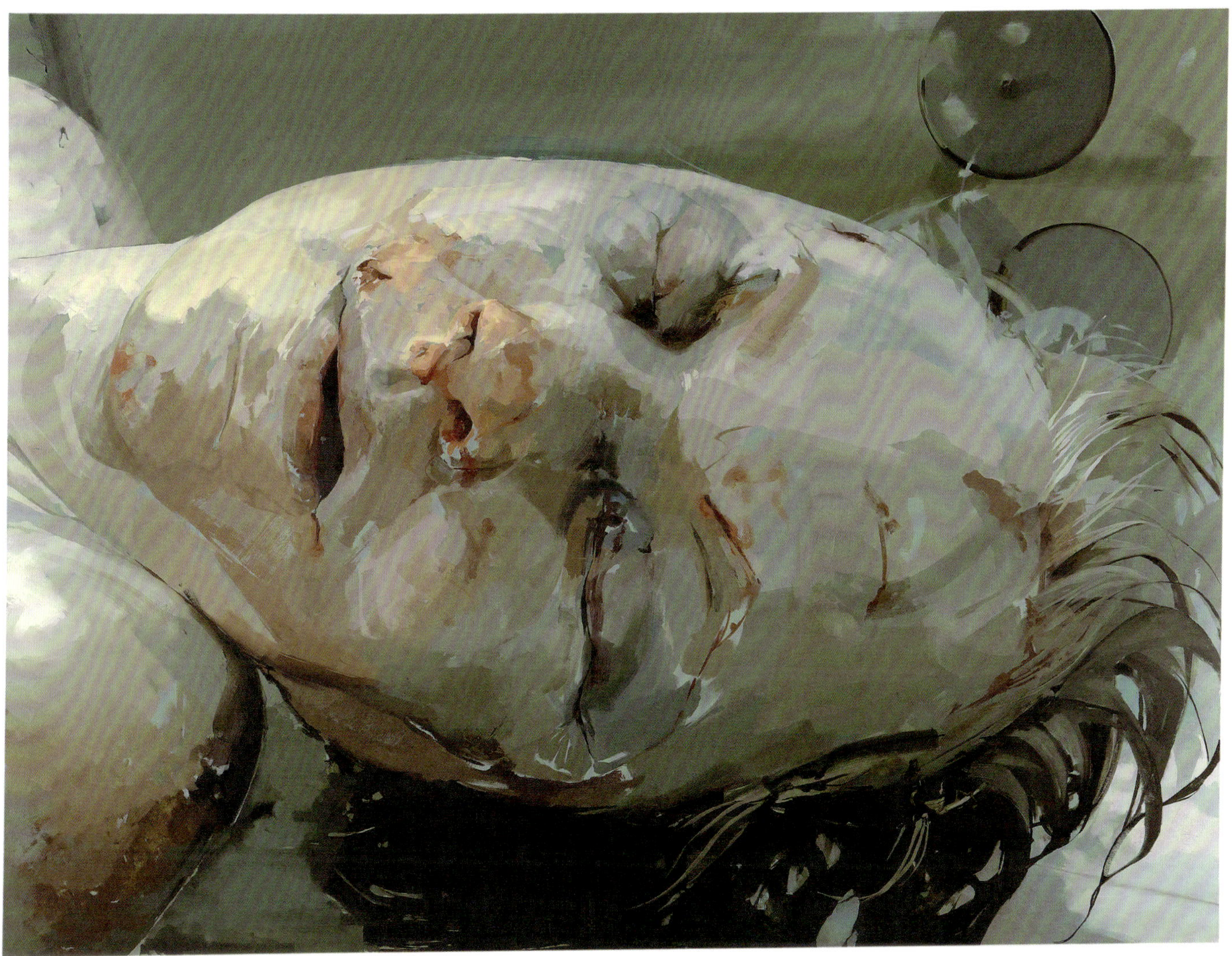

57. Jenny Saville (British, b. 1970). *Still*, 2003. Oil on canvas, 9 ft. × 12 ft. ⅛ in. (274.3 × 366.1 cm). Gift of Martin and Toni Sosnoff, 2011 (2011.516)

Saville's rejection of idealization and conventional beauty recalls the photographs of Diane Arbus, who often turned her lens on subjects society had typically marginalized and portraiture had largely ignored, including drag queens, dwarfs, giants, and nudists. In 1972 Arbus's work was the subject of a posthumous retrospective at the Museum of Modern Art, which Susan Sontag deemed a "freak show" in an essay with that title published the following year in *The New York Review of Books*. Sontag accused Arbus of glorifying ugliness and lacking empathy toward her sitters, yet Arbus's own words counter such a reading: "For me the subject of the picture is always more important than the picture. And more complicated."

Among the photographs included in the 1972 exhibition was *A young waitress at a nudist camp, N.J. 1963* (fig. 58), taken in July of that year. In her unpublished notes, Arbus likened the camp to "the Garden of Eden, after the Fall." Indeed, her teenaged subject—posing with

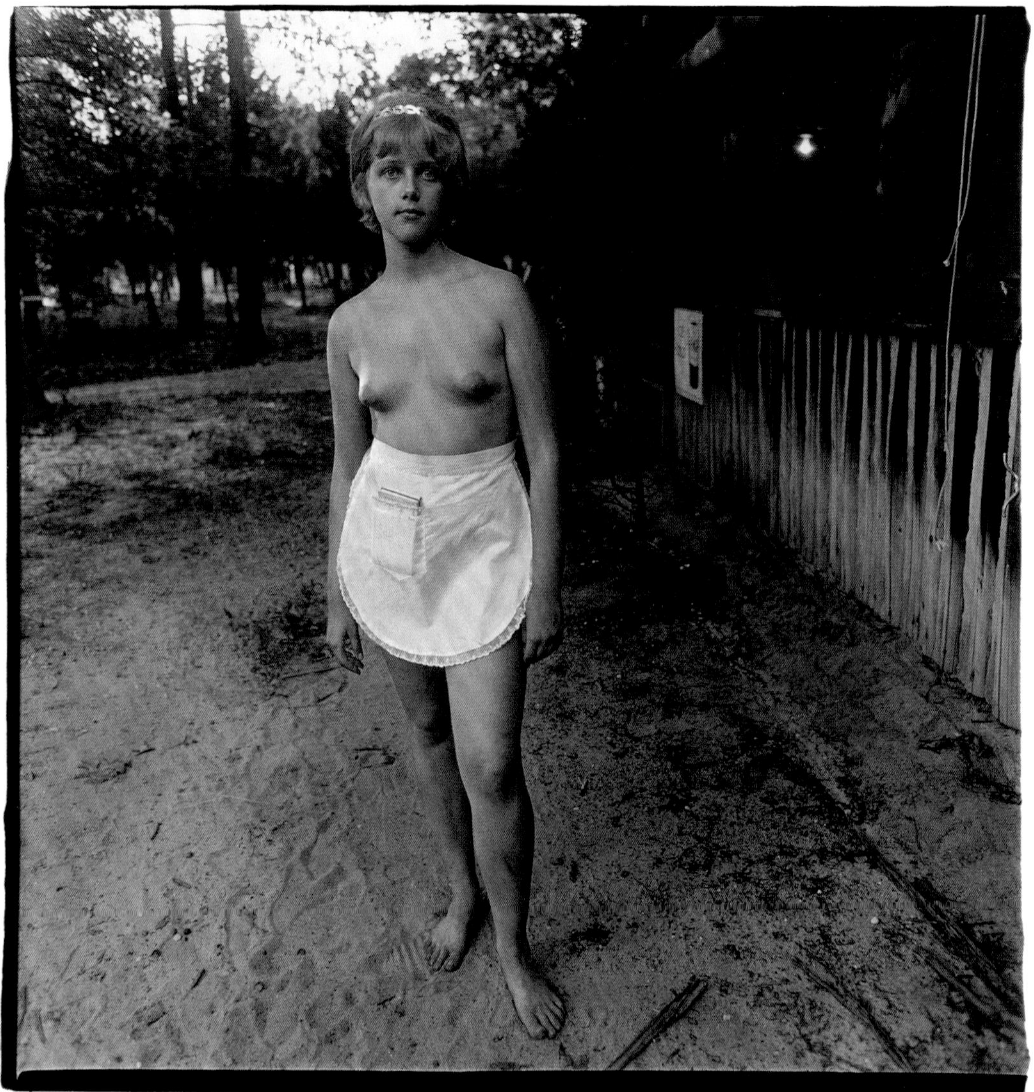

58. Diane Arbus (American, 1923–1971). *A young waitress at a nudist camp, N.J. 1963*, 1963. Gelatin silver print, image 14⅝ × 14⅜ in. (37.2 × 36.3 cm). Gift of Danielle and David Ganek, 2005 (2005.493.2)

one foot forward and weight shifted to the other side—conjures Renaissance depictions of the biblical Eve as well as the mythological Venus in the same contrapposto stance. The teenager's lace-trimmed apron, order pads neatly tucked into its pocket (a small yet affecting detail), provides the same modesty as a fig leaf in Renaissance imagery. The portrait captures the vulnerability of adolescence in the hint of uncertainty in the teenager's pose and her distant (rather than direct) gaze. She possesses none of the swagger of Van Dyck's aristocratic sitters (see fig. 21) or the self-confidence of Edith Minturn Stokes, as painted by John Singer Sargent (see fig. 22). Arbus captured both teenage awkwardness in general and this young waitress's particularity. The photographer's interest in her sitters' individuality distinguishes her work from the emphasis on social types in the work of August Sander, whom she admired (see fig. 4). As Sandra S. Phillips observed in *Diane Arbus Revelations*, "From the beginning it is clear that she was looking not for a typology, but for varieties of experience."

As Arbus did some fifty years earlier, contemporary Black artists such as Jordan Casteel have reinvigorated portraiture by challenging its traditional narratives of power and inclusion. Visible Man, Casteel's 2014 series of nude portraits of young Black men (her fellow students at Yale University), exemplifies her desire to portray "people on the periphery," as she put it: marginalized subjects in the Western art-historical canon. Focusing her painting exclusively on people of color, Casteel builds on the influential practice Kerry James Marshall established in his figurative imagery in the 1980s (see fig. 5). In contrast to Marshall's choice to render his figures in an emphatic black, Casteel favors a palette that, in her words, "allow[s] the diversity that exists within us to exist on the canvas itself" in a wide range of browns, reds, blues, and greens. Like Alice Neel, whose paintings of Black sitters she has cited as a "profound" influence, Casteel produces intimate portraits of ordinary people that emanate an essential humanism. Their larger-than-lifesize scale recalls the tradition of state portraiture (see fig. 19), conferring importance upon the sitters and commanding our attention.

The primary subject of Casteel's *Yvonne and James II* is a man she first encountered selling CDs in Harlem in 2015; James would appear in three of her paintings, including a double portrait seated next to his wife, Yvonne, and clasping her hand. In the present work, he sits alone in his kitchen, displaying the couple's gilt-framed wedding photograph in an ode to his wife, who had passed away two years earlier (fig. 59). The kitchen setting—in contrast to the aggrandizing format popularized by Van Dyck—underscores the intimacy of Casteel's portrait as well as the artist's interest in portraying her subjects at home, the better to reflect their identities. The backgrounds of Casteel's portraits are also laden with meaning. Here a reproduction of the first painting Casteel made of James is tacked to the refrigerator, making this a triple portrait that documents the sitter at three moments in his life and suggests the passage of time. The sneakers cast off in the background are Casteel's own, subtly establishing her presence in the scene; that rare gesture on her part, along with the sitter's relaxed demeanor and steady, direct gaze, underscores both her unique bond with James and the empathy that is intrinsic to Casteel's process.

Casteel works from photographs she takes herself, winnowing a hundred or more to a handful that will help her recreate a moment, as if painted from life. Photography has become essential to many contemporary portraitists' practice, whether as a tool or as an independent art form. More recent technological advances have also expanded the possibilities of portraiture. In the early 1970s Bill Viola pioneered the use of video in the genre, introducing motion and duration as well as sound. From his earliest works, Viola has been preoccupied by time and its passage, often expressed through slow motion, his stylistic signature. Similarly, in 1996 Thomas Struth began making his One Hour Video Portraits series, in which he further explores his sitters' experience of posing for photographs (see fig. 33) by prolonging the exposure to one hour. In each of Struth's real-time video portraits the subject sits still, silent and devoid of expression, while looking directly at the camera's lens, mirroring the aesthetic of his photographic portraits. These monumental video headshots are marked by the intensity of the sitters' sustained gazes and the absence of movement, save for the occasional blink and, in one instance, a stifled yawn. Through the medium of video, Struth reimagined the experience of looking at a portrait over time, activating the gaze between sitter and artist, as well as between sitter and viewer.

Recent digital technology made possible a series of portrait sculptures the German conceptual artist Karin Sander produced between 1998 and 2006. Her "1:10" sculptures are based on three-dimensional body scans of their subjects and scaled to 10 percent of lifesize, then produced in layers of plastic by a 3D printer (fig. 60). The sitters, who include Sander's friends and art-world figures, chose how they wished to be portrayed, from their pose and expression to their clothing. For that reason, Sander deemed these miniature sculptures "self-portraits," although here "self" refers not to the artist but to the sitters; their role in constructing their self-images was similar to that of the Countess de Castiglione in Pierre-Louis Pierson's photographs (see fig. 47). In *Gordon Tapper, 1:10*, Tapper, a writer, casually dressed in slightly rumpled clothing, assumes a relaxed, hand-on-hip pose. His sculpted image, its color airbrushed by a

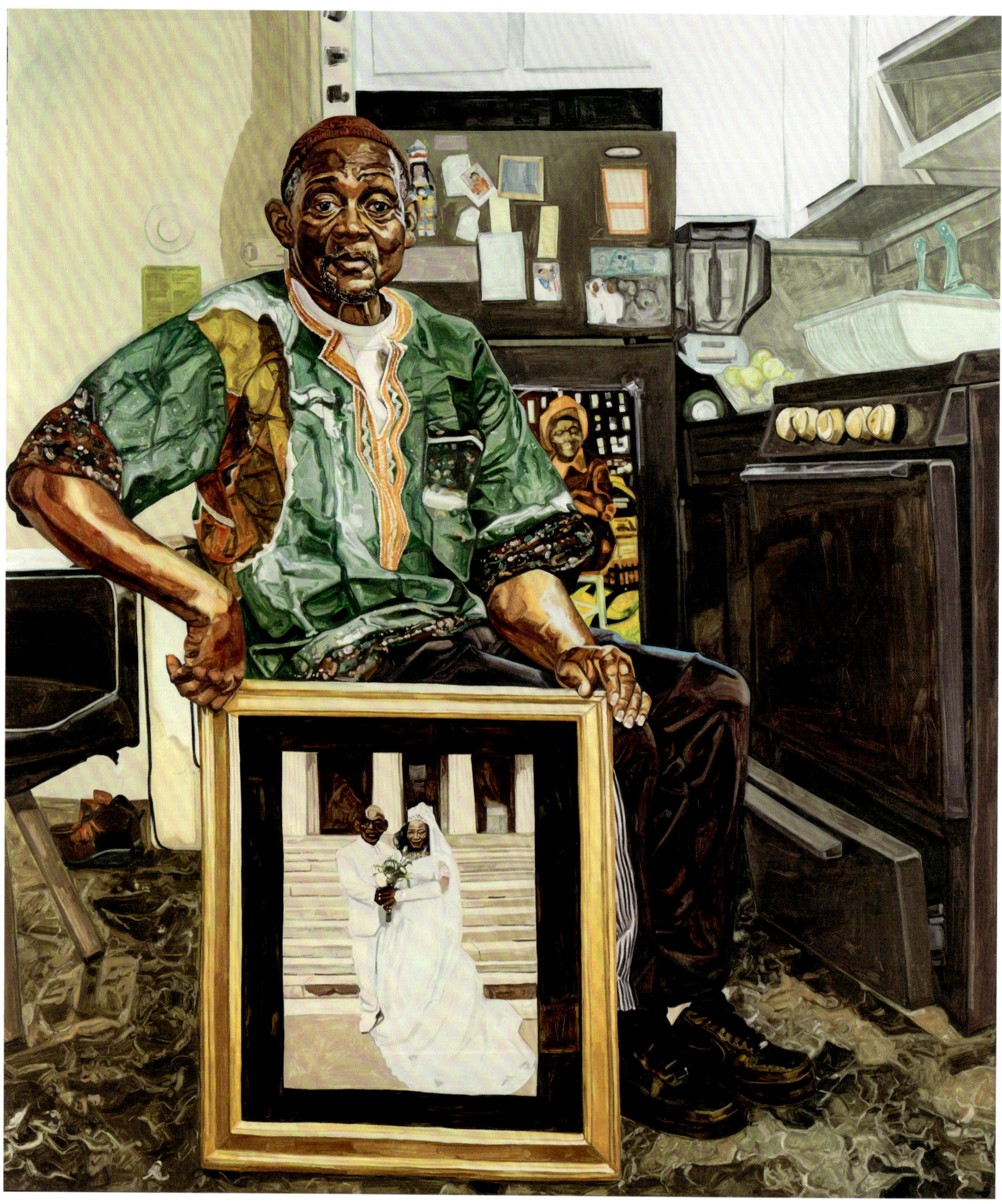

59. Jordan Casteel (American, b. 1989). *Yvonne and James II*, 2021. Oil on canvas, 90 × 78⅛ in. (228.6 × 198.4 cm). Purchase, Gina and Stuart Peterson Gift, 2021 (2021.131)

technician, is eerily lifelike despite its exaggeratedly small scale. The computerized mechanical process that generated the portrait is betrayed by the visible ridges of the layers forming the miniature plastic likeness. In fact, Sander herself never touches the sculpture; eliminating the hand of the artist, she challenges our understanding and expectations of how art is created and anticipates contemporary trends in the rapidly changing world of digital portraiture, including the use of artificial intelligence (AI), which converts text prompts into images.

Portraiture has been in the vanguard of the debate surrounding this new medium. Established artists and others producing works with AI, whether the most sophisticated algorithms or the internet's free portrait-generators, are raising fresh questions about what constitutes art and authorship. The critic Jerry Saltz dismissed AI imagery as "lack[ing] originality in the idea that generated it and the object" in 2018. That same year, an AI-generated printed portrait of a fictional subject in the style of an Old Master painting was auctioned at Christie's New York; realized by Obvious, a Paris-based collective, it was the first work created by artificial intelligence to be sold at a major auction house. Five years later, an AI-generated black-and-white portrait of two women was awarded a prestigious international photography prize. Ultimately its creator, the German photographer Boris Eldagsen, declined the prize on the grounds that "AI is not photography," while asserting AI's validity as an artistic medium in its own right.

Even as portraiture subverts our expectations in terms of subject and representational mode, its conventions of pose, gesture, and setting have endured across time and culture; they lend expressive power to depictions of African queens, Renaissance merchants, and contemporary families alike. And while the language of portraiture has expanded, encompassing abstraction and the use of symbolic surrogates, the portrait itself remains grounded in a fundamental human desire to assert identity. Over its long history, it has served as a public statement of social standing, a private form of self-expression, and a challenge to the status quo. Its multiple facets demand that we read the portrait beyond face value.

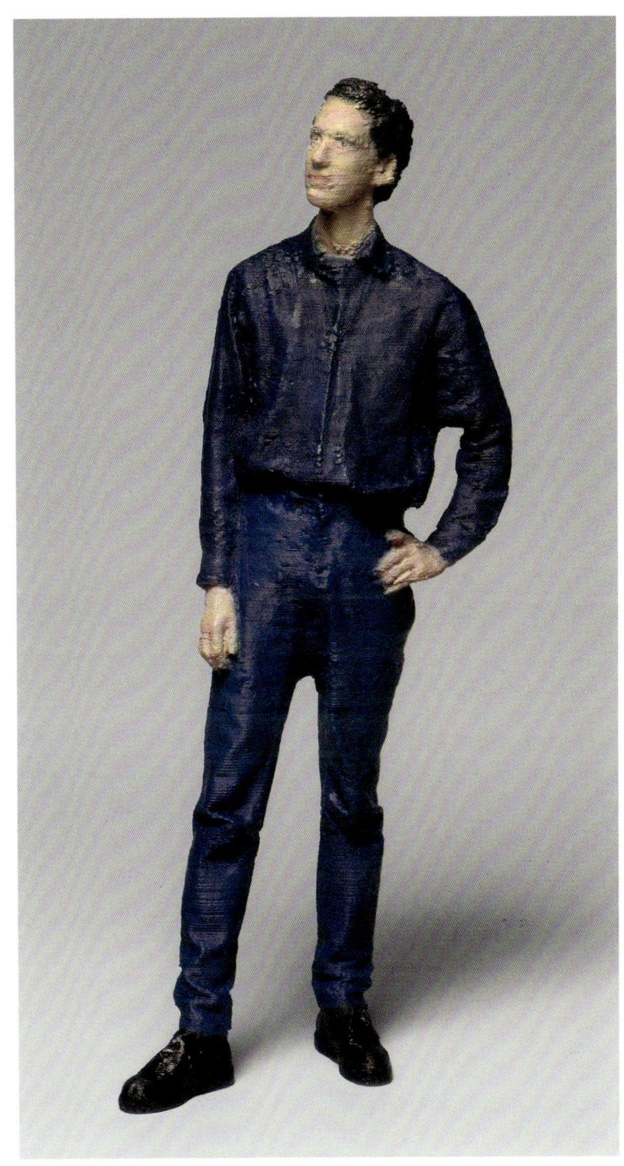

60. Karin Sander (German, b. 1957). *Gordon Tapper, 1:10*, 1999. ABS plastic (acrylonitrile butadiene styrene) from three-dimensional scan, applied color, H. 7⅛ × D. 2¼ in. (18 × 5.7 cm). Purchase, Jennifer and Joseph Duke and Anonymous Gifts, 2000 (2000.411)

SUGGESTED READING

Apraxine, Pierre, et al. *"La Divine Comtesse": Photographs of the Countess de Castiglione*. Exh. cat. New York: The Metropolitan Museum of Art; New Haven: Yale University Press, 2000.

Auricchio, Laura. *Adélaïde Labille-Guiard: Artist in the Age of Revolution*. Los Angeles: The J. Paul Getty Museum, 2009.

Bailey, Martin, Karen Serres, and Louis van Tilborgh. *Van Gogh Self-Portraits*. Edited by Karen Serres. Exh. cat. London: The Courtauld Gallery in association with Paul Holberton Publishing, 2022.

Basualdo, Carlos, et al. *Jasper Johns: Mind/Mirror*. Exh. cat. Philadelphia: Philadelphia Museum of Art, 2021.

Campbell, Lorne. *Renaissance Portraits: European Portrait Painting in the 14th, 15th, and 16th Centuries*. New Haven: Yale University Press, 1990.

Chapman, H. Perry. *Rembrandt's Self-Portraits: A Study in Seventeenth-Century Identity*. Princeton, N.J.: Princeton University Press, 1990.

Chiu, Melissa, ed. *Zhang Huan: Altered States*. New York: Asia Society, 2007.

Christiansen, Keith, et al. *The Medici: Portraits and Politics, 1512–1570*. Exh. cat. New York: The Metropolitan Museum of Art; New Haven: Yale University Press, 2021.

Clarke, Graham. "Public Faces, Private Lives: August Sander and the Social Typology of the Portrait Photograph." In *The Portrait in Photography*, edited by Graham Clarke, 71–93. London: Reaktion Books, 1992.

Cooper, Tarnya, ed. *Tudors to Windsors*. Exh. cat. Houston: Museum of Fine Arts; Bendigo, Australia: Bendigo Art Gallery; London: National Portrait Gallery Publications, 2018.

Davies, Cassie. "Interview with Njideka Akunyili Crosby." https://www.thewhitereview.org/feature/interview-njideka-akunyili-crosby/ (November 2016).

Diane Arbus: Revelations. New York: Aperture, 2022.

Eklund, Douglas, et al. *Thomas Struth: 1977–2002*. Exh. cat. Dallas: Dallas Museum of Art; New Haven: Yale University Press, 2002.

Fairhead, James. "Victorine Meurent: New Evidence from America and Paris." *The Burlington Magazine* 165 (August 2023), 817–27.

Gioni, Massimiliano, ed. *Jordan Casteel: Within Reach*. Exh. cat. New York: New Museum of Contemporary Art, 2020.

Herdrich, Stephanie L., and H. Barbara Weinberg. "John Singer Sargent in the Metropolitan Museum of Art." *The Metropolitan Museum of Art Bulletin* 57, no. 4 (Spring 2000).

Ikehara-Tsukayama, Hugo C., Dawn Kriss, and Joanne Pillsbury. "Containing the Divine: Ancient Peruvian Pots." *The Metropolitan Museum of Art Bulletin* 80, no. 4 (Spring 2023).

Inboden, Gudrun, ed. *Karin Sander*. Exh. cat. Stuttgart, Germany: Staatsgalerie Stuttgart; Ostfildern, Germany: Hatje Cantz, 2002.

Inglis, Erik. *Faces of Power and Piety*. Los Angeles: Getty Publications, 2008.

Jackall, Yuriko, et al. *Fragonard: The Fantasy Figures*. Exh. cat. Washington, D.C.: The National Gallery of Art, 2017.

Jørgensen, Lærke Rydal, and Kirsten Degel, eds. *The Cold Gaze: Germany in the 1920s*. Exh. cat. Humlebæk, Denmark: Louisiana Museum of Modern Art, 2022.

LaGamma, Alisa. *Heroic Africans: Legendary Leaders, Iconic Sculptures*. Exh. cat. New York: The Metropolitan Museum of Art; New Haven: Yale University Press, 2011.

Lamunière, Michelle. *You Look Beautiful Like That: The Portrait Photographs of Seydou Keïta and Malick Sidibé*. Exh. cat. Cambridge, Mass.: Harvard University Art Museums; New Haven: Yale University Press, 2001.

Lewison, Jeremy, ed. *Alice Neel. Painter of Modern Life*. Exh. cat. Helsinki: Ateneum Art Museum, Finnish National Gallery; Brussels: Mercatorfonds, 2016.

McCauley, Elizabeth Anne. *A. A. E. Disdéri and the Carte de Visite Portrait Photograph*. New Haven: Yale University Press, 1985.

McPhee, Constance C., and Nadine M. Orenstein. *Infinite Jest: Caricature and Satire from Leonardo to Levine*. Exh. cat. New York: The Metropolitan Museum of Art; New Haven: Yale University Press, 2011.

Ngan, Quincy. "The Significance of Azurite Blue in Two Ming Dynasty Birthday Portraits." *The Metropolitan Museum of Art Journal* 53 (2018), 48–65.

Perry, Gill. "Women in Disguise: Likeness, the Grand Style and the Conventions of 'Feminine' Portraiture in the Work of Sir Joshua Reynolds." In *Femininity and Masculinity in Eighteenth-Century Art and Culture*, edited by Gill Perry and Michael Rossington, 18–40. Manchester, U.K.: Manchester University Press, 1994.

Red Star, Wendy, et al. *Wendy Red Star: Delegation*. New York: Aperture; Dallas: Documentary Arts, 2022.

Respini, Eva. *Cindy Sherman*. Exh. cat. New York: The Museum of Modern Art, 2012.

Retford, Kate. *The Art of Domestic Life: Family Portraiture in Eighteenth-Century England.* New Haven: Yale University Press, 2006.

Roberts, Jennifer L. "The Art of Pressure." In *Willie Cole: Beauties*, 3–33. Exh. cat. Cambridge, Mass.: Johnson-Kulukundis Family Gallery; Radcliffe Institute for Advanced Study, Harvard University, 2019.

Roelofs, Pieter, et al. *Vermeer.* Amsterdam: Rijksmuseum, 2023.

Roth, Paul. "Unholy Trinity: The Making of Richard Avedon's *Andy Warhol and Members of the Factory, New York, October 30, 1969.*" In *Avedon: Murals and Portraits*, 181–92. New York: Gagosian Gallery, 2012.

Rubin, William, ed. *Picasso and Portraiture: Representation and Transformation.* Exh. cat. New York: The Museum of Modern Art, 1996.

Saville, Jenny. *Jenny Saville.* New York: Rizzoli, 2005.

Schama, Simon. "The Domestication of Majesty: Royal Family Portraiture, 1500–1850." *The Journal of Interdisciplinary History* 17, no. 1 (Summer 1986), 155–83.

Scholz, Dieter, ed. *Marsden Hartley: The German Paintings, 1913–1915.* Exh. cat. Berlin: Neue Nationalgalerie; New York: D.A.P./Distributed Art Publishers, 2014.

Shushan, Elle, ed. *Lover's Eyes: Eye Miniatures from the Skier Collection.* Birmingham, Ala.: The Skier Collection in association with D. Giles, 2021.

Simpson, Bennett, ed. *Henry Taylor: B Side.* Los Angeles: The Museum of Contemporary Art and DelMonico Books, 2022.

Spicer, Joaneath. "The Renaissance Elbow." In *A Cultural History of Gesture: From Antiquity to the Present Day*, edited by Jan Bremmer and Herman Roodenburg, 84–128. Ithaca, N.Y.: Cornell University Press, 1992.

[Stevens, Maryanne, et al.]. *Manet: Portraying Life.* Exh. cat. London: Royal Academy of Arts; New York: Harry N. Abrams, 2012.

Sylvester, David. *The Brutality of Fact: Interviews with Francis Bacon.* London: Thames and Hudson, 1987.

Welch, Stuart Cary, et al. *The Emperor's Album: Images of Mughal India.* Exh. cat. New York: The Metropolitan Museum of Art, 1987.

West, Shearer. *Portraiture.* New York: Oxford University Press, 2004.

Wolohojian, Stephan, Melinda Watt, and Michael Gallagher. "A Grand Tableau: Charles Le Brun's Portrait of the Jabach Family." *The Metropolitan Museum of Art Bulletin* 75, no. 1 (Summer 2017).

Woollett, Anne T., ed. *Holbein: Capturing Character.* Exh. cat. Los Angeles: J. Paul Getty Museum, 2021.

Zanker, Paul. *Roman Portraits: Sculptures in Stone and Bronze in the Collection of The Metropolitan Museum of Art.* New Haven: Yale University Press, 2016.

ACKNOWLEDGMENTS

It is an extraordinary privilege to write a book for The Metropolitan Museum of Art. I am grateful to Max Hollein, Marina Kellen French Director and CEO, for his endorsement of this project. I also thank Mark Polizzotti, Publisher and Editor in Chief, for his generous support of this book. From the beginning, our conversations helped to shape my thinking about portraiture. My writing benefited immeasurably from the intellectual rigor of my editor, Nancy E. Cohen. I extend sincere gratitude to my talented colleagues in the Publications and Editorial Department: Peter Antony, Elizabeth De Mase, Lauren Knighton, Michael Sittenfeld, and Dale Tucker. Designer Rita Jules of Miko McGinty Inc. made the book itself a work of art. The support of the Roswell L. Gilpatric Publications Fund enabled its realization.

My colleagues across the Museum have supported my work on this project in myriad ways. The staff of The Thomas J. Watson Library ensured that I had access to all the research material that I needed. Jeff L. Rosenheim, Joyce Frank Menschel Curator in Charge, Department of Photographs, was unfailingly generous in sharing his passion for and deep knowledge of photography. I also acknowledge the kind assistance of Jennifer Farrell, Curator in the Department of Drawings and Prints; Maxwell K. Hearn, Douglas Dillon Chair of the Department of Asian Art; and Joanne Pillsbury, Andrall E. Pearson Curator, Art of the Ancient Americas in The Michael C. Rockefeller Wing. I thank Heidi Holder, Frederick P. and Sandra P. Rose Chair of Education, for supporting my work. Throughout the writing of this book, the enthusiastic support and encouragement of all my colleagues in the Department of Education have meant the world to me. Many of the ideas embedded in these pages were developed through my teaching at the Museum, from public lectures and gallery conversations to training sessions with The Met's volunteer guides, and I am grateful for all these experiences.

Portraiture has been a through line in my academic and professional career as an art historian. My doctoral dissertation, which focused on family portraits, was inspired by Linda Nochlin's innovative reading of one such work by Edgar Degas, and my first job at The Met was as a research assistant for the exhibition *Portraits by Ingres*. The cross-cultural approach of *How to Read Portraits* is indebted to the expansive vision of Robert Rosenblum, my advisor at the Institute of Fine Arts, New York University, whose enduring influence I gratefully acknowledge. Finally, I am sustained by the richness of so many friendships, above all that of my husband, Todd.

Kathryn Calley Galitz

INDEX

Numbers in **bold** indicate pages with illustrations.

Akbar (Mughal emperor), 67, 68
Akunyili, Dora, 82, **82–83**
Akunyili Crosby, Njideka: *Mother and Child*, 80–82, **82–83**
Albert (English prince consort), 68–71, **70**
Alberti, Leon Battista, 36
Arbus, Diane: *A young waitress at a nudist camp, N.J. 1963*, 109–10, **110**
Armstrong, Carol, 90
Augustus (Roman emperor), 29–31, 49, 52, 54; marble head, 19, **28**, 85
Auricchio, Laura, 78
Avedon, Richard: *Andy Warhol and members of The Factory, New York City*, 21, 75–76, **76–77**, 78

Bacon, Francis, 44–47; *Three Studies for Self-Portrait*, **5**, 44, **46–47**, 107
Bandinelli, Baccio: *Cosimo I de' Medici, Duke of Florence*, 49, **51**, 52
Barberini, Cardinal Antonio, 86
Barney, Tina, 71, 76
Bayard, Hippolyte: *Self-Portrait as a Drowned Man*, 92
Bell, Charles Milton, 62; Crow Peace Delegation photographs, 60
Bergeret de Frouville, Madame, 86, **88**
Bey, Dawoud, 60
Bowery, Leigh, 107, **108**

Cannadine, David, 71
Casteel, Jordan, 60, 110–11; Visible Man series, 111; *Yvonne and James II*, 111, **112**, **119**
Castiglione, Countess de (Virginia Oldoini), 92–95, **94**, 111
Chapman, H. Perry, 44
Charlemagne, 54
Charles I (English king), 54–55, 86
Charles V (Holy Roman emperor and Spanish king), 49, 55
Clarke, Graham, 22
Coachman, Alice, 62
Coignet de Courson, Marie Émilie, 90
Cole, Willie: *Five Beauties Rising*, 20, **98**, **104–5**, 105–7
Courbet, Gustave, 26
Crabtree, Andrea Motley, **16**, 62, **63**
Crow Peace Delegation, 60–62

Daguerre, Louis, 92
Dallesandro, Joe, 75–76, **76–77**
Dara Shikoh (Mughal emperor's son), 68, **68–69**
Darling, Candy, 75, **76**
Daumier, Honoré: *The Past, the Present, and the Future*, **42**, 43, 99
Dawson, David, 107
de Piles, Roger, 36, 55
de Zayas, Marius, 101
Dibutades, 20, 27, 29
Disdéri, A. A. E., 68
Dix, Otto, 43; *The Businessman Max Roesberg, Dresden*, 38–40, **39**, 62
Doncieux, Camille (later Monet's wife), 22, 92
Dyer, George, 44

Edo artist of Benin: *Queen Mother Pendant Mask: Iyoba*, 19, 49–52, **50**
Eldagsen, Boris, 113
Elizabeth I (English queen), 49
Esigie (Benin king), 49

Fairhead, James, 90
Faiyum portraits, 30; Portrait of the Boy Eutyches, **3**, 30–31, **30**
Fiocre, Eugénie, 90
Fischl, Eric, 101
Ford, Ann, 55
Fragonard, Jean Honoré: *Woman with a Dog*, 90
Freud, Lucian: *Naked Man, Back View*, 107, **108**; *Sunny Morning—Eight Legs*, 107

Gainsborough, Thomas, 55; *Ann Ford [later Mrs. Philip Thicknesse]*, 55; *The Blue Boy*, 92
Gauguin, Paul, 99, 104
Gérard, François: *Portrait of Napoleon I*, **10**, 21, 29, 52–54, **53**, 60, 104
Géricault, Théodore: *Raft of the Medusa*, 108
Gisze, Georg, 36, 38, 104
Gobelins French tapestry, after Gérard's *Portrait of Napoleon I*. *See* Gérard, François
Goodridge, Sarah: *Beauty Revealed*, 78–80, **78**
Gouel, Eva, 101, **102**
Goya, Francisco de: *The Art of Bullfighting*, 90

Hals, Frans, 55
Hamilton, William, 86
Hammershøi, Vilhelm, 82
Hart, Emma (later Lady Hamilton), 86
Hartley, Marsden, 107; *Portrait of a German Officer*, 20, 101–2, **103**; War Motif series, 102
Henri, Robert, 58
Holbein, Hans, the Younger, 36–40, 43; Hanseatic League portraits, 36, 38, 49, 62, 75; *Hermann von Wedigh III*, **20**, 21, 36–38, **37–38**, 49, 62, 75; *Member of the Wedigh Family*, 38; *Portrait of Georg Gisze*, 36, 38, 104
Honus Wagner, Pittsburgh, National League (baseball card), 21, **21**, 74–75, **74**
Hunter, Sam, 75

Idia (Benin queen mother), 49–52, **50**, 52

Jabach, Everhard, and his family, **64**, 65–67, **66–67**, 76
Jahangir (Mughal emperor), 67–68
John the Baptist (saint), 108
Johns, Jasper: *Savarin 3 (Red)*, 20, **106**, 107

Kaphar, Titus, 26
Keïta, Seydou, 60; *Untitled, #313 (Woman Seated on Chair)*, **8**, 60, **61**
Kelly, Grace, 95
Kempe, Margery: *The Book of Margery Kempe*, 43
Ketel, Cornelis: *The Company of Captain Dirck Jacobsz Rosecrans and Lieutenant Pauw*, 21, 75, **77**

Labille-Guiard, Adélaïde: *Self-Portrait with Two Pupils, Marie Gabrielle Capet and Marie Marguerite Carreaux de Rosemond*, **9**, 76–78, **79**, 80
LaGamma, Alisa, 52
Lawson, Deana, 26, 71
Le Brun, Charles, 65–67; *The Jabach Family*, **64**, 65–67, **66–67**, 76
Leibovitz, Annie, 76
Lewis, Carl, 62
Louis XIV (French king), 54, **54**, 55
Louis XVI (French king), 78
Louis-Philippe (French king), 43

Malanga, Gerard, 75, **76–77**
Manet, Édouard, 26; *Mademoiselle V... in the Costume of an Espada*, **12**, 90–92, **91**; *Young Lady in 1866*, 22, 26
Margaret of York (wife of Duke of Burgundy), 36
Marie Antoinette (French queen), 86
Marshall, Kerry James: *Untitled (Studio)*, **24–25**, 26–27, 111
Matisse, Amélie, 99
Matisse, Henri: *Woman with a Hat*, 99
Mayall, John Jabez Edwin: *The Queen and Prince Consort*, 68–71, **70**
Medici, Cosimo I de' (duke of Florence), 49, **51**, 52
Memling, Hans, 33–36; *Maria Portinari*, 33–36, **33**, **35**, 40, 44; *Tommaso di Folco Portinari*, **32**, 33–36, **34**, 40, 41, 44, 49
Meurent, Victorine Louise, **12**, 22, 26, 90–92, **91**
Moche potters (Peru): bottle with portrait head, 31–32, **31**
Monet, Claude: *Camille Monet on a Garden Bench*, 92; *The Woman in a Green Dress*, 92; *Women in the Garden*, 22, 92
Morrissey, Paul, 75–76, **76–77**

Nanha: *The Emperor Shah Jahan with his Son Dara Shikoh*, 67–68, **68–69**
Napoleon I (French emperor), **10**, 29, 30, 52–54, **53**, 60, 104
Napoleon III (French emperor), 95
Nattier, Jean Marc, 96; *Madame Bergeret de Frouville as Diana*, 86, **88**
Neel, Alice, 26, 58–60, 62, 99, 111; *Elenka*, **2**, 58, **59**, 60, 74
Newton, Huey P., 62
Nochlin, Linda, 58

Okutsu family, 71–74, **73**
Oldoini, Virginia. *See* Castiglione, Countess de
Opie, Catherine, 26, 104–5

Pasqualini, Marcantonio, 85–86, **87**
Peelatchixaaliash/Old Crow (Raven), **48**, 60–62, **62**
Perry, Gill, 86
Phillips, Sandra S., 110
Picasso, Pablo, 108; *Gertrude Stein*, **6**, 26, 99–101, **100**; *Self-Portrait with Palette*, 101; *Woman in a Chemise in an Armchair*, **14**, 19, 26, 101, **102**
Pierson, Pierre-Louis, 92–95; *La Frayeur (Fright)*, 19, 94, **94**, 111
Pliny the Elder: *Natural History*, 29
Portinari, Maria, 33–36, **33**, **35**, 40, 44
Portinari, Tommaso di Folco, **32**, 33–36, **34**, 40, 44, 49

Raimondi, Marcantonio, 90
Raphael, 43, 90
Red Star, Wendy: *Peelatchixaaliash/Old Crow (Raven)*, **48**, 60–62, **62**
Rembrandt, 43–47, 80, 86; *Self-Portrait*, **7**, **45**, 92
Reynolds, Joshua, 55, 86
Rigaud, Hyacinthe: *Louis XIV, King of France*, 54, **54**, 55
Robinson, Jackie, 62
Rodin, Auguste, 55
Roesberg, Max, 38–40, **39**, 62
Rosecrans, Dirck Jacobsz, 21, 75, **77**
Rosenblum, Robert, 75
Ruan Zude: *Portrait of the Artist's Great-Granduncle Yizhai at the Age of Eighty-Five*, 40–43, **41**
Rubens, Peter Paul, 43
Rubin, William, 99

Sacchi, Andrea: *Marcantonio Pasqualini Crowned by Apollo*, 21, 85–86, **87**
Saithwaite family, 21, 71, **72**
Saltz, Jerry, 113
Sander, August, 26; *People of the 20th Century: Pastrycook*, **11**, 22, **23**, 40, 110
Sander, Karin: *Gordon Tapper, 1:10*, 111–13, **113**
Sargent, John Singer, 55, 60; *Mr. and Mrs. I. N. Phelps Stokes*, 19, 55–58, **57**, 110
Saville, Jenny: *Reverse*, 108; *Still*, 107–8, **109**
Schad, Aquilin: *La Frayeur (Fright)*, 94, **94**
Schama, Simon, 71
Schiele, Egon, 44
Shah Jahan (Mughal emperor), 67–68, **68–69**
Sherald, Amy, 26
Sherman, Cindy, 26, 95, 96; History Portraits series, 95; Men series, 95; *Untitled Film Still #21*, 26, 80, **84**, 95, **96**; Untitled Film Stills series, 95
Simpson, Bennett, 62

Sontag, Susan, 109
Stein, Gertrude, **6**, 26, 99–101, **100**
Stokes, Edith Minturn, 19, 55–58, **57**, 110
Stokes, Isaac Newton Phelps, 19, 55–58, **57**
Struth, Thomas, 76; *The Okutsu Family in Tatami Room, Yamaguchi*, 71–74, **73**; One Hour Video Portraits, 111
Stuart, James (Duke of Richmond and Lennox), **18**, 19, 21, 27, 54–55, **56**, 58, 105–7, 110
Suetonius, 30
Swift, Taylor, 58, **58**

Taylor, Elizabeth, 104–5
Taylor, Henry, 60, 62; *Andrea Motley Crabtree, the first*, **16**, 62, **63**
Terence, 38
Titian: *Emperor Charles V with a Dog*, 55

van der Goes, Hugo: *The Portinari Triptych*, 36
van Dyck, Anthony, 85; *Charles I at the Hunt*, 55; *James Stuart, Duke of Richmond and Lennox*, **18**, 19, 21, 27, 54–55, **56**, 58, 105–7, 110
van Gogh, Vincent, 80, 104; *Self-Portrait Dedicated to Paul Gauguin*, 99; *Self-Portrait with a Straw Hat*, 44, 80, **81**; *Self-Portrait with Bandaged Ear*, 96
Vasari, Giorgio: *Lives of the Artists*, 43
Velázquez, Diego: *Las Meninas*, 26
Vermeer, Johannes: *Girl with a Pearl Earring*, 90; *Study of a Young Woman*, **1**, 86–90, **89**, 99
Victoria (English queen), 68–71, **70**
Vigée Le Brun, Élisabeth, 78
Viola, Bill, 111
von Freyburg, Karl, 20, 101–2, **103**
von Wedigh, Hermann, III, **20**, 21, 36–38, **37–38**, 49, 62, 75

Wagner, Honus: *Honus Wagner, Pittsburgh, National League, from the White Border series*, 21, **21**, 74–75, **74**
Warhol, Andy, 58, 75, 95; and the Factory, 21, 75–76, **76–77**, 78
Webster, Daniel, 80
Wedigh family, 38. *See also* von Wedigh, Hermann, III
Wheatley, Francis: *The Saithwaite Family*, 21, 71, **72**
Wiley, Kehinde, 60; *A Portrait of a Young Gentleman*, 60, 92, **93**

Zhang Huan: *Family Tree*, **4**, 95–96, **97**

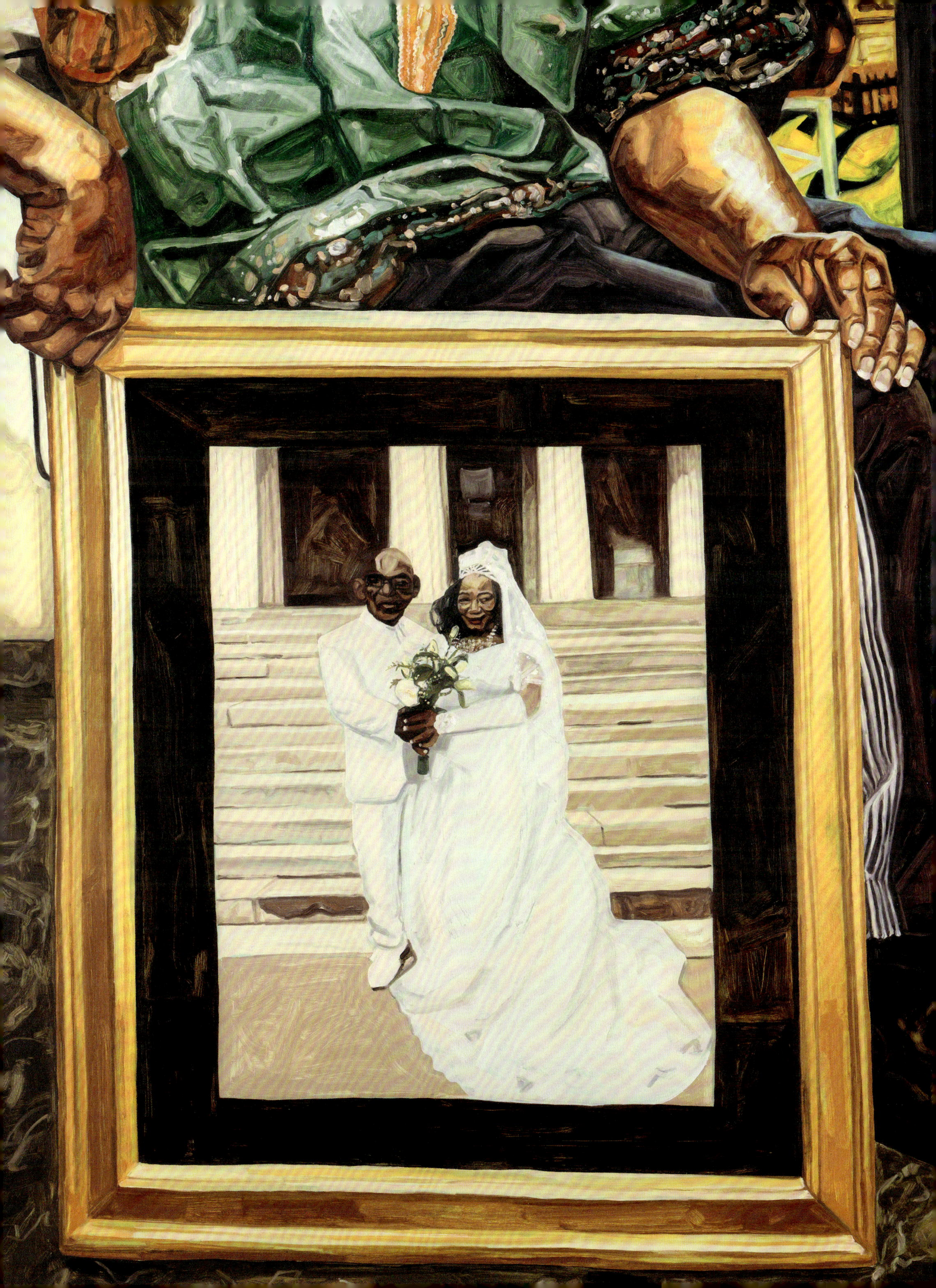

This publication is made possible by the Roswell L. Gilpatric Publications Fund.

Published by The Metropolitan Museum of Art, New York
Mark Polizzotti, Publisher and Editor in Chief
Peter Antony, Associate Publisher for Production
Michael Sittenfeld, Associate Publisher for Editorial

Edited by Nancy E. Cohen
Designed by Rita Jules, Miko McGinty Inc.
Production by Lauren Knighton
Image acquisitions and permissions by Elizabeth DeMase

Works illustrated in this publication are in the collection of The Metropolitan Museum of Art, with photography by the Imaging Department and © The Metropolitan Museum of Art, unless otherwise stated.

Additional photography credits: front cover, fig. 40: © Njideka Akunyili Crosby. Courtesy of the artist, Victoria Miro, and David Zwirner. Photo by Robert Glowacki; p. 2, fig. 24: © The Estate of Alice Neel. Image © The Metropolitan Museum of Art, photo by Juan Trujillo; p. 4, fig. 49: © Zhang Huan; p. 5, fig. 15: © The Estate of Francis Bacon. All rights reserved. / DACS, London / ARS, NY 2024. Image © The Metropolitan Museum of Art, photo by Juan Trujillo; pp. 6, 14, figs. 51, 52: © 2024 Estate of Pablo Picasso / Artists Rights Society (ARS), New York; p. 8, fig. 25: © Seydou Keïta / SKPEAC. Courtesy The Jean Pigozzi African Art Collection; p. 10, figs. 1, 12, 19, 21, 42, 45: Image © The Metropolitan Museum of Art, photo by Juan Trujillo; p. 11, fig. 4: © Die Photographische Sammlung / SK Stiftung Kultur – August Sander Archiv, Cologne / ARS, NY 2024; p. 16, fig. 27: © Henry Taylor; fig. 5: © Kerry James Marshall; fig. 11: © 2024 Artists Rights Society (ARS), New York / VG Bild-Kunst, Bonn; figs. 16, 26: © Wendy Red Star; fig. 20: © RMN-Grand Palais / Art Resource, NY. Photo by Christophe Fouin; fig. 23: Photo by Jeremy Smith/imageSPACE/ Sipa USA (Sipa via AP Images); fig. 33: © Thomas Struth. Image © The Metropolitan Museum of Art, photo by Juan Trujillo; fig. 35: © Richard Avedon; fig. 36: Rijksmuseum, Amsterdam; figs. 41, 48: © Cindy Sherman. Courtesy the artist and Hauser & Wirth; fig. 46: © Kehinde Wiley; fig. 55: © 2024 Jasper Johns and ULAE / Licensed by VAGA at Artists Rights Society (ARS), NY, Published by Universal Limited Art Editions. Image © The Metropolitan Museum of Art, photo by Mark Morosse; fig. 56: © Lucian Freud; fig. 57: © Jenny Saville; fig. 58: © The Estate of Diane Arbus; fig. 59, p. 119: © Jordan Casteel; fig. 60: © 1999 Karin Sander

Typeset in DTL Documenta and The Future by Tina Henderson, Miko McGinty Inc.
Printed on FSC-certified 150 gsm Arctic Silk Plus
Separations by Professional Graphics, Inc., Rockford, Illinois
Printed and bound by Ofset Yapimevi, Istanbul

Cover illustrations: front, Njideka Akunyili Crosby, *Mother and Child*, 2016 (detail of fig. 40); back, Vincent van Gogh, *Self-Portrait with a Straw Hat*, 1887 (detail of fig. 39)

page 1, Johannes Vermeer, *Study of a Young Woman*, ca. 1665–67 (detail of fig. 44); **page 2**, Alice Neel, *Elenka*, 1936 (detail of fig. 24); **page 3**, Portrait of the Boy Eutyches, Egyptian, Roman period, 100–150 CE (detail of fig. 7); **page 4**, Zhang Huan, *Family Tree*, 2001 (detail of fig. 49); **page 5**, Francis Bacon, *Three Studies for Self-Portrait*, 1979 (detail of fig. 15); **page 6**, Pablo Picasso, *Gertrude Stein*, 1905–6 (detail of fig. 51); **page 7**, Rembrandt, *Self-Portrait*, 1660 (detail of fig. 14); **page 8**, Seydou Keïta, *Untitled, #313 (Woman Seated on Chair)*, 1956–57 (detail of fig. 25); **page 9**, Adélaïde Labille-Guiard, *Self-Portrait with Two Pupils*, 1785 (detail of fig. 37); **page 10**, Manufacture Nationale des Gobelins, after an 1805 painting by baron François Gérard, *Portrait of Napoleon I*, woven 1808–11 (detail of fig. 19); **page 11**, August Sander, *Pastrycook*, ca. 1928 (detail of fig. 4); **page 12**, Édouard Manet, *Mademoiselle V . . . in the Costume of an Espada*, 1862 (detail of fig. 45); **page 14**, Pablo Picasso, *Woman in a Chemise in an Armchair*, late 1913–early 1914 (detail of fig. 52); **page 16**, Henry Taylor, *Andrea Motley Crabtree, the first*, 2017 (detail of fig. 27); **page 119**, Jordan Casteel, *Yvonne and James II*, 2021 (detail of fig. 59)

First printing

The Metropolitan Museum of Art
1000 Fifth Avenue
New York, New York 10028
metmuseum.org

Distributed by
Yale University Press, New Haven and London
yalebooks.com/art
yalebooks.co.uk

Cataloguing-in-Publication Data is available from the Library of Congress.
ISBN 978-1-58839-764-5